Decorative
Painting

Decorative Painting

For Fun & Profit™

Susan Young

PRIMA HOME

A Division of Prima Publishing

PRIMA PUBLISHING and colophon are registered trademarks of Prima Communications, Inc.

FOR FUN & PROFIT logo is a trademark of Prima Communications, Inc.

Library of Congress Cataloging-in-Publication Data on file

ISBN 0-7615-2045-7

99 00 01 02 II 10 9 8 7 6 5 4 3 2 1
Printed in the United States of America

How to Order

Single copies may be ordered from Prima Publishing,
P.O. Box 1260BK, Rocklin, CA 95677; telephone (916) 632-4400.
Quantity discounts are also available. On your letterhead, include
information concerning the intended use of the books and
the number of books you wish to purchase.

Visit us online at www.primalifestyles.com

Contents

Introduction

TWENTY-FIVE YEARS AGO, when my son Brit went off to kindergarten, I found myself looking for something to fill my hours. One afternoon during a chat, my neighbor told me she was learning the art of "tole painting." Perhaps I'd been living under a stone (an unpainted one), for I was not familiar with the term. However, a seed had been planted.

Shortly thereafter, I noticed a newspaper ad:

TOLE PAINTING CLASSES

THURSDAY EVENINGS FROM 6:30 to 8:00

SIGN UP!

The next afternoon I registered for tole painting classes. A novice, I had no knowledge what I was in for as the clerk handed me a list of supplies to purchase for the class. I'm sure I gulped when I saw the total on the register receipt, but I was excited about going to a painting class. I was lucky. Our teacher had a personality that wouldn't quit, and boundless, contagious enthusiasm for her craft and for what she would share. She quickly showed how to prepare our bare projects (cutting boards), offered delicious colors to squirt onto our waxed paper palettes, explained which brush to use, and demonstrated how to paint a daisy in five strokes. The rest, as they say, is history. I was hooked.

Defining Decorative Painting— A Brief History

IN TODAY'S CREATIVE CRAFTING environment, the words "decorative painting" fly off the pages of painting and craft-oriented publications. Painters, authors, and editors apparently recognized the need for a comprehensive term embodying a contemporary definition of decorative painting in general, one not limited to tole or folk art styles.

Decorative painting is an accurate term. If I were to sign up for a painting class today, likely it would be advertised as decorative painting rather than tole painting. As I pursued decorative painting, it was inevitable I would absorb a bit of knowledge. The term "tole painting" has historical roots associated with the Pennsylvania Germans. The word tole translates to tin so tole painting literally means "painting on tin." Today, decorative painting is a subject widely recognized and accepted as a diverse art form that combines a variety of media and techniques. It embraces many styles of folk art and tole painting found throughout America and in nearly every country of the world, including Japan, Germany, Sweden, Russia, Mexico, and Norway.

It includes simple techniques developed during America's early years, which utilized milk paint and a rag or crude paint brushes and stain from crushed berries. Housewives, cabinetmakers, and peddlers recognized they could brighten up theirs and others' environments. They cultivated decorative painting techniques to use on their time-worn and well-traveled blanket chests, plain cabinets—and yes, even the old tin coffeepot that once belonged to Grandma.

Decorative painting has become more sophisticated and diverse through modern technology and ever-developing techniques. But it's also become easier and less time-consuming. While we might consider a finished decorative painting project the result of specific brush-stroke techniques, it may include the methods of antiquing, graining, stenciling, sponging, gold-leafing, or rag-rolling.

When I began decorative painting, I used oils. They took days to dry and attracted everything from laundry lint to cat hair. Today, technology affords environmentally friendly acrylics and other products that are generally water-based, odorless, non-toxic for pets and people, and provide practically instant drying times. They offer so much diversity that our application options are limitless. With ease, we now paint on virtually any surface, including glass, candles, metal, and wood. And since I discovered the wonderful world of decorative painting, that stone I was living under is now beautifully embellished with weather-resistant acrylic colors.

Pride, Pin Money, and Profit

DECORATIVE PAINTING PRESENTS a working combination of opportunities when it comes to a pleasant pastime and, if desired, a profitable income. The craft and art form of decorative painting has survived for generations and only proliferates, evidence of its universal appeal.

History confirms that centuries ago people painted designs on the walls of caves. Generations later they decorated meager furnishings to enhance their often dreary surroundings to make them cheerful. People respond to this concept today with such fervor that our homes reflect our individual personalities. Decorative painting is a perfect means to this end. It easily prompts compliments to which one can respond with pride, "I did it myself."

In the new millennium, this age of super high-tech professional and social environments, our need to de-stress will continue to mount. Decorative painting, with its easy adaptation to home decoration and personal gifts, its multiple product options, and its general lack of prerequisite skill level, encourages individual expression and a sharing of our personal selves with others.

Decorative painting is a sound choice for a small business as the popularity of this craft continues to explode. The number of available publications that concentrate on painting reflect this trend. Thirty years ago instructional painting books or magazines dedicated to decorative painting were practically nonexistent; today there are hundreds. Source material is everywhere—through book clubs, magazines, television, and the Internet (see resource section). Whether you are a beginner looking for ideas, techniques, and answers to questions, or are an expert who monitors industry trends, a wealth of information exists to help get you started, keep you up to date, or launch a profitable business.

If you're concerned about costs and floor space, the investment in basic materials is minimal. Manufacturers have long followed the growing popularity of decorative painting and have worked diligently to ensure that paints and brushes are reasonably priced. You may upgrade to more expensive paints and brushes as you progress. Supplies take up minimal storage space (unless you can't resist purchasing everything you see). A small corner will do; a card table can be utilized as a worktable. A friend of mine paints on a lap tray while she watches television.

After I completed my tole painting classes, I spent every spare hour staining wood and painting. In a few weeks, the walls and end tables sported collections of my decorative painting projects. I was running out of room. Then, visiting neighbors began to express interest in a piece and would ask if I would paint a similar design for them. Oh, yes, they were willing to pay me. Pay? Me? For doing something I loved so much that I skipped meals to have more time to devote to it? Suddenly this delightful hobby was taking on a new perspective.

So, I began painting pieces for others. One early spring day, about a year after I'd finished my painting classes, a longtime friend called. She was a "serious" artist, having studied at a fine arts college, and was making a fair income selling paintings on consignment and on commission. She invited me to her home to paint with her. Though I felt we were on different levels when it came to painting, I packed my paintbox and arrived at the agreed-upon time. We spent the day at her large table, our paints spread out alongside cups of tea and sandwiches. Near the end of the day, she announced she'd be doing a spring show in the city park and mentioned that her reserved display area was too large for one exhibitor. She asked if I'd like to bring a few of my things and join her. Of course, I said yes.

The weekend of the show the weather was perfect and a great public turnout was expected. We unpacked our projects and I put my decorative paintings next to my friend's serious works. I recall how insecure I felt and how primitive I thought my offerings were compared to those of my artist friend. Visitors began to course through the park, stopping at all the booths to browse. The first couple of hours, no one purchased my items. My spirits fell lower and lower. Then I had my first customer, and another, and another. My heart soared. I was sporting a goofy smile. Passers-by must have thought I was deranged. By the end of the show, I had sold out. People liked my decorative paintings. Not only did they like them; they paid for them. I felt rich, not only because of the jingle in my jeans but because of the confidence I gained.

How to Make This Book Work for You

MY GOAL IS TO provide a book that is not only inspirational, fun, informative, and non-intimidating, but that also contains helpful insights and information based on personal experiences.

As you go through this book, I hope you enjoy the personal stories—my own and those of others who have shared unselfishly—as well as various tips, additional information, and a little humor (so important in our day-to-day lives!).

Go back and scan the table of contents for topics to see what jumps out at you. Each of you will likely be drawn to certain subjects that you'll want to flip to and read first, before you digest the balance of the book. Most of us don't have time to read everything in one sitting.

Check the resource section to locate specific publications and wonderful books on the market that address in-depth painting instructions and the legal aspects of selling. I have most of those in my reference library and recommend them. Also check Internet sites dedicated to the decorative painter, any of which may provide valuable information (but remember, too, that information in this computer age changes daily!).

Writing this book is a delightful opportunity and is a direct result of my quarter-century-long dedication to the art of decorative painting. Whether you are starting your first decorative painting project or are completing yet another that numbers in the thousands, you never know where the road will lead. There has never been a better time to begin—or reaffirm—your love of decorative painting.

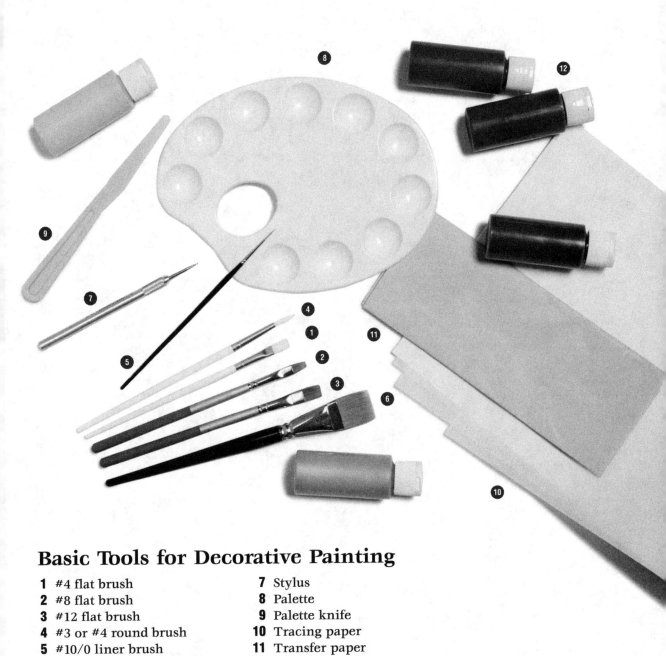

Basic Tools for Decorative Painting

1 #4 flat brush
2 #8 flat brush
3 #12 flat brush
4 #3 or #4 round brush
5 #10/0 liner brush
6 1-inch glaze or wash brush

7 Stylus
8 Palette
9 Palette knife
10 Tracing paper
11 Transfer paper
12 Tubes of acrylic paints

Part One

For Fun

The Joy of Decorative Painting

▼▼

A POPULAR SAYING GOES, "When life fails to provide a rainbow, grab a paintbrush and create your own." As a decorative painter, I have painted my own rainbows, even on gardening gloves. If you are already acquainted with this delightful activity, you are no stranger to the pleasure it provides, not only during the learning process but through the results. If you are a newcomer to this wonderful world, welcome. I promise you, it's fun. And don't be concerned—this form of arts and crafts won't back you into a corner. It never demands an exact rendering of a sample design. It won't betray you if you decide to use a round brush instead of a flat brush to paint a one-stroke daisy. Each of us will paint a rose or a bumblebee differently, regardless of pattern or teaching methodology. With that simplicity in mind, it's easier to understand what makes decorative painting appealing and enjoyable.

I wouldn't dream of tackling a craft or an art form that wasn't fun. Like everyone else, I have enough stress in my life. The last thing I need is to learn an uptight activity when I'm looking for a simple passion that will put a smile on my face. During the first part of this book, I will share the many reasons I find decorative painting fun, enduring, and rewarding.

The Popularity of Decorative Painting

Decorative painting offers you complete freedom to decide at which level to begin, to progress at your own pace, and to develop any personal goals that evolve along the way. The flexibility of this craft contributes to its popularity. You can choose from an unlimited variety of surfaces on which to paint. You can focus on decorating terra cotta pots and paper bags for wonderful gift containers, concentrate on wooden or porcelain ornaments for Christmas, end up painting wall murals, reviving old furniture, or sponging cloud formations on ceilings for others. All this might result in a home-based business venture, as it did for a friend of mine, whom I'll tell you more about later.

Evidence mounts that the craft of decorative painting is growing by leaps and bounds. As I write this, the annual Creative Painting Convention in Las Vegas just closed. This show is dedicated to the craft of painting; and it's not the only one of its kind. The "Extrav" painting exposition is a twice-yearly event. The Society of Decorative Painters sponsors an annual convention. Other events and painting seminars go on nationwide every month of the year, hosted by retail crafting operations or by recognized artists at individual studios. One has only to pick up a painting magazine for information on exhibitions, seminars, and class schedules. A friend of mine commented if she had a motor home and enough money, she'd spend a year just driving from one painting

If It Doesn't Move, Paint It

Try painting on battered tin pots, mailboxes, candles, plastic garbage cans, cast iron skillets, bisque, ceramic tiles, the blade of an old hand saw, stepping stones for your garden path, wooden kitchen spoons, cloth lamp shades, switchplate covers, watering cans, window shades, birdhouses, plant pokes, lunch bags, envelopes, filing cabinets, placemats, or floor cloths. Is your water heater an eyesore? Rough up the surface and paint a mural. The possibilities are endless. If it doesn't move, paint it. I see that the cat just settled in for a nap. Where's my paintbrush?

convention to another and still wouldn't have time to participate in them all (see resource section). She and I were discussing the number of "home shows" on television, and realized that just about every program features some form of decorative painting, whether a *faux* finish for a wall, a stenciled entry table, or a one-stroke apple painted on a kitchen tray. In observing the number of magazines, books, and websites dedicated to decorative painting, I can't recall a time when this craft was as popular as it is today. What a wonderful time to be part of this enjoyable adventure.

Spanning Geography and Generations— A Widely Practiced Craft

For generations people have been enjoying decorative painting, long before it had a contemporary definition. Decorative painting lends itself to a variety of fields, including "home dec," as the trade industry often refers to interior decorating. I remember spending the summers of my childhood with my grandparents. They had lived in the same wonderful old farmhouse for forty years or more. While the overall house was comfortable enough, the kitchen cabinetry was as old as the dwelling itself. One smothering summer's day, without fanfare, my grandmother, Muriel Clutter Colle, proceeded to empty the kitchen counters of canisters and catchall and fill the sink with hot soapy water. I decided some form of housecleaning was underway as my grandmother washed down all the cabinet doors and countertops. Then from a huge shopping bag, she retrieved a paintbrush, a bag of steel wool pads, and boxes labeled "two-step antiquing."

Within a short time, my grandmother had slathered the cabinet surfaces with a neutral basecoat, and as that began to dry, she proceeded to go back and apply a top coat in a different color. She

Did you know???

The Society of Decorative Painters (SDP) has approximately 300 chapters around the world with the number of active members ranging from 25,000 to 30,000.

grabbed a pad of steel wool and began to pull it across the wet paint, creating instant wood graining. By the time the final cabinet had been grained, the first one was dry. She had a new kitchen in time to start frying chicken for the evening meal. My grandmother expanded into florals and still lifes and continues to follow the creative spirit into her nineties. She is a decorative painter.

Earlier childhood memories are of an old peddler who rode in a wagon pulled by a mule. He made his rounds through the sparsely populated Ozark Mountains of Arkansas, where my family lived. "Clang, clang, clang," we'd hear his rickety wagon coming up the rutted dirt road to our small country home. Decoratively painted coffeepots and other tinware clattered, hanging precariously from the tailgate. He'd tie the mule to a peach tree and remove his hat before knocking. "Good morning, Missus," he would say to my mother Gaynell, "If you can spare a lunch, I'll trade you a painted pot or an illustration of your daughter."

One day in exchange for a single dollar bill, he sketched a charcoal portrait of me, softly colored with chalk pastels. He signed his work "By Golly." I've wondered many times since whether that was his real name or if he had just capitalized on the old slang expression. Fifty years later, I still possess the original sketch in my collection.

By Golly was responsible for the decoratively painted wall murals covering huge expanses of a few brick buildings in my tiny hometown of Eureka Springs, Arkansas. More than a half-century after the artist completed those murals, the evidence of his talent and labor of love remains, though the images are somewhat faded with time. But what a wonderful tribute to the long-lived craft of decorative painting and to the understanding of its continued popularity.

As I track my exposure to and love for decorative painting to childhood years, I wonder how many of you have similar memories. Drawings, paints, and brushes have always been an influence in my life. During one hot July at my grandparents' house, grandfather declared I would repaint the big iron sign at the farm's entrance. After all, what does one suggest an eleven-year-old girl do while her brothers are driving tractors? Grandfather took down the huge sign, carted it to the shade of a grove of trees, and dismantled it. He drove into the nearest town and returned with paintbrushes, mineral spirits, and several small cans of enamel in delicious colors. The next morning I was ushered to the shady grove with instructions to repaint the sign.

I was extremely nervous at first. But once my grandfather went on to his own chores, I remember thinking: How difficult could this be? All I had to do was paint over the surviving faded image of a Hereford bull and refresh the lettering proclaiming:

ROY COLLE AND SONS—
REGISTERED POLLED HEREFORDS

I had no clue what a polled Hereford was, but I took one look at those cans of glossy paints and instantly became addicted to the task at hand. For days, every morning after breakfast I rushed to paint in the solitude of that shaded grove. But don't think that my grandfather didn't check to be sure I'd cleaned my brushes thoroughly.

Thirty-five years later I returned one last time to the old farm for my grandfather's funeral. As I watched for the turnoff to the tree-lined drive, I spotted my proudly painted sign. It had survived in spite of not having been repainted since my adolescent attempt at what is called folk art, one form of decorative painting. Decorative painting lasts through generations, leaving a legacy.

The Reward of Making Something from Nothing

I once read that painting is the most practical of crafts because, with very little skill, materials, and time, we can obtain rewarding results. Some of my favorite "something from nothing" projects are made from a paint-stirring stick, free from home improvement centers when you buy a gallon of paint. I've worked up several designs using this item. They are perfect for the beginner but are also fun for an intermediate painter; you can almost do these designs in your sleep. They are great bazaar sellers. I don't feel guilty when I ask the guy in the paint department for extra stir sticks; after all, I'm paying for the paint. He always smiles and hands me an extra half-dozen. See chapter 5 for a fun and simple stir-stick project.

In the attic, basement, or garage you'll often find family hand-me-downs or antiques. Inherited items have sentimental value, so I hesitate to classify their potential as something from nothing; but you may be sitting on a treasure trove of free painting surfaces. What do we do with items we don't want to part with, but remain in a box or gather cobwebs? Altering the finish or painting decorative designs on heirloom surfaces may negate their collectible worth, but may enhance their aesthetic appeal. It's a personal choice whether to paint on these treasures, a decision that may require some thought. Personally, I'd rather give an old piece a happy new life and enjoy it daily than leave it in the attic unadorned, unseen, and unappreciated.

I love the thrill of spying a garage sale find or a cast-off at the side of the road and hauling it home with visions of painting it. One treasure sits begging me to start it once this book is finished—a doll's wardrobe or armoire. While an oval mirror that once was glued to the front is missing, the tiny wardrobe is in excellent condition and the little doors and drawers demand to be painted. I look forward to transforming this piece, which cost me 50 cents at the garage sale, into a hand-painted treasure. It may become a jewelry box for the vanity in the master bedroom. One day it may be a keepsake to a granddaughter or perhaps a great-granddaughter. I hear the whispers of a blonde-haired little girl telling her best friend, "Grandma Susan made this for me." I already feel rewarded though I've yet to pick up my brushes.

Little Loot, Lots of Love

Most of our calendars are marked with several special occasions every month—birthdays and anniversaries, retirement parties, housewarmings, wedding celebrations, and baby showers. Many of us have careers and families, extended and blended. Our problem is twofold: our time is at a premium and so is our pocket money. We, as decorative painters, have the perfect solution—our own private gift shops literally at the tips of our fingers (or the tips of our brushes). Once I began painting, it didn't take long to build up quite a wide variety of projects. I don't know when the lightbulb came on, but I soon realized I didn't need to rush to the mall before it closed. I already had the perfect item sitting right on my painting table. Shopping from home had taken on a whole new meaning. I have a scrapbook filled with thank-you notes from friends and relatives who have penned over and over again how much my gifts have meant to them over the years.

A Gift from the Heart

When I first entered the outside workforce, which I have since betrayed to pursue decorative painting and write about it, I had the privilege of working for a great manager. I wanted to give him a Christmas gift that was "professionally correct." Knowing the fellow was an outdoors type who liked to hunt, I painted an oval wood plaque with cattails and the silhouette of a mallard duck and added the lettering, "Boss of the Year." Looking back, I'm not certain that duck even resembled a duck. But my manager proudly placed the plaque on his office wall and told me it was the most thoughtful gift he had ever received. Money can buy beautiful gifts that we appreciate, but a gift painted from the heart is priceless.

The Benefits of Decorative Painting

In the introduction, I talked about my first painting class and the cutting board project. I'm sure my hand shook as I prepared to apply my first daisy petal. With each successive brush stroke, I became more confident and the strokes grew easier and quicker in application. The evening I finished my cutting board, I couldn't wait to take it home and display it on the kitchen wall. In my eyes, that first project was beautifully painted.

A Salvaged Treasure

One of my favorite projects is an old spice rack found on top of a neighbor's trashcan at the curb. It was dark brown wood and had collected a bit of kitchen grease and dust. With a good soapy scrubbing and a thorough drying, it received a couple of basecoats of spray acrylic. Then the fun began as a small paintbrush adminis-tered an apparel of olive green bay leaves and basil. Metallic gold paint was the finishing touch for this now delightful piece, saved from the landfill. I was going to give this project as a housewarming gift, but when it was completed I selfishly found that I couldn't part with it.

Accomplishment—I Did It Myself

Friends who came for tea or to have lunch noticed my cutting board. How could they not? To paint the daisies, I had used my favorite color, turquoise. I loved telling my friends, "Oh, I painted that." I couldn't wait to get to the craft store and buy more paints and brushes. Eventually, I set up a seven-foot table in what was then called the den (now it's a great room). I won't relate the ordeal of furniture rearranging in order to accommodate my newfound passion; but in no time at all, I was painting gifts for relatives and friends for every occasion and for no occasion at all. My home personifies decorative painting: mailboxes, birdhouses, switchplate covers, and trinket boxes. I always enjoy the sense of achievement and self-confidence that comes with completed projects. After all, I did them myself.

Relaxation—Relief from a High-Tech World

The world we knew even twenty-five years ago was a complete contradiction to today's microchip, nanosecond, Internet-paced cosmos. Compare the ways our grandmothers and great-grandmothers spent their average days to how most of us now spend ours. One of my first newspaper columns about today's approach to crafting focused on longings for simpler times, if only for a portion of our frenetic routines. In recent years the excitement of high-tech computerized environments teased and tempted us to the point of being consumed, forgetting how to create with our hands unless by a remote control or a mouse. As we run the daily race to achieve advancement in our careers and are forced to absorb more technology, we begin to yearn for simple and pleasant pastimes that allow us to slow down the pace and relax.

Did you know???

The original emblem of the Society of Decorative Painters was adopted in 1973 at the first SDP convention. The design, by Joan Johnson, has stood the test of time and remains the society's logo.

People today are discovering decorative painting as a diversion from the daily grind. Picking up a piece of pine and a sanding block to prepare a painting surface is a great stress-reliever. There is something calming about brushing a delicious color onto a birch cutout or a plain plywood birdhouse. There is something joyful when a Santa face appears as if by magic from the end of the bristles of a brush. After a hectic day, sleep comes easier after I've spent a couple of hours painting a creation from the heart and watched its personality emerge from my own fingertips.

Enjoyment Unlimited

I recently was looking for a different project and suddenly was pulled toward one of my father's old typewriters that dates back to 1925, complete with its battered black case. Though I'd run my hands over it many times to dust it, I'd never approached it as a painting surface. Yet I knew I wasn't interested in the antique value of this typewriter, only in the nostalgia I had for this old machine and its inspiration for me. So I made the decision to transform it.

The entire piece received a soapy wipe-down and careful drying. After basecoating the case with flat black acrylic and sealing it, I painted the top with one-stroke violets and a few simple green stroke leaves. Then I added my father's name and dates of birth and death with permanent white paint. Both the violets, with their green leaves, and the white-inked inscription are stunning on the black background. I chose to display the typewriter and newly painted case on an old cabinet, accompanied by an old bottle of ink and a quill pen I found at a garage sale long ago. Whenever I walk past this vignette I feel close to my father. This decorative painting project was one of my most enjoyable, though far from my most difficult. The original typewriter ribbon, the last one my father used, remains in the machine; and when one pushes the typewriter's carriage return, the little bell still goes "ding." My father, who died in 1962, was a painter and a violinist; and though he never pursued it seriously, he was also a talented writer. When I walk by that typewriter, I can hear the sound of the keys as he sat at the kitchen table in his undershirt, pounding away. Would Dad enjoy seeing his typewriter case painted with purple violets? I think he would. I sure do.

The Art of Self-Expression

Decorative painting allows you to express your own personality and style. You can dare to be different and be recognized for it. When I decided to use acrylics to paint purple violets on Dad's old type-writer case, that was my personal painting choice. I wanted to express my feelings for the piece and knew where I would display it. Dad likely would have preferred an oil painting of mallard ducks and cattails set against the illusion of a small flowing stream. He would have enjoyed coming up with his own idea, just as I did, which is another advantage of decorative painting. It's a perfect pathway for communicating your individual personality and unique creative style. You and I could each be painting plums on a wood plaque. Yours might be in shades of dioxazine purple; mine might be navy blue. We don't all view subjects in the same way, whether we're looking at an apple or at the world. Decorative painting encourages creativity and self-expression without limits.

What If I Make a Mistake?

Some of my favorite painted projects started out as mistakes. One in particular involved a simple pine plaque that I sanded, sealed, and base-coated to perfection. I eagerly began to paint the design. For whatever reasons, the more I painted the worse the result. I let the piece dry and proceeded to sand off the paint. I had so much ugly paint on that pine plaque, I realized I'd be sanding longer than my patience allowed. Frustrated, I cut a piece of artist's canvas and glued it securely, covering my ruined surface. The second effort was a success; the canvas inlay appears to have been done deliberately. The piece is one of my absolute favorites, and I won't part with it.

There are simple guidelines to help us avoid problems we might encounter in decorative painting. The information available today is easily absorbed and, with a little thought, mistakes are unlikely. The best advice when beginning a project is to read the instructions thoroughly, particularly concerning surface preparation, basecoating, and sealing when required. Doing a little homework in advance can make a big difference in your results. Even so, we may find ourselves facing an occasional challenge. Perhaps a piece of wood wasn't as dry as it should have been; maybe the weather is a factor in paint drying time. We can follow every tip, hint, and instruction to the letter and still make a mistake.

Most problems can be easily corrected or camouflaged, but I do recall one experience that gave me a sinking feeling. I had enthusiastically painted a pillar candle for a baby shower gift. It turned out beautifully. I applied a gloss varnish to protect my painted design and left it to dry overnight. The next morning, I packaged the candle in a particular kind of plastic wrap. Later that day I noticed the plastic wrap appeared quite bonded to the painted design. You guessed it. I unwrapped the candle and the design came off with the plastic. What if the recipient, in front of her guests, had opened her gift to find a plain candle and what resembled a wrinkled teddy bear decal? Thankfully I discovered my mistake in private, painted a second candle, and swaddled it in tissue paper.

That learning experience was neither the result nor the fault of the candle product or the manufacturer whose paints I used. I had no knowledge of how to prepare a wax surface, paint on it, or protect it. At that time, little or nothing had been written on candle painting, and there was no specialty product for that application as there is today (see Resource Guides). Our sources of new information and innovative products have made decorative painting so much easier. Now, every magazine and book devoted to decorative painting includes columns or chapters on problem solving, which address hundreds of questions concerning surface prep, paints, enhancing mediums, and brushes. All we need do is read the instructions and product labels before we begin a project. Our success as decorative painters is virtually guaranteed.

Handy Hint

Read all instructions ahead of time when tackling a painting project. Every author has his or her own writing style, and you will save time if you have the basics under your belt. Also, check the supply list before starting the project. You don't want to get half way through and realize that you've got every color except Mint Julep.

Getting Started

▼▼▼

DECORATIVE PAINTING TECHNIQUES are not limited to
using a particular category of materials. Today's decorative painters
draw upon acrylics, oils, alkyds, watercolors, and a variety of pencils, chalks, and enhancers. They paint on wood, plaster, plastic,
paper, terra cotta, wax, porcelain, fabrics, and glass. Each medium
and surface you choose for decorative painting will offer different
effects and results because each possesses distinct characteristics.
Though I started out painting with oils years ago, today I am in love
with acrylics.

Acrylics are colored pigments that have been combined with
water or a binding agent. They come in bottles or jars and are a modern marvel. You can also purchase tube acrylics, which are pure pigments that are not pre-mixed. In my early days of pursuing this craft,
I used jar acrylics for undercoating a design, priming a porous surface
as one might use gesso (commonly, a white matte sealer and primer),
or for creating a background color on canvas. Then I would paint my
actual designs with oils on top of the dry acrylic background. It never
occurred to me back then (and no information was readily available
to tell me) that acrylics could be used for detailed decorative painting.

The few books in my small neighborhood craft store, inspiring as they were, only provided instructions for using oils.

Of course, it wasn't long before someone either decided or discovered that acrylics were a perfect medium for decorative painting. Artists and crafters who had already made names for themselves hesitated to leap from oils to acrylics. After all, oils took days to dry; and we had plenty of what is called "open time" to blend and brush. In those earlier days, acrylics possessed a reputation of drying in literally a couple of minutes. Having painted with oils, which would barely dry within two days, how could one possibly shade and highlight an apple in two minutes flat? Not to worry; it can be done. In this fast-paced world, quick drying time is less a pressure and more a benefit to increase the fun of learning easy decorative painting techniques. While most acrylics still dry fast, they may be encouraged to dry less quickly. How? We now have premium paints that naturally dry more slowly, as well as additives that when mixed with acrylics extend their open time. We even have water-based oil paints. All my life I remember hearing, "oil and water don't mix." Modern technology has changed that.

Which type of paint should you choose? Certainly you can paint with oils. Or you can begin with acrylics and switch to oils, or begin with oils and switch to acrylics. Alkyds may be your paint of choice as you experiment with decorative painting. Alkyds achieve similar results and have the same pigments as oils, but have a binder allowing a faster drying time (see glossary). Many artists and crafters within the decorative painting field alternate between media to achieve a variety of effects and (more important to them) to keep their skill levels honed.

Color Your World

For the beginning decorative painter, I recommend good quality acrylics as your paint of choice—regardless of the project or surface you choose. Acrylics are wonderfully inexpensive and their adaptability to many applications makes them easy and fun to use. Here are some examples of ways to use acrylics:

- *Decorative painting in general.* Use for practically any surface, including leather, drywall, paper, tin, ceramics, plaster, terra cotta, concrete, and wood, whether for basecoating or doing design work.
- *Stenciling.* Fast, easy, and quick drying; use right from the bottle with stencil brushes.
- *Watercolor technique.* Add water to your acrylics to create a sheer wash of color.
- *Faux finishes.* Rag-rolling, sponging, and marbleizing effects can be achieved with acrylics.
- *Fabric painting.* Just add a fabric-painting medium and embellish everything from your baseball cap and running shoes to your bedsheets, table runners, and kitchen curtains.
- *Airbrushing.* Thin your acrylics with water or what is called an extender, which also acts as a thinner. (Note: This process requires some specific instructions for certain paints.)

Today's painting palette not only includes a kaleidoscope of colors but also special-effect paints, which offer everything your heart—not to mention your imagination—desires. Acrylic paints are classified as multipurpose, all-purpose, metallics, glow-in-the-dark, stencil, tempera, wood stains, transparent washes, stone textures, snow textures, glitters, and gloss enamels—and that's not the entire list.

Because all these products are water based, you'll encounter no nasty odors or serious environmental threats when disposing of palettes or cleaning your brushes. Not only are acrylics fabulous to use, but from personal experience I can tell you that brushes used for acrylic paints are less expensive overall than brushes generally recommended for oil paints. All you really need to get started is a little information (which this chapter will provide), a few basic acrylic paint colors, and a half-dozen good-quality synthetic brushes. These supplies are easy to find, easy to use, and won't break your piggy bank.

There are wonderful paint colors on the market today. The color choices number in the hundreds, and several manufacturers offer quality paints. I have a preferred product line (DecoArt) based on personal experience; certainly you will choose your favorite brands and colors as you progress. When I buy paints, I truly am like a kid in a candy store; if only I could choose all of them!

The following colors will get your paint inventory off to a good start. You can add other colors as you expand to specific designs and projects. These particular colors, from the Americana product line by DecoArt, are among my favorite paints.

Titanium (Snow) White	Lamp (Ebony) Black	Flesh Tone
Pumpkin	Burnt Sienna	Cadmium Red
Royal Purple	Sapphire Blue	Burnt Umber
Buttermilk	Kelly Green	Ice Blue
Hauser Green Medium	Hauser Green Light	Hauser Green Dark
Primary Yellow	Gooseberry Pink	Cranberry Wine (Transparent)

Different companies may manufacture similar colors, but the color names are not always consistent among different manufacturers. It can be confusing to look for a particular color, such as Pumpkin, when all you can find on the shelf is Tangerine. That's okay; it will work. Your palette doesn't always have to be an exact match. As you gain experience, you'll choose to paint designs in colors totally opposite from those named in the project materials list. One of my favorite pieces is a Santa whose robe I painted in Gooseberry Pink, although the original designer's instructions called for a traditional red.

With the increased popularity of decorative painting, at least one company (Tru-Color Systems, or TCS) is now marketing a comprehensive sourcebook, which is probably the ultimate color-matching reference guide. It allows you to choose a color name and find an equivalent color from five different paint manufacturers. The book, which costs approximately $20, may be purchased from TCS if your local retailers don't carry it.

Many project books and magazines featuring decorative painting include some form of color comparison chart or list. When I see one, I clip it out and put it in my reference notebook. Some craft stores also give customers free color comparison lists or charts that paint manufacturers provide, or you may find them hanging on a peg in the paints section. If you are unable to locate a color comparison list, contact major paint manufacturers. They are more than willing to send free helpful information.

Even if you are a beginning painter, a color comparison list is a good reference tool to have in your library for those times you want to recreate a design in its original colors. For example, if I only have DecoArt paints in my paint rack and want to follow an artist's instructions to use the color Straw (by Delta), I can refer to a comparison chart and see that Golden Straw (by DecoArt) will give me the same result.

Defining Opaque and Translucent Paints

One topic I did not encounter when I first began painting (it hadn't even surfaced back then) concerned the differences between "opaque" (maximum coverage) and "translucent" (somewhat transparent). While my lack of knowledge did not cause problems then, I've since realized that this bit of knowledge can be useful. When choosing a paint color for base-coating an item, I want the highest possible degree of opacity—paints that possess sufficient pigment to allow good coverage regardless of the surface to which it is applied.

Several colors of paints are more translucent and are wonderful for shading and adding depth when they are floated over an opaque color. At least one major paint manufacturer now includes the word "transparent" on the labels of applicable colors, information I greatly appreciate. The word transparent tells me that a particular color will better serve me as an embellishment to my work rather than as a background application. In other words, I might love the color I see in a paint bottle, but now understand that a translucent color won't perform successfully as a basecoat but will work beautifully to shade a crimson apple.

Happiness Is Holding a Beautiful Brush

Let's talk a bit about paintbrushes, the most important of your tools. I can't place enough emphasis on purchasing the best quality brushes that you can afford. A good brush will make all the difference in your work. It feels comfortable in your hand, gives you a controlled and neat stroke, and will outlast an inferior quality brush. You will save money by purchasing higher quality, more expensive brushes when you first take up painting, rather than continually replacing cheaper ones as you progress. Most important, a poorly made brush will frustrate you from the beginning because it won't perform to your liking. A cheaper brush might work fine the first few times you use it; but you'll soon find the bristles won't hold their shape and you won't want to pick it up to paint. Regardless of your skill level (but especially if you are new to decorative painting), you don't need that kind of frustration. Even as an experienced painter, I refuse to try to manipulate a brush that's out of control. I have a jar full of brushes that may not be used again; I've come too far to let an unruly brush spoil my violets!

I often observe during painting classes and seminars a few students struggling while practicing their brush strokes, perhaps thinking or even saying out loud that they were unable to master the techniques. It wasn't the students' fault; the problem lies with the fact that they either chose or were sold inferior quality brushes. The harder they worked, the more discouraged they became, all because of poor quality brushes. Once they had good tools in their hands, they saw immediate improvement and began to smile. A quality brush can make all the difference in your approach to decorative painting, beginning with the very first practice strokes. If you are starting out with acrylic paints, purchase fine quality synthetic brushes. For decorative painting with oil paints, I recommend red sable brushes. Regardless, buy the best grade affordable.

> ## Handy Hint
>
> Be sure to buy the highest quality brushes you can afford. You will save time and money in the long run.

Buying and Using Your Beautiful Brushes

If you've never purchased brushes for decorative painting, the process can be daunting. You stand in front of the store display facing a hundred brushes from which you must choose. You already know you should buy the best quality you can afford. Other issues spring up: How many do you buy? How big? How tiny? What brand? Several companies produce excellent quality synthetic composition brushes that are ideal for use with acrylic paints. I recommend Robert Simmons, Loew-Cornell, and Royal-Langnickel, which personal experience tells me are among the best investments.

When selecting the right brush, consider the type of paint being used, the surface on which you are going to be painting, and the effect you wish the brush to achieve. For our beginning brush inventory, we will need a few flat brushes, one round brush, a liner brush, and a wash brush. My favorites for getting started include the following:

#4 flat

#8 flat

#12 flat

#3 or #4 round

#10/0 or #1 liner

1-inch glaze or wash

You'll find dozens of brush sizes available, from #00 through #20, and a variety of special effects brushes abound, including fan, rake, and deer foot. There are also angular shaders (which some artists refer to as rose petal brushes) and filberts (which have been christened "cats' tongues"). Specialty brushes aren't required in order to begin decorative painting, but as your skill and interest levels increase, you will undoubtedly begin adding them to your brush collection. For now, the six brushes listed are adequate for beginning decorative painting. You may also want to add a stylus (a double-tipped instrument held like a pencil and used to make fine lines) to your toolbox.

The round brush will be used primarily for stroke work, including daisy petals and similar shapes. It has the ability to paint thin lines or thick, relative to the pressure applied to the brush. It can also be teased into thinking it's a flat brush; but for the moment, think daisies and comma strokes.

The flat brushes will be used to fill in areas of the pattern design you are painting, including basing in colors (think "coloring book" painting), and for shading and highlighting by either double-loading your flat brush with two colors of paint or with paint and water to "float" highlights and shadows. Don't panic! Contrary to what you may have heard or read before, there is no real science in learning how to double-load, float, shade, and highlight.

The liner is a nice little brush for eye and face details, for adding embellishments such as "stitches" to lend a country accent, or for filler flowers, dots, and lettering. If the idea of using a liner is a little scary in the beginning, you can always use a fine-line marking pen and stylus in combination and accomplish the desired results. But you should still have a good liner at the ready.

The 1-inch glaze or wash brush is a tool I consider a utility brush and will be used for applying basecoats, sealers, and varnishes. Some decorative painters and well-known artists like to use disposable sponge brushes for these utility purposes. My personal feeling is they are difficult to control and tend to lay down uneven coats of paint. In particular when used with varnishes, they are likely to cause bubbles during the application. They aren't that quick to clean after use so while they may be touted as inexpensive and disposable, I prefer to avoid them.

I recommend if possible that you purchase three 1-inch wash or glaze brushes and that you keep each one separate for specific purposes. They will last you for a few years with proper cleaning, as they don't collect combined product materials. By using separate brushes dedicated to individual applications, you are less likely to get a surprise during project finishing. During my early days of painting, I had been using the same 1-inch brush for basecoating, sealing, and varnishing. Though I'd been performing what I felt was a thorough cleaning after every use, that poor brush was exposed to a lot of product and was bound to complain sooner or later.

Once, when preparing the finishing touches to a big project, I dipped my seemingly clean brush into the varnish and began to apply it to my painted surface. As I continued the top coat application, I saw a faint tint of red mixing with the varnish. Immediately, I "floated" the painted surface with clear water and patted it dry. Luckily, I saved the actual painting on the project but, more important, I learned

Handy Hint

Use a different brush for the tasks of:

- Sealing
- Basecoating
- Varnishing

Label the handle of each brush so you can easily identify its purpose. No more streaky surprises. The brushes will last you three times longer, and the time needed to clean them will be reduced. Regardless of the medium you are using or the number of brushes you have, keep those brushes CLEAN, CLEAN, CLEAN!

something. I've always prided myself in thoroughly cleaning my brushes, thanks to my grandfather's lesson years ago. But that day I realized a brush can appear clean even when it is not. For certain applications this is not a crisis (indeed some wonderful effects are achieved with a technique known as "dirty brushing"). However, when applying a sealer or a top coat of varnish, the last thing I want is any hint of residue creeping down the bristles of my brush and onto my lovingly painted project.

How to Keep Your Synthetic Brushes Like New

■ *Remove sizing from new brushes.* When you purchase new brushes, they come with a sizing agent that coats the bristles. The sizing keeps the hairs of the brush in place during shipping and store display. When you get your brushes home, remove this sizing using clean cool water and gently working the bristles with your fingertips.

■ *Avoid getting paint all the way up to the ferrule (the metal sleeve) of the brush.* If you do, rinse the brush and reload it using a little more caution and a bit less paint. Paint that has made its way up into the ferrule is impossible to remove. It causes short brush life through bristle breaking, shedding, and splaying, and contributes to painting surprises later, including strange streaks of color and unwanted particles on your perfect work.

■ *Never leave your brushes soaking in the cleaning basin.* No matter how tempting this might be, especially during a painting session in which you may be using the brush again and again, don't leave it in the water container between uses. It isn't necessary to do a thorough cleaning during your sessions unless you're changing colors. Just swish the brush gently and remove it from the basin. It will remain wet enough for a reasonable amount of time that paint won't dry in the bristles. Exposing brushes to water for long periods of time causes their wooden handles to swell, split, chip, and crack. Before you know it, your nice brush handles are loose in their ferrules. This will make it hard to control the brush since the bristle end will wobble.

- *When finished painting, rinse brush well in cool water.* Stroke bristles across a bar of mild soap or use a product recommended for cleaning paintbrushes. You may also use a small amount of mild liquid detergent. Work some of the soap into a lather with your fingertips, gently removing all paint from your brush. Rinse brush well in cool water. If you're uncertain whether the brush is clean, repeat the process.

- *Reshape and "size" your brushes.* After rinsing brush, reapply a small amount of soap or cleaning product and reshape brush to its original flat or round form, leaving in the soap to act as a sizing.

- *Carefully store brushes.* Store brushes upright in a brush holder, recycled jar, can, or coffee mug, or lay them flat on your work surface. Never store your brushes with bristle ends downward! It's virtually impossible to restore a round or liner brush to its original shape once the bristles have been bent. You may as well throw away the brush.

- *Rinse before using.* Before using brushes again, gently rinse out any soap or brush cleaner residue.

Handy Hint

When you purchase brushes, some of them may come with a little plastic sleeve over the bristles. Its only purpose is to protect the brush during packaging, shipping, and store display. Once you remove this sleeve, do not attempt to put it back on. It is easy to break and splay the brush bristles by trying to replace the sleeve.

More Tool Talk

Linda Maretich and her husband, Ivan, operate their small home-based business in Salem, Ohio, "Linda's Ewenique Boutique of Crafts." Their individual and combined talents produce a variety of painted crafts, including one-of-a-kind decorative wood pieces for yards, walls, and doors. Linda reports that she comes up with the "I want" ideas and Ivan does the cutting, sanding, and assembly; she gets to do the fun part—painting. Of course, their essential tool list includes a selection of good paintbrushes and a large assortment of paints. It also consists of saws and sanders, a drill press, and even a nail gun.

"Besides the obvious essential tools of a good workspace and quality brushes, good tools have been a comfort to me," says Pama Collée of Glenwood Springs, Colorado. "I feel I can do anything."

Your own tool list will start with the basics, but as your skill level progresses or your area of interest changes, your individual needs and preferences will become more defined. For example, after exploring several categories of decorative painting, I gravitated to more small gift items and home-decorating accents. Consequently, my must-have list includes dozens of pristine detail brushes and special effects tools, while fellow painter and crafter Susan Nelson of Cats 'n Stuff says she can't live without pigment pens in a variety of points, everything from fine line to brush tip.

Along with a few quality brushes, you will need additional tools to outfit your painting workspace. You can start out quite simply and inexpensively, as many commercial products are available for specific functions. Additionally, you can often find alternatives that cost you nothing, serve the same purposes, and may already exist in your own household. Some tools are required and others are just nice to have. Let's look at a general tool list for decorative painting.

Essentials

Stylus. You hold this double-tipped tool like a pencil and use it either to transfer a traced design to your prepared surface or dip into your paints to make little dot fillers or flowers. The two tips are different sizes.

Black permanent marking pens. Fine and medium will get you started. After much experimentation, I still prefer Micron Pigma pens. These pens are inexpensive, last a long time, and offer superior performance even on wood and clay. You can buy expensive technical pens that require manual filling with ink and, even worse, require manual cleaning. Some mornings I view just rinsing out my coffeemaker as a nuisance, so I'm sure not going to bother squirting a syringe through an ink pen!

Sandpaper or sanding pad. Sandpaper comes in various grades or grits, from extremely rough to very fine. Before you seal or base-coat a piece of wood to prepare it for painting, sand down all rough spots and ragged edges. I prefer sanding pads available from my favorite craft catalog because they last a long time and come in packages of three. One side of the pad is a medium grit and the other is fine. I have yet to tackle a project that these pads can't manage, and they are very easy on the hands.

Tack cloth. This sticky rag is used for removing sawdust and sanding particles. These can be purchased ready to use or you can make your own using a mix of linseed oil and varnish. Store the treated cloth in a sealed glass jar when not in use and keep it away from children.

Palette. A palette can be a pad of waxed paper sheets, a plastic bubble palette, a scrap from a slab of marble, a purchased

BETTY'S STORY

Betty Clendening of Williford, Arkansas, began painting for pleasure when she and her husband retired and moved to their farm in the Ozark Mountains. "I never started out to sell my art," she says. But a person offered to buy a painting and then ordered two custom ones for Christmas gifts to her husband.

Betty said she felt apprehension about doing those special paintings. However, upon finishing them and seeing how much the couple loved them, her confidence soared. Soon Betty was selling at craft shows and putting up a Web page on the Internet. That Christmas she did quite well, paying for her supplies plus extra.

Betty's paintings reap profits as well as personal satisfaction. Her reputation as an artist has been established, and she regularly receives sponsor awards and garners Grand Champion and other ribbons at county fairs,

palette made especially for acrylics, or a piece of glass. You will need some type of surface to serve as a palette for dispensing your paints for ease of use. No particular item is required; but since acrylics tend to dry rapidly, the Sta-Wet Palette has become invaluable to me. It's comprised of a small shallow tray that holds a thin sponge. Saturate the sponge with water and then place a water-soaked sheet of palette paper on top of the sponge. The tray includes a lid, so that when you are finished painting you can seal your paints

which result in photos and write-ups in local newspapers (a great advertising resource).

Betty acknowledges her supportive husband, who is willing to put up with the smell of paint and is thrilled over each achievement. Evidence proves she has successfully made the transition from painting for fun to painting for profit. "Each year I can see my income increase by 10 percent or more," says Betty. Her expansion plans include submitting projects to magazines, publishing a book, and teaching classes in landscape painting.

Betty's advice is, "If you want to be a full-time artist, prepare to put in many hours beyond those spent actually painting, but don't over extend yourself. Be careful that you never lose your love for painting for if you lose that, you sacrifice the ability to create freely and it will show in your work."

and, because of the wet sponge, your acrylics will remain workable for days at a time. This palette is available at craft stores, through painting supply catalogs, or by writing to Masterson Art Products (see resource section).

Palette knife. This reminds me of a butter knife. There are straight-bladed and angle-bladed knives. Both work fine so it's a matter of personal choice as to what feels good in your hand. A palette knife is handy for mixing paints on your palette.

Spray bottle. This comes in handy to apply a misting of water on your acrylic palette if paints appear to be drying too fast and losing their open time.

Paper towels or cotton rags. These are handy for blotting and wiping your brushes. Use good quality paper towels or well-used rags (the softer the better). Abrasive fibers will eat at your brush and shorten its life. Over time, a rough cleaning towel can be as detrimental to your brushes as painting on a concrete garden stone.

Tracing paper. This is used to make an outline of the pattern in order to transfer it to your project. Any transparent tracing paper will do the job. If you anticipate using the pattern more than once or want to save it in a project file, a good quality paper can be used over and over again with a little care. Tracing paper can be purchased in padded sheets or by the roll.

Transfer paper. Sometimes referred to as graphite paper. I recommend two products: Saral or Super Chacopaper. Both allow for a reasonable amount of erasing and do not leave waxy lines. Some painters simply use their tracing paper pattern instead of transfer paper. On the reverse side of the pattern with ordinary white chalk. The tracing paper is placed right side up on the project and a stylus is used to transfer a chalk outline rather than transferring a graphite outline. The method you use is a personal choice. I find chalking to be messy during the pattern transfer process. The procedure may have evolved when painters discovered that carbon paper tended to smear. Carbon paper was a common and inexpensive product for pattern transfer but it also left pattern lines too dark and difficult to cover. Chalking became a reasonable alternative. You may want to experiment with this method.

Scissors. You'll need a couple of sizes, for trimming up tracing and transfer papers and cutting sheets of paper toweling.

Water container. There are round and square plastic products available at craft stores made specifically for rinsing brushes. I use a product called Brush Basin, available through a catalog and in some craft outlets.

Brush holder. There are a variety on the market, including those made of wood, plastic, and folded canvas sleeves. Some water basins have a few slots on one edge that will accommodate a half-dozen or so brushes, keeping them conveniently located while you are working.

Brush soap or cleaner. I prefer The Masters Brush Cleaner and Preserver; but you can use a plain bar of gentle face soap or a small amount of liquid detergent placed in your hand. I have used all three types of cleaning products on my brushes. The Masters Brush Cleaner and Preserver does an excellent job and, if necessary, can be used to rescue a brush that has dried paint in it. The key is to thoroughly wash your brushes when you are done painting for the day and to gently reshape them and let them dry by lying them flat on your worktable or standing them in a container with bristles upright.

Spray matte medium. Matte spray is invaluable for sealing lettering or outlining done with a black pen or ink. Even if a marking or liner pen is labeled permanent, don't ever trust it, in particular if you're going to use a brush-on varnish. Once your outlining or lettering is applied and dry, lightly mist your project with a spray matte finish. I prefer Krylon 1311, which has saved me much grief over the years by preventing ink smears when I brush final coats of varnish on to my projects. I can almost promise you that without matte spray you'll be in tears more than once. Additionally, should you want a matte finish on your project, apply several light mistings as your final protective top coat instead of any type of varnish.

Extender. These products extend the drying time of acrylic paints. There may be times when you are working with acrylics and doing a fair amount of brush blending that you will want more open time. Extender keeps your acrylics "wet" longer, slowing down their drying time. I prefer to use DecoArt's Americana's "Brush & Blend" with my Americana acrylics.

Water-base varnish. Used over your finished painted projects as a final protective top coat, varnishing also brings out the detail in your work. It adds a spark and intensifies or deepens acrylic colors, most of which when fully dry are visually flat and dull. You may choose from gloss or satin varnish depending on the desired effect.

Unnecessary—But Nice

The following items are nice to have and come in very handy, but you do not need these before you can begin your new hobby.

Paint bottle storage. As you accumulate more colors, you'll want a method or space to keep your paints organized and convenient to your workspace. There are wood and metal racks and tiered turntables on the market. Several kinds are advertised in painting magazines.

Drying board. About the size of the cardboard backing from a pad of paper, this board is flat on one side but a mass of tiny points on the other. You place freshly painted items carefully onto the points to dry. This product is a big help when painting round or egg shapes. No messy fingers and no rolling around.

Paper cutter. This small to mid-size platform has a sharp pull-down blade that's convenient for neatly trimming patterns, as well as tracing, transfer, and canvas papers.

Light box. Lay pattern and paper onto the top of this box, turn on the switch, and trace your pattern. Especially handy when you want to duplicate a pattern on plain paper before transferring it to tracing paper or to ink a permanent file copy of a favorite pattern.

Bookshelf-size music system. Your favorite oldies station or a favorite tape or CD adds to your fun and is a nice addition to your work area.

Portable television with built-in VCR. Not only is this wonderful to have for keeping up with news bulletins or for listening to a favorite program while you paint, but you may wish to purchase learning videos to help develop your skills. Today's TV/VCR combinations are so easy to use and take up less space than ever (mine is a few years old and is bulky, but still fits on my paint table). I treated myself to the convenience and inspiration of being able to watch and listen to an instructor as I'm painting. I just pop in a tape and I'm "in class."

> **Handy Hint**
>
> Pick up a large white ceramic tile—the type used for flooring—at a hardware store. Glue a felt pad to the back so it won't scratch your work table, and you have a permanent, easy-to-clean paint palette for very little money.

Beginning on a Budget

Here are some hints for using common household items while you decide what you need or until you want to go shopping for more professional items.

- Choose a clean, wide-mouth jelly or pickle jar or a large, plastic margarine tub to serve as a water basin for rinsing brushes.

- Recycle foam meat trays (washed in hot water with an antibacterial dish soap) to use as wet palettes. Place a layer of dampened paper toweling in the bottom to hold moisture. Cover paper toweling with a coffee filter folded in half, and squirt your paints onto the coffee filter in small amounts. Coffee filters are inexpensive, lint-free, and easily replaced when your palette gets messy. When you've finished a painting session, just enclose the meat tray in plastic wrap. Your acrylics will remain workable for quite some time.

- A disposable plastic knife from the deli or fast-food restaurant can be used as a palette knife.

- Recycle a plastic spray bottle that once held a hair-care product; the small narrow size makes a great mister for your painting table (and you'll be sending one less item to the landfill!).

- An old ballpoint pen can be used as a stylus tip when transferring patterns. The familiar shape is easy to control and the fine point helps beginners maintain neat outlines.

- Toothpicks can be used as dip-dot tools for creating small flower fillers and borders, or for adding detail to permanent pen lettering.

- To avoid washing or disposing of paint rags, use paper towels to blot and wipe brushes. Keep a stack of paper towel squares beside your water basin. I cut each sheet of paper towel into four pieces, stacking them. If you cut up an entire roll at one time, you have a long-lasting supply of toweling. Using smaller pieces is more economical than wasting entire sheets (and is more beneficial to the environment).

- Instead of a tack cloth with oil and varnish, simply use a water dampened sponge. ✓

- The paper varieties of shop or automotive towels can be used for general cleanup and for drying your hands. They're strong, soft, virtually lint-free, and with a quick rinse can be re-used, saving money as well as space in the landfill. I sometimes use them to wipe sanding dust from my smaller projects, eliminating the need for conventional tack cloth, which contains oil and varnish. I like being free of concerns about potential environmental hazards related to product odor, storage, or disposal.

- Brushes can stand, handle-end down, in a clean aluminum can, a ceramic mug, or a pickle jar, rather than in a special brush holder.

- A kitchen turntable or lazy Susan, the kind sold for spice cupboards or small jars, makes a great organizer for paint bottles. This item is inexpensive, takes up little space on your worktable, and can easily fit several bottles. Just give it a spin and choose your colors.

Handy Hint

Recycle a tall round cardboard snack can (the kind potato chips come in) as a great storage container for brushes. With the snap-on plastic lid, the can serves as a nifty brush tote if you're going to class or to a friend's house to paint for the day. Just quickly suds, rinse, and dry the can before use. Remember: always store your brushes bristle end up.

Selecting Super Supplies

Selecting the proper materials for intended applications can determine how successful your project will be, in everything from basecoating to stroke work to final finishing. Many project books and magazines provide practical hints and tips on purchasing supplies and their specific uses. Take the time to read any information presented, as it may prevent your buying an item you don't need or won't like, particularly if you are at a beginning or intermediate skill level. Some craft catalogs also include excellent descriptions and explanations about their supplies. Two of my favorite mail-order catalogs are almost like having decorative painters' dictionaries at my fingertips.

Today, we have such a variety of wonderful supply sources available that it's easy to locate and purchase quality materials. The product lines of acrylic paints and paintbrushes in our contemporary craft stores are typically quite good; most are exceptional. I shop a variety of craft outlets from the more expensive to the discount centers; all offer many of the same name brands. I recommend you do a little homework before you purchase supplies, take advantage of available information by reading as much as you can. Keep a small notebook to list items you need or want or new products you see advertised in magazines or on television that interest you. Take notes on ad prices so you can recognize good deals. Bring your notebook with you when you go shopping. Many stores (though not all) employ informed salespeople whom you can ask questions if you are unsure of a product's application. I also have to hand it to many of today's manufacturers, which provide product labels that are excellent sources of information.

"Save Me a Nickel!"

That's what I tell my husband, Dennis, when he leaves on all the garage/workshop lights while he's taking a break from rebuilding the engine of his race car. You can save yourself a few nickels by being cost-effective in purchasing your tools and supplies. There is the logical approach, which includes watching for sales inserts in your local newspaper. The large craft retailers—Michael's, Ben Franklin, JoAnn's, and Hobby Lobby, to name a few—issue sale fliers as often as weekly, usually included in Sunday editions of the paper. These generally include excellent seasonal sales and promotions. Linda Maretich is a firm believer in hitting off-season sales when prices are slashed by as much as 75 percent and says that's when it pays to shop for supplies. Another great tip from Linda is to watch the classifieds for small crafts businesses that might be relocating, going out of business, or liquidating partial inventory.

Mail-order catalogs are a convenient way to shop, and often offer products you can't find locally. Some times I prefer mail order because it saves me time on the highway and the hassle of traffic. If you live in an outlying area or your town has no large craft retail outlet, then catalog shopping is an easy way to obtain paints, brushes, and related supplies. Be aware, though, that mail-order operations may not offer the lowest possible prices, compared to local retailers. That's one reason Susan Nelson believes it pays to be self-educated on competitive prices so you can recognize smart buys. She recommends that you not only compare prices in competitive catalogs, but check catalog prices against those of local retailers. Susan adds that some catalogs offer as much as a 15% discount when you order a minimum dollar amount or comply with other guidelines. Comparison shopping and buying in bulk can save you money.

Be selective rather than impulsive when doing your catalog ordering. As a practicing decorative painter, self-discipline is not easy. I react to catalog offerings the same way I react to a rack of paints in the store: I want one of everything.

One of my favorite ways to save money is to browse those catalogs with coupons included in their pages, or which offer other enticements like free shipping. Coupons may be good for up to 50% off such items as wood birdhouses, papier-mâché surfaces, and brush-tip pen sets.

▼▼▼▼▼▼▼▼▼▼▼▼▼▼▼▼▼

Handy Hint

Avoid impulse ordering. Make your list of items, writing down everything your heart desires. Place your list in the catalog and close the book. Leave it for a day or even three. Then retrieve the list and review it. You will be amazed that what you just had to have on Monday, by Wednesday you don't need after all.

▲▲▲▲▲▲▲▲▲▲▲▲▲▲▲▲▲

When ordering from catalogs, be aware that shipping costs can add $5 to $10 to your total invoice. Some vendors offer free shipping if an order exceeds a minimum dollar amount or if you order by a certain date. I always take advantage of this kind of savings by building up a substantial item list over several days or even weeks so I can phone in one large order. If I order three or four times annually and eliminate shipping costs each time, I've saved $20 to $40.

When it comes to saving a nickel, craft painter Claudia Gentry of Dryden, Michigan, is one of my favorite examples. She states, "I love to find furniture and other items for next to nothing and transform them with paint. I find supplies at garage sales, flea markets, and goodwill operations for as little as a dollar. I end up with one-of-a-kind treasures for very little investment plus the added bonus of having fun while I saved money. You can't put a price tag on that." I couldn't have said it better.

I hope this section of the book succeeded in presenting a basic overview of painting supplies, tools to purchase, household items you can use to make do, and toys to wish for as you continue on this joyful journey.

Setting Up
Your Personal
Workspace

▼▼

IT'S TIME TO PLAN and set up your personal workspace, to carve out a corner somewhere just for you and your paints. It doesn't have to be a large area; you'll be amazed how much can be achieved in a small spot.

When I first began painting, I chose the utility room as my workspace. My first worktable was the top surfaces of my washer and dryer! As strong as my desire was to paint, I wasn't ready to accept tubes of oils, jars of additives, and half-completed projects cluttering up and taking over the living area in the house (my family and friends will tell you I have always been a neurotic neatnik). The utility room wasn't large, but it had bright ceiling lights, a huge window above the washer and dryer, small countertops on either side of the appliances, and overhead storage cabinets. Since it was also somewhat isolated from the rest of the house, I thought this would be a perfect workplace. Remember, I started with oils, and some of the product additives had distinct odors, as did the paints themselves. Besides I loved the idea of claiming a little room for my own, even if it was associated with doing laundry. It was going to be my personal painting retreat, and I was already viewing that utility room as my first "studio."

I cleared out one overhead cabinet to store paints and other supplies. As a beginner, one shelf was all I needed, but I loved opening that cabinet door and seeing my few painting tools. I went to a local discount store and purchased a kitchen stool to use for a chair and a plastic drop cloth to cover the tops of my washer and dryer. I came home, unrolled the plastic, pulled up my stool, and was ready to grab my brushes. Never mind that each time I needed to do the family laundry, I had to transfer my half-dry projects to the countertops and roll up the drop cloth. Never mind that when the laundry was done I had to put the drop cloth back down and rearrange my half-dry projects on top of the washer and dryer. What was important to me was that I had created my own personal place to paint.

One wonderful summer afternoon, having spent the morning proudly painting my first apples on several wood plaques, I knew I needed a break. I also knew I needed groceries. I cleaned my brushes (thoroughly!) and put my supplies into the cupboard. Of course, I left my freshly painted apple plaques to dry, carefully arranged on the tops of the washer and dryer. Then I headed for the grocery store.

Upon my return home, entering through the utility room door with my arms full of brown bags, I paused to admire the work I'd left behind. I couldn't believe my eyes. My apples were no longer awesome. All over the plastic drop cloth, across the countertops, down onto the floor leading all the way through the kitchen and into the den were little red paw prints. It had not occurred to me that our kitten, Daffy—though trained to stay off tables and counter surfaces—would vault the washer and dryer and walk across my paintings!

Fortunately, curiosity did not kill the cat. I followed the little paw prints and found kitty hiding in a corner, looking forlorn and confused. Thankfully, because of the taste and the smell of the paint, he had not licked his paws clean but instead was sitting there

Handy Hint

Have a piece of glass cut to fit the top of your painting worktable. Patterns and ideas can be placed under the glass and will be safe from splatters and drips, and the glass top is a breeze to keep clean with any household glass cleaner

waiting, holding up first one front foot and then the other as if to say "now what?" I forgot about putting away the groceries. I had a painting crisis on my hands—er, paws. I had to think for a moment and, all jokes aside, realized that one does not use turpentine on a cat. Common sense prevailed. Peanut butter! Peanut butter contains natural oils and Daffy loved the taste. Using peanut butter dabbed on a paper towel as though it were a cleansing lotion, by the time all was said and done kitty was none the worse for wear; and he enjoyed a tasty treat during the final cleanup process. Long ago my workspace ceased to be confined to the tops of my washer and dryer; and Daffy lived to be twenty years old in spite of his surprise encounter with decorative painting.

Acrylic Paints Are Pussycats

This may be a good moment to calm safety concerns and to mention that water-based acrylic paints and acrylic products are completely nontoxic. These products offer exceptional peace of mind in terms of our own health and that of our children and pets. If the innovations that have resulted in so many wonderful acrylic products had been at my fingertips when I painted at my washer-and-dryer worktable, there would have been no fright over red oil paint on a confused kitty's paws.

Unlike some oil-based mediums, acrylics contain no harmful chemicals, skin irritants, or harsh fumes. If you look at the label of any water-based acrylic product, whether it's a gel formula for glazing or staining wood, a crafter's paint in a primary color, or a varnish, you'll see a round symbol on the back of the container. The symbol includes the words "AP Nontoxic" with the notation "Certified by Arts and Crafts Materials Institute" and "Conforms to ASTM D-4236," which is a product safety standard requirement.

This doesn't mean you should drink the paint. My husband continues to frown at me for licking the bristles of my paintbrushes to shape them (I *do* rinse them first!). He should know by now I've already got paint in my veins. A little more won't hurt.

I market several pattern packets though the studio and by mail order. Even though all of my endorsed products are water-based acrylic paints and varnishes, I consistently include the following message in small print:

"PLEASE KEEP VARNISHES, ETC., FROM CHILDREN AND PETS."

While we are on the subject of safety, note that most aerosol products are *not* harmless due to the propellants used to disperse the medium. Use only in a well-ventilated area and keep from flame. One of my favorite products is a spray matte sealer, used not only for surface prep but also for a protective top coating. I always take my projects outdoors when I'm using spray mediums. Be sure to keep these kinds of products up on a high shelf away from children.

> ▼▼▼▼▼▼▼▼▼▼▼▼▼▼▼▼
> ## Handy Hint
> Saliva is a great bristle shaper. (Don't practice this little habit unless you use only non-toxic acrylic paints.)
> ▲▲▲▲▲▲▲▲▲▲▲▲▲▲▲▲

My worst "environmental disaster" with acrylics was when I dropped a 2-ounce glass jar of blue paint (with the lid off, of course) onto my brand-new kitchen carpet. The words "water based" were never so important. As with the peanut butter on the paws, common sense prevailed. I grabbed every old sheet and towel I could find, saturated the carpet with cold water, blotted it up, saturated, blotted, saturated—you get the idea. All traces of paint disappeared so I never told my husband. There was no evidence so I didn't have to admit to the crime.

Paint Where You Live— Live Where You Paint

Decorative painters are as unique in their creativity as they are in their choices of where they brandish their brushes. Claudia Gentry (mentioned in the previous chapter) told me that when she first started craft painting, she always worked on her kitchen table but soon realized she needed a dedicated workspace. "With all the steps to complete a project, I was always having to move my unfinished pieces from the kitchen table," she shared. Being the enterprising and pragmatic person that she is, Claudia found a solution that not only has endured in its functionality but remains personally satisfying. "I was at a garage sale and spotted a school desk that fits flat against the wall, with tapered sides and a knee space in front," she said. "At the same sale was an old television stand with a Formica top, so I brought home both pieces." After cleaning up her finds, Claudia transformed the television stand by decoupaging Victorian scrap art onto the top, spray painting the legs metallic gold, and adding new casters.

The desk became a worktable placed along a wall in the great room, and when not in use the television stand, which became a supply table, rolls under the desk for easy storage. Claudia enjoys working in her great room because the location provides easy access to kitchen functions and allows her to oversee and be near to family activities. She enthusiastically summed up how she feels about her workspace when she recently told me, "My work area is always inspiring me to do something creative. I think it's the coolest setup in the world." By the way, the desk and television stand that now function efficiently as Claudia's personal workspace cost her a total of six dollars.

Not all decorative painters object if the kitchen table disappears; or perhaps they mind just a bit, but their senses of humor negate any concerns. Remember Linda and Ivan Maretich who operate their small home-based crafts business, Linda's Ewenique Boutique of Crafts? Linda related that while the woodworking and basecoating is usually done in their basement, the kitchen has temporarily become her personal painting space for applying details to their variety of decoratively painted projects. Jokes Linda: "What table? Is there really a table under all that stuff?"

In the Introduction, I mentioned a friend who paints using a lap tray while she watches television. She has a small side table by her chair for her paint bottles and water basin, but her actual work is done from the lap tray, a good example of what can be accomplished utilizing a small work area. She says, "I do my best work while sitting in my favorite recliner, and when I get tired I rinse my brushes, park them, and lean back and take a nap." Though I could perch on a kitchen stool and paint at the washer and dryer, I could never paint while sitting in a recliner.

For a few years I did my decorative painting at a plain desk placed in an area of the kitchen, which the builders' plan referred to as ESK (eating space in kitchen). We never used the space for that purpose as it was too narrow and turned out to be only a rather dark and uninviting passageway between the actual kitchen and the utility room. So I appropriated it as my personal artistic alcove, thinking it could be transformed into PSK (painting space in kitchen). With some strategically added lighting and a well-placed shelf or two, I was confident it would serve my needs, which it did quite well for a while. I wrote and sold my first major magazine article on "painting at home for profit" while designing and writing at that workspace.

But, over the course of time, the location began to feel confining. And as my skill and interest levels progressed, I began to add to my paint and brush inventories almost daily. Storage for supplies, project books, and unfinished wood pieces was nonexistent in this space. Kitchen traffic patterns and the noises of the refrigerator, washer, and dryer were beginning to pinch my creative nerves. I

Creative Space

"An appropriate workspace is probably *the* essential tool. The kitchen is most suited for cooking. Bathrooms are for caring for our bodies. Bedroom spaces are primarily for sleeping. Writing comes naturally at my desk. Hence, creativity comes most easily in the space corresponding to the creative energies. Therefore it's most important to have a permanent space dedicated to the creative spirit."

—*Pama Collée,*
artist, writer, and designer,
Glenwood Springs, Colorado

also found that, being so close to the cooking center, I was continually jumping up and down to check on a pot roast, forsaking the wooden Santa on the worktable who sat patiently awaiting his painted trousers.

Perfect Painting Place

Well, when it came time to move out of the kitchen passageway, I realized I was at a crossroads concerning my personal painting space. I was ready to embark on my biggest project so far, driven by my love of decorative painting. And so I began a thought process that would result in building my own studio, separate from the house. The prospect was exciting!

After much deliberation I contacted a local outlet of a company specializing in prefabricated yard barns (Heartland Industries) and arranged to have one of their buildings constructed in my backyard. "No, I really do not want a barn for parking the tractor mower; I want a painter's studio," I explained with fervor to the sales representative, James Mills. He looked at me with disbelief for at least a split second. But with a sketchpad in front of us, and with his professional and helpful questions, we simply modified the company's standard specifications concerning the type of entry door and also allowed for additional windows. I wanted lots of daylight. After all, this was going to be a studio.

Within a matter of days, the building contractor arrived with all the materials and completed the shell of the structure. Overnight, I had a 10-foot-by-16-foot building just a few steps away from our back deck. We did a lot of the interior finishing work ourselves to save money. We put fiberglass insulation in the walls and then installed panels of light-colored decorative wallboard. A sheet of easy-care vinyl kitchen flooring was bonded over the plain plywood floor. We contacted a licensed electrician friend to help us add a separate circuit to the breaker box in our garage; and we dug the trench ourselves for underground electrical cable with a rented auger—after checking on local utility company code for in-ground depth requirements. The structure is considered portable since it's not on a permanent foundation; the county in which I reside requires no building permit for this type of construction. I did advise my insurance agent that we had constructed a portable out-building and of its intended purpose. I was happy to learn our existing homeowners policy covers a non-permanent structure and its contents for up to 20 percent of our home's value; my studio and its inventory fits within that criteria.

The studio has a window air conditioner, portable baseboard heating, and an 8-foot overhead shop light. I have two or three electrical outlets on every wall for work lamps, tools, a bookshelf stereo, and for plugging in seasonal decorative lights. While there is no access to running water other than a garden hose, I'm only steps away from the back door to the house so have no problem keeping a gallon bucket of clean water beside my painting table for refilling my water basin to rinse brushes.

The furnishings cost me little or nothing. I moved existing desks and bookcases from that kitchen passageway and relocated them to the studio. To fill the bare walls, I found inexpensive bookcases made from hard white plastic at a discount store. For about a hundred dollars, I outfitted every wall in the building with plastic shelving. Then a friend called, saying she was going to toss an old drop-front desk, and if I wished to pick it up I could have it gratis. When I went to collect it, she said she also had a tall dining room hutch she no longer wanted. The glass doors, broken out long ago, had been replaced with wire mesh; and some enterprising soul had painted the entire piece with white gloss enamel—which for some reason was still sticky in certain spots. Did I want the hutch, too? "Hurry, Dennis," I said. "Let's get this stuff into the back of the truck!"

Building a Perfect Painting Place

Approximate Expenditures

Prefab building shell w/house-type door and extra windows	$2,100
Exterior paint and caulk	$75
Auger/trencher (rented)	$75
Wiring and electrical supplies	$90
Permanent light fixtures (ceiling and outside motion sensor)	$120
Air Conditioner and baseboard heaters	$375
Vinyl flooring	$150
Insulation, paneling, baseboards and trim	$500
Contracted labor	$600
TOTAL	$4,085

Just when I didn't think I had room for one more piece of furniture in the studio, impulse led me to a nearby antiques mall that was going out of business. I spied a display pegboard about seven feet tall by four feet wide, securely mounted on a roll-around platform that served double-duty as a bottom shelf. The unit had been painted white and decoratively stenciled with blue morning glories all across the top. The price, which I could barely read, was written on a piece of masking tape. Was that $100.00? No. It was $10.00. I bought it. It's a perfect fit.

I generally frequent the studio mainly during spring and summer months, because even with baseboard heating, the temperature in winter cannot be uniformly controlled. However, except for paints and brushes, I leave all my supplies, displays, completed projects, and artist samples in the studio year-round. During the late fall and the winter months I work from my home office, having set up a painting center comprised of a computer desk and hutch combination, purchased inexpensively from friends who were moving and didn't want it. The desktop provides adequate room for decorative painting projects. There are enough shelves for paint bottles and brushes, three work lamps, a li_____en my portable TV/VCR. Extra supplie_____ot used on a daily basis are hidden out_____e desk and hutch are located on the w_____-puter system, which is where I do mo_____t of decorative painting, and is adjace_____a telephone, and a bookshelf stereo. I enjoy convenient creativity, in a room totaling a mere 110 square feet. Now, all I have to do is figure out how to write at the computer desk and paint at the worktable—simultaneously.

When I asked Susan Nelson of Cats 'n Stuff about her workspace, she told me she has three work areas, including one set up in a spare bedroom that she uses primarily for fabric crafts, sewing, and decorative painting on fabric. She also utilizes a porch that features a large table and shelves, where she cuts and paints fabric pieces as well as stores her paints and drawing supplies. In addition, the basement of the house includes a work area where Susan can saw, sand, and paint wood projects. Susan says, "All of these work areas have direct or nearby access to sinks, running water, and electricity." This is an excellent example of how to make more than one area within your home function as an efficient workspace.

Use your creative imagination to visualize where you'd like to work and why; write down your ideas and make sketches of the possibilities. Take a little time to experiment with setting up a space, then try it out. If it doesn't function comfortably, pick another corner and start again. I've relocated my acrylics so many times that they migrate by themselves from room to room while I'm sleeping, looking for a permanent home. How do I know? I have bottles of paint I can't find.

Creative
How-To's

▼▼▼

AS A BEGINNING PAINTER, you will gradually come to enjoy gathering knowledge about product properties, specialty brushes, brush-stroke techniques, and the new acrylic paints and other artists' media that seem to surface almost daily. Resolve that over time at your own pace, you'll study the available books, magazines, and videos and will attend classes if you have the opportunity.

When I took my first painting classes, as enthusiastic as the instructor was, little was actually communicated about the variety of painting techniques, terminology, or descriptions of the products we were using. We were given a list of supplies to purchase and were required to show up prepared to paint, which of course we expected to do. There was no overview about brush control or the proper way to prepare a surface for painting. The instructor had even prepared most of the wood surfaces for the students prior to class.

It may have been done to save time, as staining a wood piece was achieved using a slow-drying oil-based product. It may have been done to save the disorder of a dozen eager painters bogged down in sawdust and sticky paint brushes. Without a doubt, that early experience as a beginning decorative painter provided a fond memory of being in a hands-on classroom with an environment of "just view it and do it." It was a great way to get right to the brush, which is what we as decorative painters can't wait to do, whether we are beginners or have a little experience. As much fun as the class was, and as grateful as I am for the fire it built in me for decorative painting, I didn't learn much about insuring long-lasting quality results.

In recent years I have encountered more and more instructors who are taking time to fully demonstrate painting techniques before a student is allowed to pick up a brush, and some decorative painting teachers even distribute handouts that include glossaries, definitions, and general product information. Along those lines, I will provide you with more detailed descriptions of basic brush strokes, simple painting methods, and background preparation techniques—particularly for wood items, which lend themselves to such a variety of effects. We'll also touch on the basics of preparing several other surfaces, transferring patterns, and performing finishing techniques.

If you are an accomplished painter who is already successfully executing your craft, you might be tempted to skip this chapter. Please don't. Even after painting for several years, I still like to review techniques and procedures, both old and new, as they continually change. While I view my introduction into decorative painting as satisfying and joyful, the processes and products diversify rapidly.

I consider myself a creative soul rather than a technical person, but I believe that taking time to understand and practice even the most basic project preparation steps can prevent a disappointing painting experience. Remember, too, that in this era of information saturation, every imaginable subject, even innovative painting techniques and products, is considered an emerging technology. By now

Painting on the Web

Check out these Web sites, which provide a sampling of some major paint manufacturers' wares:

www.decoart.com

www.deltacrafts.com

www.duncancrafts.com

www.plaidonline.com

the phrase "welcome to the computer age" is a cliche. We've already been here for quite a while. So it stands to reason that even decorative painters have new and exciting resources available. I'm not exaggerating when I tell you I own literally hundreds of decorative painting pattern books. I still have the first one I bought (*For Whom the Brush Toles* by Priscilla Hauser). I painted every pattern in that book. We can now buy decorative painting patterns on CDs, which your computer transfers into full detail and color—not only to your monitor but to your printer. Instant patterns. Every time I pick up current issues of my favorite painting magazines, I'm bombarded with advertisements for new paint colors, specialty paints, and painting mediums and CDs for my computer system. Practically every paint manufacturing company has a Web site.

Being something of an "old dog," and one who isn't completely keen on new tricks, I understand so much technology and information can be intimidating; but as I examine and test these innovative products, I marvel at their ease of use and flexibility. The good news is many new specialty paints and mediums have eliminated the steps required to prepare some surfaces. What a timesaver! The new colors are so delicious one almost wants to taste them. What fun! I prefer to stay on top of the new decorative painting technologies; though I do wonder how many more paints will fit on my closet shelf. (which looks as though it will crash a lot sooner than my computer system will!).

As you gain some general knowledge from this book, you may have questions not addressed here; or new curiosities may surface while you read various passages and chapters. By all means tap into the wealth of information so readily available and generously shared by decorative painters, artists, authors, editors, and paint and other product manufacturers. You'll find innumerable solutions, ideas, and products through a variety of books, magazines, and videos at reasonable prices—whether from the Internet, your local bookstore,

Magazines with a Painter in Mind

The publications listed below are among several dedicated to the decorative painter.

Tole World

Painting

Let's Paint

PaintWorks

Quick and Easy Painting

Decorative Woodcrafts

Decorative Artists Workbook

You will find many projects with wonderful full-sized patterns and detailed instructions for every level of experience. I can't part with my back issues so I now have hundreds, some dating back to premiere editions published a decade ago. (If my house ever catches fire, there'll be no saving the place!)

supermarket magazine rack, or mail-order catalogs. Take advantage of these valuable resources. Everything is out there waiting.

Right Steps for the Right Prep

Decorative painting techniques in general lend themselves so well to many surfaces, particularly wood pieces, most of which are not only unique, but are designed to be functional within the home. Wood items are easy to find, fun to paint, and generally very inexpensive. While I've chosen to concentrate on general procedures for preparing wood surfaces, as we explore this chapter you will find lots of information and quick tips for prepping and painting other surfaces, including metals, terra cotta pots, candles, and even denim.

To prep previously painted or stained wood surfaces. If the old wood surface is in decent condition and does not have a slick or gloss varnish finish, you can usually paint right over the old coatings with an acrylic or a flat latex, using either spray or brush-on applications. If the piece has been stained and has no apparent varnishes or other finishing sealers, you will need to apply a sealer/primer to prevent the stain from rising or bleeding through any newly applied basecoats. One particular sealer/primer product is KILZ, found at most home improvement centers. I've used it on everything from birdhouses to kitchen cabinets. It's available in spray and brush-on forms. Once sealer/primer is applied and dry, lightly sand all surfaces and wipe clean with tack cloth or a dampened sponge or shop towel. Let project dry and apply your choice of basecoat, either a quality acrylic or flat latex house paint.

If the existing paint is chipped, peeling, or has a slick surface, you will need to sand down as much old paint as possible, roughing up the surface with a medium grit paper and finishing with very fine paper. Some decorative painters prefer to complete the sanding process by making a final pass with a pad of ultra fine (number 0000 grade) steel wool. If the item has many coats of old varnish or what appears to be gloss enamel, your best bet is to remove the paint with a stripping product, most of which are more user-friendly today than they were even a few years ago. Follow manufacturer's directions for application and disposal of material. After stripping and drying the wood piece, lightly sand, wipe clean, and proceed to apply your basecoat.

To prep new (raw) wood prior to staining or painting. Sand all surfaces with sandpaper. Depending on the type of wood or the size of the piece, you likely will need to sand first with medium or fine grit and finish with very fine paper. Remove all dust with a tack cloth or a slightly dampened sponge or shop towel. Allow to dry.

To stain new wood. Today we can choose from a wide variety of wood-staining products, from acrylic gels in two-ounce bottles found at the craft store—which are especially handy for smaller ornaments and gift items—to the larger cans of oil-based products available at home improvement centers. As a decorative painter, you will be quite pleased with acrylic-based wood stains. They are easy to use, provide superior results, and can be cleaned from your brushes with a quick soap and water rinse.

Do not apply a sealer or other similar medium to new wood before staining, as the wood will not absorb the stain properly, if at all. Leave your wood raw prior to staining, but note you will usually want to apply a sealer *after* the staining process is complete (I'll explain why later).

Once your raw wood piece has been sanded and wiped clean, use a 1-inch wash brush (I refer to it as a utility brush) to apply a generous coat of stain. Work quickly in long strokes to cover your surface. Immediately rub down the stain with an old rag or lint-free paper shop towel. If the color is not as dark as you wish, an additional application will intensify the effect. After the stain is completely dry, lightly mist the surface with two or three coats of spray-on matte finish sealer. The reason for applying a sealer at this time is that the wood, though stained, is still basically raw and is usually quite porous. If you neglect to apply a sealer, the paints you use will be absorbed into the stained wood too quickly. The sealer allows you more open time and insures the color choices for your design will remain true. When the sealer is thoroughly dry, lightly sand the surface with very fine sandpaper and wipe clean. You are now ready to transfer your pattern to the wood piece, a process that will be covered later in this chapter.

To pickle new wood. Usually when we think of pickled wood we think of a whitewashed effect, as if it had been bleached, but pickling doesn't have to be done in gradations of white. There are several easy techniques for achieving a pickled effect.

One method that doesn't require purchasing a specialty product is to simply dilute acrylic paint with water, approximately two parts water to two parts

Handy Hint

Following are the three easy steps to two-tone staining:

1. Apply gel-based acrylic stain onto wood piece with a soft lint-free rag, wiping down well.

2. Allow to dry slightly.

3. Using soft water-dampened cloth, rub out areas you wish to lighten.

paint, which will result in a transparent color wash. Brush the diluted paint onto your project in even strokes and allow the wood to absorb the color. This method requires longer drying time and may raise the grain of new wood to a greater degree than certain other techniques. You should therefore allow extra time for drying and sanding. Make sure wood is thoroughly dry before transferring your pattern.

Another easy technique is to use a product that combines white stain and sealer. An excellent one is "White Lightning," manufactured by J.W. Etc. It can be used on all wood, including new ("green") wood, as its sealing abilities prevent sap from weeping. Just apply the product to new wood with a brush, allow to dry, and lightly sand. Transfer your pattern and paint.

This next procedure is also uncomplicated and allows you to customize your pickling color. At least one major acrylic paint manufacturer markets a white pigmented gel-based stain. Just apply to smoothly sanded new wood straight from the bottle to achieve a whitewashed effect. If you wish a pickled look in a custom color, simply add enough acrylic paint in your color choice to white gel stain until you get the preferred shade. The more acrylic color you add, the darker the pickling. Now, isn't that easy?

For a different effect that adds striations, or streaks, of color, you may also paint your wood surface with white gel-based stain and, while it is still slightly wet, dip a piece of soft rag into a small amount of acrylic color of choice and rub into the stain where desired.

Perhaps the easiest of all methods to achieve a pickled or softly faded effect is by using the wonderful acrylic transparent washes such as Heavenly Hues from DecoArt. These washes come in many colors so there's no mixing of color or water, and there's no guesswork about the finished effect. Simply brush the color wash of choice onto new wood, right from the bottle. While the paint is wet, wipe down with a damp sponge or rag until you get the look you want. If you've removed too much paint, reapply and wipe again. Allow to dry and sand lightly if necessary. Wipe surface clean, transfer your pattern, and paint.

To base-coat new wood in a solid color. Some artists always seal new wood before applying any paint. A fellow painter maintains that applying sealer to new wood prior to base-coating is a waste of product and time. Several years ago, a well-known decorative painting instructor told me that sealing new wood before painting might keep the basecoat from adhering properly as the paint can't embed into the pores of the wood, so I generally do not seal new wood prior to base-coating. However, there are exceptions to every rule. I certainly seal all wood that will eventually be used as an outside display piece. I also want to warn you, if there are any knotholes in your wood or if your chosen raw surface may not have been dried or cured (known as green wood), you may eventually find beads of sap or other discoloration seeping up through your painted project. Note that if wood is green, basecoating with plain acrylic paint will not seal knotholes, eliminate sap from surfacing, or prevent wood from warping if exposed to weather.

Simple Alternatives to Basic Basecoating or Plain Stains

There's certainly nothing wrong with applying only a simple stain or acrylic paint as your project background. Most designs have so much detail in them that a plain uncluttered background is exactly what you will choose. But do tuck into a little corner this reminder: A few wonderfully simple painting methods can lend a special touch of variety to your painted pieces. These techniques include spattering, sponging, stippling, color banding or accenting, and glazing.

Spattering. This technique offers more than one effect depending on the choice of colors and the paint consistency used for spattering. Also called "flyspecking," spattering can add contrast and interest by brightening up a plain solid color basecoat. For example, a project with a flat yellow ochre background might be spattered with Straw or Snow White to add some spark. But this same approach can have the opposite effect. A wooden box basecoated in a dusty blue would become a more subdued subject if flyspecked with charcoal gray to add shadows and soften the blue.

Yet another variation using the same technique could be a wood-stained tavern board, with a darker color simply spattered over the stain. If I want an aged or antique wormwood effect, I do my flyspecking in two steps. The first application is done with thinner paint, and my brush held a few inches above my project. The second application is very brief, using slightly thicker paint, and the brush is held more closely to my project, which deposits larger, sparsely applied spatters on top of the smaller flyspecks. It really does give the appearance of authentic wormwood.

To spatter or flyspeck, choose an old toothbrush or use a spattering tool such as the ones manufactured by Kemper. The product is available though most craft catalogs or in retail craft outlets. To use the toothbrush, you simply drag a fingernail or palette knife across the paint-filled bristles and let the paint fly. With the Kemper tool, you rotate the stiff bristles and built-in sleeve; the sleeve flicks the paint-loaded brush, which throws out flyspecks. I found the toothbrush method easiest to control, and it didn't cost me any money—even though my thumbnail ended up covered with Prussian Blue.

Regardless of which you decide to use, thinning your paint with enough water is the crucial factor in getting the right look. Most decorative painters prefer an inky consistency. You may want to experiment a bit. Once you've thinned your paint and have an old toothbrush or spattering tool in hand, grab a brown grocery bag, a scrap of colored poster board, or a sheet of colored printer paper for practicing the technique. To spatter:

1. Load your toothbrush or spattering tool into the thinned paint.

2. Rotate the handle of the Kemper tool, or if using a toothbrush pull a fingernail or palette knife across the bristles.

3. Practice holding the brush at different heights, angles, and with different consistencies of paint to see which effects please you, depending on the look you want.

Spatter Matters

You may spatter your entire project before transferring and painting your design. If you choose this method, keep in mind the spatters may leave you with tiny raised bumps under what will become your finished painting—unless you do a little sanding or do some undercoating of your design with gesso or acrylic before transferring the final pattern details. An alternative is to paint your entire project, and when it is dry, cut a piece of plain tracing paper to shield the decorative design. Lay the tracing paper on top of your painted detail and then spatter only the background. You will achieve the special effect you desire for the project background without spattering over your detailed painting.

Sponging. This is extremely simple and the effects are wonderful. Though many decorative painters use what is called a natural sea sponge (and you certainly may do so), I've had good results with pieces torn from a plain kitchen sponge. The technique is really easy. To enhance a background after your basecoat has dried:

1. Dip a piece of sponge in clean water and squeeze out all excess.

2. Pick up very little amounts of paint, right from the bottle, on two or three edges of sponge.

3. With a light touch and continually turning the sponge "every which way but loose," apply paint sparingly all over your project surface. The reason you want to keep rotating your sponge is so you don't get a row of identical pattern marks when using this technique as a background effect. (Certainly, there may be times when a pattern repeat is your goal, such as trimming the edge of a box lid or a serving tray.)

   If you apply a sponge technique to a dry background surface, you will get a bolder and sharper pattern, even with very little paint on the sponge. For a very soft, almost blended effect, wash or blot a small amount of water over your background surface and then sponge on your paint. For a completely different result, while your background is still wet from the base-coat application, immediately pick up a clean damp sponge and lift off some of the color. It'll never turn out the same way twice—which is another joy of decorative painting.

Fun with a Sponge

When experimenting with sponge painting effects, you might use any of the following:

- Natural sea sponge

- Torn or cut pieces from old kitchen sponge

- Piece torn or cut from a car-washing sponge

- Compressed sponges that come in thin sheets, cut into shapes and immersed in water

- Cosmetic or makeup sponge using original shape

Stippling. Stippling is also referred to as pouncing or dabbing with a brush. If you have an old 1-inch wash brush (utility brush) that has become slightly flared and splayed and the bristles refuse to go back to a sharp edge, don't throw it out. Keep it as your stippling or pouncing brush to use for background effects on larger projects. With very little paint on the tips of dry bristles, you can achieve a soft mottled basecoat rather than a sleek brushed-on look. Choose a paint color a shade lighter than your basecoat, or mix a small amount of white into the base-coat color. Load the old brush sparingly, hold the handle straight up and down (perpendicular), and gently pounce the lighter color all over the background.

Color Banding or Accenting. I call it color banding or accenting because I don't like the word "striping." Because I can't really paint a straight line, the idea of painting a stripe makes me shake in spite of all my wonderful script liners and my perfectly shaped flat chisel-edged brushes. I suppose, as several artists have proclaimed, that with enough practice you and I can learn to perfectly pinstripe with a liner, or swagger a half-inch stripe with a #12 flat. Well, I love shortcuts; they are part of the fun of decorative painting. Sometimes I like to add a stripe or a border accent around a papier-mâché heart ornament, to the rim of a terra cotta pot, or to the lid of a wood recipe box. An easy way to do this is to use painter's tape (available at home improvement centers) or with household tape (the kind that looks "frosty"). To color band, or trim your project with a border stripe:

1. Basecoat the entire surface as desired and let dry thoroughly.

2. Decide where you want your stripe or trim (how far inside from the edge of your project). If necessary, make a few light dots with pencil or chalk pencil and use them to line up your tape.

3. After applying painter's tape or frosty tape along your marks, firmly smooth down the edges of your tape to prevent paint from seeping underneath.

4. Paint along the edges of the project up to the adhered tape using your choice of contrasting color or accent color. You may have to apply two or three coats, letting it dry between applications.

5. When paint is dry, gently strip off tape. You should have a neat line. If the paint lifts in a spot or two where the tape wasn't firmly pressed down, just do a little touch up with a liner brush.

Finished projects such as small plaques and boxes can also be accented with dip-dots made with the tip of your stylus (or brush handle) dipped in paint and applied uniformly all around the border. You can also do a series of small brush strokes, whether comma-shaped with a round brush or checkerboard style using a flat brush. These are easy and require no patterns. (Refer to Basic Brush Strokes in this chapter.)

Glazing. This term is also referred to as a color wash or a floated finish. It simply means a translucent layer of color applied to a dry basecoated surface. Remember when I discussed the difference between opaque and translucent acrylic paints? Translucent paints act as wonderful enhancers to provide special effects, including glazing, with very little effort. If I had a project board base-coated with Santa Red and wanted to apply a glazing effect, all I have to do is lay on a wash of Cranberry Wine, which I know from the manufacturer's label is a color with translucent characteristics. To glaze:

1. Make sure your basecoat is dry.

2. Apply the coordinating top coat, which will be your glaze coat, with a 1-inch brush (utility brush) making long strokes over the surface, brushing out most of the glaze. Allow to dry and transfer pattern.

3. For a unique effect, apply glaze coat as above but leave a fair amount on the surface. Then crumple a discarded plastic bread wrapper or piece of kitchen wrap, and pounce onto the wet glaze in a random pattern. Let dry and transfer pattern.

Transferring the Pattern Design. Make sure your stained or base-coated surface is thoroughly dry and smooth. With tracing paper and a fine-tip pen, trace your pattern onto the tracing paper. After tracing your design, place the tracing paper on your project, positioning it where you want it on your surface. You may wish to tape the pattern down with small bits of painter's tape or plain masking tape. Slide your transfer paper (such as Chacopaper) under your tracing paper, making sure the transfer side is face down on the surface of your project. Using a stylus or ballpoint pen, lightly go over the pattern lines on your sheet of tracing paper. Your design is now transferred to your project.

Taping down your pattern allows you to peek under your transfer paper and see if your design is successfully transferring. As soon as you begin the pattern transfer process, look to see whether your design is showing on the project. If not, check to be sure you have the correct side of the transfer medium facing down. I know this sounds simple enough in practice, but I can assure you I have been known to trace an entire pattern then lifted off my transfer and tracing papers, and—guess what? My tracing paper but not my project sported a blue outline. So take a peek early on in the transfer process, and it may save you some time and frustration.

Antiquing Effects. I'm not much of a fan of "antiquing," particularly the darker values. After I've deliberately chosen soft pastels or vibrant primary colors, I don't see any reason to muddy things up unless I've got something to hide. Certainly it depends on the colors you've chosen to paint your project and on the finished look you de-

---

Handy Hint

Instead of using an acrylic paint labeled transparent, try a ready-to-use transparent wash such as Heavenly Hues by DecoArt. This is an acrylic product that can be applied over basecoats to create an added layer of color and impart depth to a plain solid background. Brush it on top of your thoroughly dried basecoat, then lightly wipe off any excess to create highlights where desired, or you may achieve a mottled effect by distressing with crumpled paper or plastic wrap.

sire. Some decorative painters specializing in primitive looks utilize various antiquing methods to add an old-world warmth and authenticity to their works. I've seen some beautifully antiqued decorative paintings that looked as though they survived colonial times, complete with the effect of burn marks from a stone hearth. To antique or not to antique is a matter of personal choice. Experiment and see whether you like the results.

You may purchase a product in craft stores or from specialty catalogs called "Folk Art Mud," an antiquing glaze that works on wood, metal, and other surfaces. The result imparts a well-aged look. You may also make your own antique-finishing medium with a technique known as "mudding." Briefly, the original process called for mixing burnt umber or other dark oil pigment into a glazing medium. Then once the mud was applied it was ragged (wiped down) with linseed oil and took at least 24 hours to dry, depending on the humidity. Even if I were willing to undertake the process, how and where would I safely store and dispose of oily rags? It's not difficult but does take a bit of time (and I'm too busy already!). Yet I like having this knowledge even if I'm not going to use it. As we've learned, one joy of decorative painting is the flexibility we have in choosing our own interpretations. Through the learning process, we each develop individual signature styles.

Transferring Without Tears

If you check while tracing your pattern and find it's not showing up on your project, verify whether:

- You have the right side of the transfer medium face down against your project.

- Your transfer medium is not old and faded from overuse or dry and brittle from storage.

When transferring your pattern, particularly to wood pieces, *never* press down firmly with your stylus, pen, or pencil. It is all too easy to make indentations or depressions in your project, especially with pine or other softwoods. Unwanted lines from most transfer papers can be removed one way or another, or (as a last resort) can be painted over or inked over. But if you make indentations on your wood, you're stuck with them. About the only way to save the piece is to sand it down completely and start over.

Thanks to today's technology, the modern decorative painter can achieve the effects of old-world antiquing in mere minutes, with easy cleanup. Once your project is painted and dry, apply a small amount of a dark acrylic color of choice to a clean dry rag and wipe down the entire surface. Turn the rag and continue wiping off as much color as desired, leaving darker shadows around the edge of the design or the outer portion of the project background.

Another method is to use the gel-based stains in one of the available wood tones. Apply a thin coat with a brush and wipe down with a soft cloth before stain dries. Allow more stain to settle into any cracks or imperfections to enhance the authentic antique look.

If you wish to achieve a colored patina or tinted antiquing with a particular hue rather than a mud look or a wood tone, apply a transparent wash acrylic such as Heavenly Hues by DecoArt. Just brush on straight from the bottle and wipe off any excess with a damp sponge or rag until you get the effect you want. Again, allow a little excess paint to remain in crevices or cracks in the wood.

Crackling Effects. It's easy to achieve a cracked or weathered wood effect with an acrylic crackling medium. This is a wonderful look for birdhouse roofs, mailboxes, wood candle sconces, plaques, and more. The product works on any surface that will hold acrylic paint, and it takes three simple steps.

1. Basecoat the project with the acrylic paint of your choice and allow to dry.

Handy Hint

- When using crackling mediums, do not use metallic acrylics as a top coat. However, they present an elegant effect when used as a basecoat (for example, a metallic gold basecoat with a flat black top coat).

- When you apply your top coat, the heavier or thicker it is, the larger the cracks.

(continued next page)

2. Brush on one coat of crackling medium and let dry. This will take 30 minutes to an hour.

3. Apply a top coat of acrylic in a contrasting or complementary color to your basecoat, then just watch the magic.

Final Finishing Techniques. Varnishing is the method of choice to finish most painted surfaces including wood, terra cotta, and metal. I have even varnished over designs painted on candles. Most importantly, varnishing protects your work from the effects of handling, displaying, and weather exposure. It also brings life to your projects. The colors seem to come forward, literally standing out from the flat surface and every detail appears intensified. Varnishing really adds a spark to projects.

Oil-based varnishes are available for use with oil painting mediums and wood stains. They are so slow to dry that two or three applications may take days. Cleanup requires mineral spirits. Of course, with acrylic paints, you're going to use an acrylic-based varnish, which to me is truly a modern miracle.

Water-based acrylic varnishes are forgiving, simple to use, easy to clean up, and the savings in time is amazing. Several applications of varnish can be applied in a few hours. I've actually applied two or three coats of varnish to painted wood pieces between 8:00 and 10:00 in the morning and by noon had them wrapped for mailing. I've yet to receive any feedback from my friends or customers that they found a sticky mess upon opening up their packages. I recommend first of all labels, especially as a beginner. Then where drying or curing times are concerned, let your own experience be your

Handy Hint

- You can control the direction of the cracks by brushing across the project for horizontal crackling, or by brushing top to bottom for vertical crackling.

- If you like the result of antiquing, rub a dark stain over the dried crackled project, letting the color settle into all the cracks.

- Crackled finishes are not recommended for outside use even if sealed with varnish, as the cracks do compromise the weather resistance of the surface.

guide. Keep in mind that humidity, air flow, and temperature are all factors in drying time, as it is for any acrylic product. Consider how thick is the varnish application as well as the size of the item being finished. Are you laying down a generous flowing amount onto a 2-foot tavern board, or just quickly whisking a final top coat on a 2-inch lapel pin? Your varnished piece might dry in 15 minutes, or it could take an hour. For small painted items and projects that will be displayed only indoors, I like DecoArt's Americana varnishes. They are available in quick-drying matte, satin, or gloss, and are non-yellowing.

As you prepare to finish your project, whether the varnish you've chosen comes in a bottle, jar, or can, do not shake the container! The last thing you want is bubbles in your varnish. They are extremely difficult—read that as impossible—to eliminate. My experience has been that the binders in most acrylic-based varnishes don't separate out even if they've been on the shelf for an extended time. If varnish needs to be mixed, use a craft stick or a paintbrush handle and gently stir, avoiding bubbles. Then let the product sit a few minutes to allow any air to dissipate.

You may use the varnish right from its container. I prefer to pour an amount of varnish onto a wax paper palette or into a small jar lid, depending on the size of my project. I can see immediately if there are bubbles or particles in the product. Dip your 1-inch brush (or any brush of your choice) into the varnish and begin to apply to your project surface. I have used two methods for applying varnish smoothly and evenly. Both work; it's a matter of personal preference and experience. To varnish, either:

■ Begin at the center of the project and work outward, going in one direction with the brush until the entire surface is coated. Quickly brush out any drips or runs.

■ Or begin at one edge of the project and pull the brush across to the other edge, repeating until the project is covered. Again, quickly brush out any drips or runs.

With either method, once the first application has thoroughly dried, you may add a second or even a third coat of varnish, making sure each is dry before applying the next. When brushing out any drips or runs, use a light feathery touch to just whisk across the top of the varnished surface. Don't be alarmed about minor brush marks; they will settle out.

Note: While some artists have told me they use sponge brushes for applying varnishes, I have found they are more prone to introducing tiny bubbles in my finishes. I also feel sponges are nearly impossible to use for smoothing out drips and runs without leaving ridges in my varnish. For those reasons, I prefer to use a synthetic 1-inch brush. You may wish to experiment on practice projects and choose which method works for you.

Focusing on a Great Finish

■ Apply water-based varnish in a generous amount relative to the size of your project.

■ Use a good soft synthetic brush and execute your strokes as quickly as possible, keeping in mind that acrylic-based products dry fast.

■ When your first application is dry, check for any bubbles or particles. This is rare, but if you see anything you can't live with, lightly sand surface with a very fine sanding pad or paper and wipe clean.

■ Apply second and, if desired, third coats of varnish, allowing to dry thoroughly between applications.

If you are varnishing a large flat piece, such as a wood tavern sign or a metal tray, try pouring a little puddle of varnish in the center of the project, then with your brush work it quickly outward to all the edges. This way, you don't get any brush marks, and because the varnishing was done in one application, everything dries uniformly and you are not struggling to hurriedly brush additional varnish into a "wet edge."

Beating the weather—outlasting the elements. The best line of thought is "nothing lasts forever." While some wonderful polyurethanes are available at home improvement centers, as are products labeled marine or spar varnish, over time these may turn yellow and discolor your project. These products are largely oil based so you will need mineral spirits to clean your brushes. Also, the chemical composition in these products likely will not be compatible with your acrylic paints. Though it's tempting to find a cure-all for high humidity and rainy weather, exterior water-based acrylic varnishes will serve you as well or better than trying to mix product lines. Be aware that mixing products can destroy your project. If your basecoat and design is painted in acrylic and then is finished with an incompatible medium, you are wide-open for cracking, flaking, and even melting of your painted design. This can be heartbreaking after all the work you've achieved. If you're painting with acrylic paints, stick with acrylic varnish or other acrylic finishes. A great advantage to water-based acrylic varnishes is they do not yellow with age and so will preserve the clarity and depth of color in your painting. Though oil-based polyurethanes have a reputation for lasting a long time, most yellow with age. Believe it or not, water-based acrylic varnishes can be coaxed into living a long cheerful life even when a painted project is continuously exposed to the weather.

When your outdoor project has been completely sealed, basecoated, and decoratively painted, just apply several coats of exterior water-based varnish to all surfaces, including the back and edges, allowing to dry thoroughly between applications. Then, once a year, use a very fine grit sandpaper or steel wool pad to gently go over the entire project surface. Buffing lightly will help remove any oxidation and discoloration. Wipe clean. Don't be alarmed about a scratchy or cloudy appearance. Fresh varnish will eliminate that. Apply three or more coats of exterior gloss varnish. For a bit of extra protection, apply a coat of automotive wax to your outdoor projects. Just wipe it on over the thoroughly dry varnish and gently buff with a soft cloth.

Preparing metal for painting. Speaking of mailboxes, I painted my first one many years ago while I was still enthused from my beginning painting class. It didn't turn out badly, but wasn't exactly my finest effort because I took no time to prepare the piece. I had no understanding of the importance of proper surface preparation, though I was surely inspired to go public with my newfound painting skills.

When I painted that first mailbox, it had already been on the post for a few years and had seen all kinds of weather. However, once I decided I wanted a painted mailbox, that old black oxidized one looked like a perfect target. I loaded a cookie sheet with several bottles of acrylics, a water basin, my brushes, and headed for the street one July afternoon on a mission to enliven that old black mailbox. I squirted out my paints and proceeded to freehand what was to be a meadow of wildflowers. First, I didn't clean, or prep, the mailbox surface. Second, the temperature was about 100 degrees in the shade so my paints dried almost before they touched the tin. Third, I didn't varnish the design when I was finished. But I had my painted mailbox, and was really proud of my achievement—for about six months, at which point the meadow of wildflowers began to flake off and finally disappeared with the wind.

Preparing and painting on generic metal surfaces is not difficult. Here are the basics steps:

1. Wash piece in hot soapy water.

2. Rinse in a solution of ¼ cup vinegar and one quart of water.

3. Let dry for 24 hours or place in a 200-degree oven for half an hour and let cool.

4. Lightly sand the surface with very fine sandpaper and wipe clean.

5. Spray with flat metal primer or base-coat, if desired, with color of choice.

6. Apply pattern and paint as desired.

7. When paint is dry, varnish with several applications of exterior varnish.

8. Once a year, lightly sand and renew varnish and apply a paste wax if desired.

Handy Hint

DecoArt offers a product called No Prep metal paint, which is especially formulated to be used on metal surfaces. It requires no primer and works for interior and exterior projects. It performs on practically all metal surfaces, including tin, galvanized metal, aluminum, brass, and wrought iron. Sealing and varnishing are not required. The paint is available in 35 colors—and yes, in those wonderful, convenient 2-ounce squeeze bottles.

Practically Painless Prepping and Painting for Sundry Surfaces

Porcelain. Virtually no preparation is needed; just sand very lightly and wipe clean. You do not want porcelain overly smooth or it will lose its tooth and your paint won't adhere. Mist with matte spray. Base-coat, transfer your pattern, paint, and varnish. Note: When painting on porcelain, do not use graphite or carbon as any extra lines are impossible to remove. Use Chacopaper. Apply satin or gloss varnish when painting is dry.

Denim, duck cloth, and fabrics. Most instructions call for pre-washing your items, especially if they will receive a lot of use and frequent laundering. If you pre-wash, do not use fabric softener in the washer or the dryer. For all fabric painting, I like bottled paints manufactured for that purpose including So-Soft by DecoArt; but you can use any fabric paint on the market. If you wish to use regular acrylics, mix them with a fabric or textile medium following the manufacturer's directions. Some paints require heat setting with an iron. For items such as canvas or denim tote bags or aprons, I like to spray my finished design with matte sealer.

Canvas cloth or artist's canvas. Base-coat surface with acrylic paint or gesso and allow to dry. Base-coat both front and back to prevent warping. Transfer the pattern and proceed to paint your design with regular acrylics. Note: A control medium can be mixed with acrylic paints to slow down drying time and to give the illusion of an "oil painting." Follow label directions as too much control medium can cause paint to crack.

Candles. Lightly buff surface to be painted with paper towel. Wipe down with rubbing alcohol. Spray with a matte sealer and let dry. Base-coat background area that is to receive design, using two or three coats of acrylic and allowing paint to dry between applications. Carefully and lightly transfer your design and then paint. Mist with matte sealer and apply varnish of choice over painted portion of design. I am still enjoying candles I painted 5 years ago using this method and they remain beautiful. Caution: Do not place plastic wrap on candles unless you are certain of compatibility; some wraps adhere to varnish and your design will immediately become a puckered piece of plastic rather than classy candle art.

Terra cotta, patio stones, and rocks. Using a stiff brush and soapy water, clean surface thoroughly. Let dry. Spray with several light coats of matte sealer. Transfer design and paint as desired. You may varnish only your painted design, or the total surface with exterior varnish of choice.

> ## Handy Hint
>
> DecoArt offers a candle-painting medium that allows acrylics to easily adhere to candles. Just mix equal parts of medium with acrylic paint. Brush or sponge onto candle surface.

There are specialty paints on the market formulated expressly for stone, concrete, terra cotta, and similar materials. These paints are permanent and weatherproof and were designed for long-lasting endurance, especially when used on outdoor surfaces. DecoArt's line of Patio Paints offers close to 50 colors; the sky is not the limit when it comes to blue.

Glass, ceramic tile, dinnerware. Wash items well, wipe with rubbing alcohol and allow to dry. Carefully transfer pattern or freehand designs. Use paint labeled "gloss acrylic enamel" to paint designs. Though this product cleans up with soap and water, do not use water to thin paints while working. Use a clear medium intended to be compatible with the product line. Follow label recommendations. Allow paints to cure for 24 hours and then oven bake at 325 degrees for 30 minutes. Turn off the oven and let the project cool before removing. Note: For dinnerware, paint only on areas that will not be in contact with foods or beverages.

Basic Brush Strokes

I don't believe in a lot of jargon when it comes to brush strokes, and I feel this part of the learning experience should be neither intimidating nor incomprehensible. Some years ago I attended what was perceived as a prestigious decorative painting seminar. The instructor, prior to any other demonstrations, donned her magnification visor, loaded a brush barely the size of two eyelash hairs and begin to paint with finesse and flourish. I don't know about you, but for me that concept doesn't represent the true joy of decorative painting. I won't even own brushes that small—not that any craft store carries them.

Brushes in Brief

Here's what you need to know to get started with the three basic brushes:

1. Your round brush will be used for strokes such as the daisy petal, left comma, and right comma.

2. Your liner brush will be used for fine detailing as well as lining. This includes some little tendrils and curlicues. And when you feel brave enough to do some pin striping, you'll use the liner for that, too.

3. Your flat brush may be used for daisy petal shapes, for short line strokes, and for "S" strokes, as well as left and right comma strokes. You will also learn to use it for half-circle and "U" strokes, which are wonderful for painting folk art flowers and realistic roses.

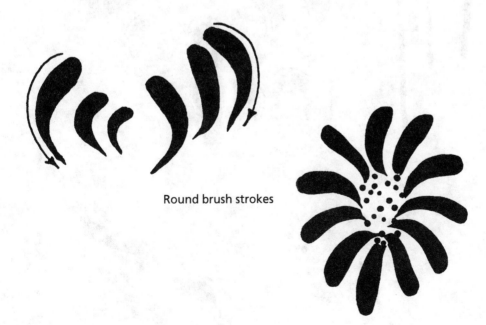

Round brush strokes

Liner brush strokes

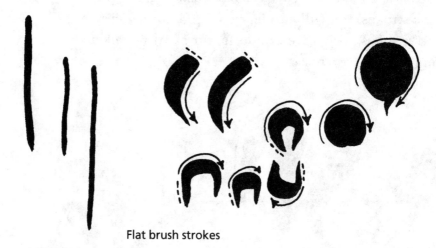

Flat brush strokes

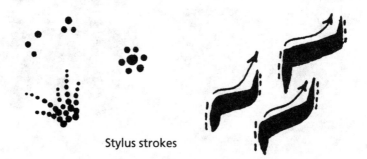

Stylus strokes

Tips for Beginners

Now you are ready to paint like a pro. Just follow these final tips and start painting!

- Study the basic brush stroke figures.

- Make sure you have a good quality brush in hand.

- Thin your paint slightly with water before you begin.

- Load your brush so it's "nice and squishy"—but don't get paint up into the ferrule!

- Practice on a piece of plastic, glass, waxed palette paper, or even tracing paper.

- If you don't like what you see, throw away the paper, wipe the plastic or glass clean, and begin again.

Don't get discouraged. One can eat an elephant the same way one eats a bag of popcorn—one piece at a time. Most mistakes can be easily corrected or hidden, and, if nothing else, they provide an education. Though my first painted mailbox didn't last, I can say with pride I learned how to give the second one longevity.

Creating Your Painting Projects

▼▼

IF YOU'VE LOOKED AT THE BASIC BRUSH strokes and began a little practicing, you have started to make friends with your brushes by now. Certainly practice will increase your comfort and confidence. The expression "practice, practice, practice" might be a cliché; but in reality, practice is one of your most constructive tools for truly enjoying decorative painting.

Years ago when I painted at my washer-and-dryer workspace, there was a wall-mounted phone adjacent to my countertop. I fondly remember from that era two priceless friends, Martha Dover and Betty Hardgrave, who would call me almost daily and talk for hours. I got into the habit of keeping a paintbrush, a tube of paint, and a pad of paper beside the phone. I never missed a word, but also never missed a chance to work on my brush strokes. It was easy to squeeze out a little paint and squeeze in a little practice time.

Whether you have a lot or a little painting experience, it's time to begin choosing projects and exercising the creative spirit—and begin practicing your brush techniques at the same time. Practice doesn't have to be pointless. You can experiment on an actual project as well as on a sheet of plastic or tracing paper—and it's a whole lot more fun because you're actually creating a painted item. If the project doesn't turn out perfect, so what? You're gaining knowledge and developing your own personal style as you go along. But what if you're painting on a piece of wood and suddenly you hate how it looks? You can always sand off the paint and start over; donate the project to the school craft bazaar; or even throw the piece into the garbage can (yes, I've done that a time or two out of sheer frustration!). I already related how I got around what felt like a disaster at the time by gluing a piece of artist's canvas over my goof.

As Claudia Gentry told me, "I believe all problems encountered are a learning experience and you shouldn't fear trying to paint anything. Sometimes having a piece not perfectly painted is very charming and adds character." Claudia admits she may hesitate momentarily over choosing a particular color or design, but she concludes: "The nice thing about painting is if you make a mistake you can always sand, repaint, and start over."

Each time you paint another project, your comfort zone and confidence level will increase. Decorative painting, particularly in the beginning, should not be viewed as an endurance race toward achieving perfect stroke work, contrary to what some teachers tend to tout. Rather it should be a deliberate, joyful journey to self-expression and personal satisfaction. The impeccable stroke work will come later, if you wish that to be your goal. I do have dreams of eventually becoming a Certified Decorative Artist, as recognized by the Society of Decorative Painters (see Resource Guide). I have yet to perfect my stroke work however. To tell you the truth, I'm a lazy painter.

One of my regrets (small, but nonetheless a regret) is that I didn't save more of my beginning pieces when I first started decorative painting. Be sure to save some of your first attempts even if you think they should be hidden in a

Handy Hint

Practice your painting on paper lunch bags, or greeting card stock made from craft or watercolor paper. You not only increase your skills and develop techniques, but also acquire a supply of unique, easily identified lunch bags for your family to use; and you'll enjoy having a stack of personalized cards for mailing to the special people in your life. Note: Mist paper surfaces lightly with spray matte sealer before you apply pattern and paint. Lightly spray again when painting is dry.

box under the bed (which is where I used to keep the few projects I saved). Six months or six years later, you will see exactly how far you have progressed. You will continually say to yourself, "I can't believe I did that."

Deciding on Designs

Perhaps your initial objective is to paint for personal satisfaction (hobby interest, decorating your home, crafting creative gifts) or maybe you're already thinking about selling your projects at boutiques and bazaars. One of your first considerations is choosing an object and then deciding on a design or pattern that will fit the subject. After a little painting experience, many times the light bulb will just come on at the moment you see a particular pattern or a blank wood piece. But in the earlier phases of decorative painting your first question may be, "How do I create or choose a specific design?"

I posed that question to Susan Nelson in Rochester, Minnesota, and she really got to the heart of the matter: "Start out with what you know and are passionate about," Susan responded. "For me it's cats, nature topics, flowers, and gardening." I wasn't surprised at all that Susan's list of passionate subjects began with cats. Her stationery items that advertise her home-based business, Cats 'n Stuff, also include the imaginative and attention-getting message "Home of the Purple Cat."

There are probably as many reasons for choosing specific designs as there are decorative painters. For some, it's a matter of keeping up with current fads and jumping on that bandwagon; or for the trendsetters, it's the challenge of trying to stay one step ahead. When I think about staying one step ahead, I'm reminded of a cute story. Bill and Fred were avid outdoorsmen. One night on a camping trip they had prepared their tent, removed their shoes, and crawled into their sleeping bags. Toward dawn they heard a ferocious growl and woke to see a huge bear heading right for the tent. Bill leapt straight up, grabbed his shoes, stuffed his feet into them and headed for the tent flap. Fred yelled, "Wait a minute, Bill. You can't outrun that bear!" On his way out of the tent, Bill yelled back: "I don't have to outrun that bear, Fred. I only have to outrun you." The moral of the story is that, by outrunning your competition when it comes to innovative designs, you will increase your reputation as an up-and-coming artist. By presenting new designs before others have had a chance to think of a similar concept—and believe me, if you hesitate, they will beat you to it—you can carve out your personal niche in the decorative painting marketplace.

For some involved in the creative field, it's a matter of following their own intuitions, goals, or expressing lifelong ambitions. Claire and Shaun Kelly showcase their products through their business, the Village Craft Gallery in Bullhead City, Arizona. In addition to developing and selling their original works, they are on an enthusiastic mission to promote and elevate decorative art and craft forms to a higher standard. The Kellys, in working up their prototype projects and designs, insist on quality materials and good business practices. But they also rely on their own creative self-expression and strive to lend their personal touch to the items they produce and exhibit. As Claire explained, "Being an artist is all about feelings; and expressing those feelings through designs."

Trendy or Timeless

Following current market trends is one of the easiest ways to stay on top of—or even a step ahead of—popular design elements, specifically new colors and home-decorating themes. Spend an afternoon and browse a couple of big furniture stores. Do the same at a local shopping mall and visit not only the swank fashion shops but also walk through the trendy home accessory boutiques and the candle stores. Take along a few index cards for handy scribbling. Fashion shop displays might be three to six months ahead of the current season. It may barely be Christmas, but if you look past the holiday reds and greens, you'll spot the up-and-coming colors of spring, already Easter-parading in the aisles.

When paint manufacturers introduce a new pastel color line, I can't help but notice I already have clothes and shoes in nearly identical tones. When browsing the furniture stores, do the items and accessories embody mostly muted tones of heather gray or olive green? Did a vignette grab your attention with its arrangement of a denim sofa and a flanking pair of club chairs upholstered in royal blue and school bus yellow? Are lamp bases and clocks trimmed in expensive metals, or do they sport pickled color-washed country style woods? The end-table accessories may offer pastel porcelain figurines, or clusters of crackle-finished birdhouses, resin frogs, and hand-painted terra cotta pots. Not long ago, the home decorating trends spoke in colors of deep forest greens, burgundy wines, and navy blues. Years ago, animal print themes were extremely popular. They never completely disappeared, and they're again making a strong showing in home decor and women's fashions. As I write this, there's a renewed interest in wildlife, rain forests, birds, and gardening. Take your cues from everything that's going on around you.

Remember that a lot of design themes and color schemes run in cycles. Someone said it best in a song: "Everything old is new again." I continually get requests for patio and kitchen accessories painted in jewel tones, such as ruby and sapphire, as well as animal prints and earth tones. I was selling frogs, dragonflies, and ladybug accents as far back as 1978. Twenty years later I'm selling them again, not only as custom home decor items, but also as themes for decorative painting projects, three of which were recently published by national crafting magazines. Suddenly it seems that frogs and ladybugs are new.

In addition to watching home and fashion markets through retail merchandising, magazines and catalogs are wonderful sources of information. With printing deadlines set generally six months in advance of availability to the buying public (for certain seasonal magazines as many as nine months in advance), you can understand how these publications are way ahead of the rest of us in predictions of color trends and themes. Some rainy afternoon fix a cup of tea, pull out your index cards or a notebook, a favorite pen with exquisite ink; and grab a stack of current magazines. In addition to those that concentrate on home improvement and decor, it's great fun to browse the ones that specialize in showing current crafting trends.

Revisit the list of magazines dedicated to decorative painting. Purchase current issues of those magazines to help you stay on top of coming trends. My point here is certainly not to sanction copying designs and projects that legally belong to the original artist (and may get you into trouble for copyright infringement). Rather, it is to encourage decorative painters to develop the habit of truly seeing instead of merely looking. This insight will become indispensable if you turn your decorative painting skills into a business, whether for pin money or for serious profit. And remember when it comes to finding ideas and inspiration, there's always more than one way to skin a cat (sorry, kitty!).

Five Tips for Choosing and Creating Designs

1. Concentrate on subjects about which you are personally passionate, and you'll paint passionately!

2. Research styles and themes that have survived the test of time—classics never go out of style.

3. Observe current and predicted trends, then design your own interpretations of what's hot.

4. Develop and maintain an ongoing inspirational file of pictures, photos, and magazine articles.

5. Jot down ideas as soon as they surface; if you hesitate, they're lost.

To Market, To Market

I don't think I know one decorative or craft painter who sooner or later isn't bitten by the bug to try marketing his or her painted works, original designs, or both. Our reasons range from running out of room in our residences to imagining that a weekend spent working a booth at a bazaar would be wonderful. Perhaps more than one friend or relative, upon seeing or receiving our creations, has commented, "You really ought to sell those." We begin to consider that we could make a few dollars if only to be able to buy more paints, brushes, and wood. Many of us begin to daydream that we can make our living doing something we love. Regardless of which bug it is, sooner or later it will bite you.

Though I've painted for years, I recall periods of time during which I placed this pastime on the shelf. During a few chapters of my life, the topic of decorative painting was edited out of the text. I had a hectic family life and was careening down a career path. My beloved avocation took a vacation. But when I picked up those brushes again, I knew they were home for good. And so I was painting at night after the household was asleep. Occasionally I would rise at 4:00 in the morning and paint for a couple of hours before going to my corporate job. One crisp October morning, on an impulse I packed a basket filled with whimsical Halloween pumpkin lapel pins, cross-eyed ghosts, and green-warted witches and carted them to my office.

Trying to be discreet, I arranged my treasures on the top of the credenza and taped a piece of typing paper on the wall: "What's this? A BOO-tique, of course." I was not aware of consciously trying to determine whether my coworkers would extend only complimentary commentary or would pay for my frivolous fall offerings. They paid, and I sold out. I had in essence successfully tested the waters.

Linda Maretich of Linda's Ewenique Boutique of Crafts, when discussing what appeals to people, commented: "I try to make things that are unique and not just what are considered the in thing. I present items no one else is offering and concentrate on the one-of-a-kind and the humorous." Another key aspect of marketing to friends and customers is to first consider their interests, color scheme, and display space. If Linda feels she doesn't have enough information to develop a requested project or design, she asks questions to get a feel for what her friends and customers might want, need, or just enjoy seeing. She concluded, "Listen to funny things people say and incorporate that." Linda, one of the most spontaneous people I've ever known, also possesses a relentless sense of humor. She has a gift for translating her perspectives on life into her projects. It is obvious her customers readily respond to her interpretations—usually with big smiles and a willingness to open their wallets. When it comes to testing the waters, Linda has done that not only figuratively but literally. She occasionally takes selected items to what she refers to as "show and sell"—offering them to the peer group at her water therapy sessions.

Inspiration and Ideas

Sometimes I can't sleep at night because designs begin to dance in my head. In a state of half-sleep, I think: "What a great project that would be! I'll write it down in the morning." Experience bears out 99 percent of the time that when the dark of night has gone, so has the idea.

Every decorative painter and creative crafter likely possesses a treasure trove of ideas, preserved in some manner. I'm no different. Currently I employ several loose-leaf or three-ring binders for recording my spontaneous ideas. I keep a notebook and pen at my bedside, and I've learned to ignore the temptation to wait and "write it down in the morning." Otherwise, as with a fanatical fisherman, there's always a big one that gets away.

If you haven't started an inspirational journal, notebook, or other type of idea file, do so. It will become invaluable to you as a decorative painter and designer. Keeping and adding to your collection of magazine articles and photographs that appeal to you will not only generate new ideas, but also will serve as a creative jump start when you feel you've hit a brick wall. The urge to paint or design a particular theme is there, but you need something to inspire the brush or the pen. To begin your idea notebook or file, simply start going through magazines and commence cutting and tearing. You don't need to develop your actual filing system just yet. A shoebox or a couple of file folders will get you started. Don't overlook any possible sources for reference materials. Learn to develop an eye for ideas. Once you get into the habit, you'll be amazed at what you see. You might be looking through a home-decorating magazine featuring elegant furniture. Are you seeing only furniture? What about the mixed colors in that huge flower arrangement on the end table? What shades of paints are combined in the room?

Wait a minute. I've got to run to the trashcan and retrieve that full-color catalog packed with close-up photographs of tulips and other flowering bulbs. What did I just say about developing an eye?

Once you have amassed a nice clutter of collected ideas, then you can begin sorting and placing them into labeled file folders, or by gluing related subject groups onto sheets of paper for inserting into a loose-leaf binder. If you want to use an index system to separate categories or topics, set up your own plan, making it as simple or as detailed as you wish. I started by clipping or tearing out ideas from magazine pages and taping or gluing them (a glue stick works great) onto the pages of spiral notebooks. I don't update those particular notebooks these days, but I have preserved them for historical reference. It's great fun to look back and see how far I have traveled on my decorative painting journey. As I progressed in building my idea

Sources for Building Your Inspiration File

- Newspapers and advertisements
- Home-decorating and gardening catalogs
- Painting, crafting, and gardening magazines
- Greeting cards, stationery, and gift wrap
- Photographs—yours and others'

file, I realized I needed the convenience of easily sorting and relocating pages to a specific index or within a seasonal topic. So I replaced the spiral notebook method with standard three-ring binders and use three-hole-punched paper as a base for gluing on tear-outs. Now I can easily retrieve a page or two from the binders to inspire a project and then return the pages when I'm finished. I prefer the loose-leaf binder method, but there are many other options. An idea file, regardless of the system, is one of your creative tools. Each of you will find what works for you.

I've separated my idea binders into only ten generic categories using colored plastic tabs for Easter, Halloween, Christmas, Fall, Winter, Spring, Summer, Gardening, Animals, and Miscellaneous Holidays. When it comes to detail, I'd rather spend time on my painting and not on my filing system, so I thought utilizing a small number of general topics was the ultimate in simplicity. Then I asked a fellow painter, who is also an avid gardener, if she employs some method for saving and referencing creative ideas. She emphatically assured me she did and that she also prefers labeled file folders. When I inquired what some of her categories were, you can imagine my double take at her quite serious response: "Well, there's one for flowers—and then there's one for everything else."

Artist, writer, and designer Pama Collé related: "I collect my ideas in a traditional scrapbook style and maintain them in several three-ring binders. They are filled with pictures clipped from many sources, primarily magazines. I glue-stick the pictures to sheets of colored papers that are inserted into page savers. Index tabs include angels, animals, flowers, scenery, seasonal (other than Christmas, which deserves a separate binder), and vegetables."

Linda Maretich told me she doesn't keep a notebook but instead utilizes a card-file system of three-by-five–inch unlined index cards. Linda uses the cards for sketching designs, listing sources of ideas, and pasting small pictures of items from catalogs and magazines.

She files her cards by groups, topics, and subjects covering more than 30 chosen categories. Linda related, "For me, this is easier than a large notebook. I can just grab a section of cards for the topic I need." A little bird told me Linda's magazine collection is approaching 500 and she currently subscribes to a dozen craft and painting-related publications. No wonder her well of inspiration never runs dry!

Now that you've recovered from the statistics of Linda's idea archive, meet Johnnie Elma Anderson of Midland, Texas. Johnnie is a decorative painter, crafter, and talented essayist who possesses her own particular approach to the search for ideas. Recently I asked Johnnie if she had any favorite magazines for fostering creativity. "No, I don't refer to any particular books or magazines," she answered. "I do what my imagination dictates and I alone decide the outcome of my projects."

Claudia Gentry told me the contents in her idea notebook come from many sources. Like most decorative and craft painters, she tears pictures of favorite items and project sheets from magazines. "I also have a cork bulletin board at my art table and I post cutouts of painted items I like," said Claudia. She expressed her delight in browsing specialty catalogs that showcase expensive hand-painted furniture featuring appealing color schemes and detailed designs. These types of catalogs offer a different perspective, particularly for the decorative painter interested in furniture makeovers. Incidentally, painted furniture is very popular and this trend affords the decorative painter a money-making opportunity. Even the most depressing plant stand or spice rack will respond to a little sandpaper, a good primer, and a basecoat. Add a few brush strokes, and in minutes you have a magical and likely marketable transformation. You may well decide your creative niche will be furniture makeover, ultimately going into business for yourself, perhaps working with interior designers or displaying your painted furniture in home decor specialty shops, and even taking custom orders.

That aside, you have literally at your fingertips the reward of creating heirlooms for others or, perhaps most rewarding, for your own home. Claudia summed it up nicely when she said, "Learning some basic painting skills allows you the creative ability to adapt ideas to suit your own style. That brings you a lot of personal satisfaction and at the same time enables the benefit of not paying hefty prices for uniquely painted objects."

Doodle Diaries and Joyful Journals

My loose-leaf binders of ideas are always at my fingertips and have become invaluable sources of inspiration when I've drawn a blank. I consider them my painting tools along with my paints and brushes. While cleaning a closet (yes, I really did), I came across another tool I had completely forgotten. It's a sketchbook from seven or eight years ago, filled with pencil doodles and line drawings of projects that never made it past the sketchbook page (so far). In addition were quotes that I love—silly sayings and notes to myself written in colored inks. One page is filled with an ink sketch of my 30-year-old dining-room table, hurriedly set for an unplanned after-work Halloween dinner party. Notes about the festive decorations and the list of attending guests appear in the margins along with pencil images of the table centerpiece and the ghosts that haunted the chair rails. Discovering that sketchbook was like reuniting with a familiar friend. A greater surprise was the realization that the contents emerged during a time in my life when I had thought I was too busy with my career to

Jump Start Those Creative Juices!

- Keep a "gratitude attitude journal," and make at least one entry every day.
- Pull out one of your idea notebooks or file folders and just browse.
- Go feed the birds.
- Make a cake from scratch.
- Write a letter to your mother and your grandmother, if you are still so blessed to have them.
- Pour a glass of champagne.
- Drive to your local card shop or gift store and just wander around.
- Retrieve that box of chocolate-covered cherries you weren't going to eat.
- Listen to classical music.
- Call a fellow painter and talk shop.
- Take a nap.

(continued next page)

paint. Each entry had been signed and dated. The creative spirit had not been absent after all; it was just waiting to be called on.

While doing research and asking questions on subject matter for this book, I found exactly what I had expected concerning the topic of inspiration. In addition to an idea file built from many sources, practically every decorative painter relies on personal sketchbooks and journals. Susan Nelson of Cats 'n Stuff told me, "I maintain several notebooks of project sketches. Primarily filled with drawings, these logs also include handwritten entries about ideas to improve my products, the discovery of a new or more efficient technique, ideas for advertising, and notes to myself."

Just a few paragraphs earlier, I mentioned painter and essayist Johnnie Elma Anderson of Midland, Texas. Johnnie keeps what she refers to as a "Gratitude Attitude journal," and her goal is to list at least five things on a daily basis for which she is grateful. In a recent letter, Johnnie expressed that her journal helps her maintain a balance in her personal life and certainly it serves as a creative tool to encourage her self-expression and provide inspiration. She wrote, "When I come up empty, whether it's to do with a painting project or with life, my journal entries are a reminder my temporary roadblocks are little pebbles and not huge boulders."

Claire Kelly, who with husband Shaun operates the Village Craft Gallery in Bullhead City, Arizona, expressed that her most essential tools are pen and paper. "I get up every morning and make notes in my journal," says Claire. "Writing gets my creative juices flowing."

Jump Start Those Creative Juices!

- Browse through your doodle diary and remind yourself of your own creativity.
- Take the camera out to your flowerbed.
- Light a scented candle and place it on your painting table (unless you're using a medium that's flammable, in which case you know better!).
- Remember something funny from your childhood.
- Quit procrastinating and start doing the laundry instead (did I say that?).
- Paint a silly project—freehand a green frog on a patio stone and place it in the garden.
- Express your creativity through a different avenue, such as embroidery or cross-stitching.

Let the Fun Begin!

Speaking of creativity, it's about time to head for the painting table. The soon-to-follow sampling of projects will inspire you, and I hope will make you smile. You can see full-color photos of the finished projects in the center of the book. Before we begin, take just a moment to review these basic steps to help insure your success.

1. Lightly sand wood if desired or if surface is rough.
2. Wipe dust with damp towel and let dry.
3. Basecoat or stain wood with color of choice or as project instructions indicate.
4. If wood grain raises after basecoating, you may wish to lightly sand again and wipe clean. An additional basecoat may (or may not) be needed after this sanding.
5. Transfer your pattern to the dry base-coated surface.
6. Paint your design as desired or as project instructions suggest.
7. Add lettering, dip-dot accents, or spattering if using these techniques on your project.
8. If using a marking pen, spray project with matte sealer and let dry. Then varnish if desired or according to project instructions, using two or more coats, allowing each coat to dry thoroughly between applications.

I have purposely taken a different slant with the instructions for each of the following projects. As you begin to collect books and magazines dedicated to decorative painting, you will be exposed to a variety of editorial modes. This is my opportunity to introduce you to examples of different instruction formats that you will recognize as you browse through the many popular painting magazines. You'll find particular publications give project instructions that are very basic and easy to follow. Others may make you wonder, especially as a beginning painter: "What am I doing here?" Don't worry. The feeling of being overwhelmed will pass. In my early days of acquiring publications and beginning my search for projects to paint, I hesitated over many because the format of the printed instructions intimidated me. It never occurred to me back then that with a little extra concentration, I could have executed nearly any project. All I had to do was read.

Years later when I began to submit designs and written instructions for publication (yet another avenue you may wish to pursue), it was not difficult to conform to various editorial preferences. Through exposure and execution, I had slowly but surely received an education.

Review List of Basic Supplies

Following is a list of basic supplies you'll need for most basic projects.

- Acrylic paints as listed in instructions or your choice
- Paintbrushes
- Old toothbrush or spatter tool (optional)
- Spray matte sealer
- Sandpaper or sanding pad
- Water container for rinsing brushes
- Paper towels
- Paint palette (paper plate, meat tray)
- Stylus or ballpoint pen
- Tracing paper
- Transfer paper
- Varnish, water base

Handy Hint

When choosing a painting project, read through the entire materials list and instructions before beginning. Doing so will familiarize you with the complexity or simplicity of the project. It will provide you an opportunity to recognize any unfamiliar terms or techniques you may not feel prepared to attempt just yet. Also, by reading through the article in advance of starting the project, you can determine whether you have the required supplies on hand.

Let's Paint!

We'll start with something easy to achieve that lends itself to your own creative spirit. There are absolutely no rules with this one and, depending on how much detail you want to add or how many little embellishments (wreaths, brass charms, etc.) you wish to glue on, you can have a basic Santa in about 30 to 40 minutes.

Stir Up a Santa— Quick with a Paint Mixing Stick

Project 1

This project is super easy and the wood is free! It's perfect for the beginning painter but every skill level will enjoy it because it brings a smile. This stick Santa can be painted many ways. I always do some in traditional red but also make them up in green, blue, and tan. You may glue on brass charms, tiny jingle bells, dried foliage, or other embellishments. Include a name or a message for personalization. Paint up a batch and take them to the school craft bazaar or to the office and watch them disappear. If desired add a date and your signature with a black or white permanent pen; or add TO and FROM as appropriate for Christmas package tie-ons. The special recipients will enjoy their unique Santa keepsakes.

Stir Up a Santa

Materials

- Wood paint-stirring stick, free from home improvement center
- Paint brushes:
    1-inch wash (utility)
    #8 or #10 flat
    liner brush
- Old toothbrush (optional)
- Black permanent marking pen (optional)
- Sandpaper (optional)

Paints

- Red (any shade will do)
- Flesh color
- White
- Black (optional, if using marking pen instead)
- Matte spray sealer
- Varnish (optional)

Handy Hint

In addition to using plain white acrylic paint for Santa's beard and hair, daub on a bit of white textured paste, such as Sno-Tex Texturizing Medium from DecoArt. Apply it over the white beard and hair areas. It's an easy way to add a fun embellishment to your Santa, Christmas, and winter projects.

Instructions

1. No preparation is necessary, unless you wish to sand the stir stick before painting. If you choose to lightly sand, wipe clean and let dry before applying paint.
2. Using your one-inch brush, base-coat the stir stick with two or three coats of red, allowing to dry between applications.
3. When red paint is thoroughly dry, with flesh color and the #8 or #10 flat brush, paint a circle or oval in the top one-third area of the stir stick. It will take two or three applications to cover.
4. Using liner brush and black paint (or permanent marking pen) add dot eyes and nose within the flesh color oval. Let dry.

5. Using your #8 or #10 flat brush and white, paint Santa's hair and beard area.

6. With white paint and the liner brush, make little eyebrows and a mustache.

7. Thin a bit of white paint and using old toothbrush, give Santa a spattering of snow.

8. If desired, personalize with name or date. Lightly spray with matte sealer to protect pen work.

   Optional: You may varnish if you choose. Note that once varnish has been applied, it will be difficult to add any personalization later.

2 Classroom Angel

This classroom angel project is just darling. What teacher or other school employee wouldn't love to receive this as an end-of-school-year gift or as a Christmas present? The project is for an intermediate level painter; but I think a beginner could manage it by leaving out a bit of the detail. Since this design incorporates several small pieces, plan on spending at least a couple of hours on this project, depending on your paints' drying times. The time invested also hinges on how much detail you wish to add. The project's instructions were written for the intermediate painter in mind, and are representative of the article structure you may find in painting magazine how-to articles.

Wood Items

- Angel (1), 4½-inch by 3½-inch or your choice from craft store or catalog
- Apples (3), 1-inch from craft store or catalog
- Star (1), ¾-inch from craft store or catalog

Handy Hint

I paint up several Santas at once and leave them unvarnished. When the need arises for a personalized gift, ornament, or party favor, I quickly add names, dates, or other lettering with a permanent pen and then finish them with varnish. Since acrylic water-base products dry in a wink, I can varnish Santa and tie him to a gift package before he has a chance to blink.

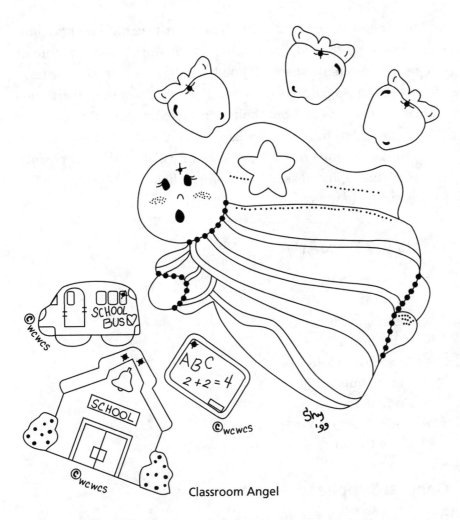

Classroom Angel

- School bus (1), 1½-inch by 1-inch laser cut wood design (or other)

- Schoolhouse (1), 2¼-inch by 2-inch laser cut wood design (or other)

- Slate or chalkboard (1), 1-inch by ¾-inch laser wood design (or other)

- Craft wire of choice, 24-inch length

Sample project features laser cutouts from West Coast Wood Craft Supplies. These particular laser designs are copyright items and may be ordered from WCWCS for your use; but you may purchase similarly shaped blank cutouts at any crafts supply store or cut your own generic shapes if you have the tools. Many intermediate and advanced painters own scroll saws and cut their own wood from basic patterns or from their own sketches. Note that this project design in its entirety is not copyrighted; you may use it for fun and profit. (Author's note: WCWCS has furnished written permission to photograph and sketch this project in its entirety for publication as author desires.)

Paints (by DecoArt)

- Primary Red
- Lamp Black
- Primary Yellow
- Titanium White
- Emperor's Gold
- Flesh Tone
- French Vanilla
- Light French Blue
- Kelly Green

General Supplies

Paint brushes in #4 flat, #10/0 liner, ½-inch flat wash; stylus; wood sealer; fine grit sandpaper; paper towels; disposable palette; water basin; thick craft glue; water-based varnish; wire cutters; small nail and hammer or hand drill with small bit; tracing paper; transfer paper.

Instructions

1. *Prepare Surfaces.* Lightly sand with fine grit sandpaper and wipe clean with damp paper towels. With small nail and hammer or drill, place holes in pieces. Transfer basic pattern lines as desired using transfer paper and stylus.

2. *Paint the accessories, starting with the school.* With Primary Red, Kelly Green, and Lamp Black, paint school, bushes, and roof and bell tower as shown in photo insert. Paint the doors with Titanium White, adding Primary Yellow trim around doors and Lamp Black door handles. Using Emperor's Gold, paint the bell. Use stylus and Titanium White to add dots to the bushes at each side of schoolhouse. With liner and thinned Lamp Black, add sign lettering.

> *Paint the bus.* With Primary Yellow, Titanium White, and Lamp Black, paint bus. Refer to photo. Use Primary Red and Titanium White for bus tail- and headlights. With liner and thinned Lamp Black, add lettering to bus.
>
> *Paint the chalkboard.* With Primary Red, outline chalkboard. Use thinned Lamp Black and fill in chalkboard; let dry. Using liner and Titanium White, add lettering.
>
> *Paint apples and star.* With Primary Red and Kelly Green, paint apples. Paint star with Emperor's Gold (two coats recommended). When apples are dry, use stylus to pull highlights with dots of Titanium White. Refer to photo or pattern.
>
> *Paint the angel.* Basecoat angel's dress with Light French Blue using ½-inch wash brush. Basecoat wing area with French Vanilla. Paint face, hand, and feet areas with Flesh Tone. Let dry.
>
> Using French Vanilla and liner brush, apply stripes to angel's dress. With stylus and French Vanilla, apply dots at wrist, neck, and hem of angel's dress. Refer to photo. Let dry. Thin Titanium White and, with #4 flat brush, apply streaking to angel's dress and wing. Optional: highlight feet, hand, and face. With liner and Lamp Black, add eye and mouth detail. Using #4 flat brush and small amount of Primary Red, float or smudge indication of cheeks and nose. With stylus and Titanium White, add highlights to eyes.

3. *Finishing*. Glue gold star to angel's wing. Varnish all pieces with two coats of gloss varnish, allowing to dry between applications. When project is completely dry, thread wire through holes, arranging wood pieces as desired.

 ## Lots 'n Lots of Terra Cotta Pots

Pots are hot! Terra cotta pots never seem to lose popularity because they can be used as more than just simple plant holders. Terra cotta pots are classics, the necessary materials are readily available, and they are terrifically inexpensive to make. If you make a boo-boo, you haven't ruined a $12 piece of wood so there's less about which to feel nervous. If you don't like your painting results, sand off the paint (or not), apply a fresh basecoat, and start over. Terra cotta pots, like brown paper bags, make great no-stress practice surfaces.

This project includes coordinating pieces that look great in a kitchen, sunroom, or on the patio. The three small pots look very nice on a windowsill and are wonderful when planted with herbs or small ivies. The large pot works well sitting in the corner of a countertop, with a large green plant. It can also be used as a utensil holder for all your cooking spatulas and spoons rather than one of those ugly plastic containers from the discount store. Instructions are written for the upper-level beginner through intermediate, but all skill levels can enjoy painting their versions of these designs. Plan on three to four hours for the three small pots and at least a couple of hours for the large one. Note that the large pot design is a little more realistic and therefore slightly more difficult to paint.

Surface Material

- Terra cotta pots, 4-inch size (3) and 6-inch size (1) with saucers in complimentary sizes

Lots 'n Lots of Terra Cotta Pots

Paints and Varnish

■ **Acrylic paints by DecoArt:**

Light Buttermilk
Lemon Yellow
Yellow Ochre
True Red
Burgundy Wine

Hauser Medium Green

Hauser Light Green

Deep Teal

Orchid

Dioxazine Purple

Burnt Sienna

- Satin or Gloss Varnish

Brushes

- #12 flat
- #6 or #8 flat
- #10/0 liner
- 1-inch wash or glaze

Other Supplies

- Sandpaper (optional)
- Paper towels
- Palette surface of choice
- Water basin
- Tracing paper
- Transfer paper
- Compressed sponge, 1-inch square, or piece of kitchen sponge cut to 1-inch square
- Masking tape or painter's tape, ¾ inch to 1 inch wide
- Stylus
- Black or Green permanent markers (optional)
- Krylon spray matte sealer

Instructions

1. Surface preparation. Terra cotta generally requires no prep, which is a time-saver. If the pots are dusty, give them a wipe down with a damp rag. If there are

Handy Hint

- Terra cotta pots, once basecoated and sealed or varnished, make great surfaces to apply decals and rub-on transfers. These products are easy to use and provide a hand-painted appearance without taking the time to hand-paint.

- Try basecoating the pots in your favorite color combinations and applying a stencil technique in the design of your choice. Stencils come in all themes. You can use your regular acrylics (use paint sparingly) or purchase stencil paints. The colors are delicious, creamy, and easy to use.

(continued next page)

rough edges, you should lightly sand them down and then wipe them clean. If pots are obviously dirty, wash in hot soapy water, rinse, and allow to thoroughly dry, which could take overnight as terra cotta is a porous surface and absorbs moisture. When pots are dry, basecoat pots and saucers per the following instructions.

2. With 1-inch wash brush and Light Buttermilk, basecoat the center sections of all four pots and also the interior portion of ONLY the large pot saucer. Two or three coats are recommended. Allow paint to dry between applications.

3. Using masking tape or painter's tape, mask off a 1-inch stripe around the *center* portion of the rim of the large pot, wrapping tape securely around the rim. Refer to photo or pattern outline. Using a smaller flat brush (#8 or #12) for better brush control, basecoat the top rim of the large pot, working along the top and bottom edges of the masking tape with Hauser Medium Green. Set aside to dry and remove tape. You will have a band of the natural terra cotta in the center of the pot rim. Paint the exterior of the large pot's saucer with Hauser Medium Green. Set aside to dry.

4. On one of the small pots, paint the pot rim and exterior of its saucer with Hauser Medium Green and allow to dry. Leave interior portion of saucer unpainted. For the second small pot and its saucer, basecoat the pot rim and exterior of the saucer with Yellow Ochre. Leave interior of saucer unpainted. Set aside to dry. Using Dioxazine Purple, for the third small pot, basecoat the pot rim

Handy Hint

- When painting terra cotta pots, don't worry about blending perfectly. Remember that decorative painting is all about the personal touch, whether your result is fine art or folk art.

- If you absolutely hate what you've done and don't want to fix it, break up the pot (wear safety glasses) and use the shards in other pots for drainage. Or break the pot in half lengthwise, and place it, broken side down, in a flowerbed so it resembles a little tunnel. Letter a small sign: TOADS WELCOME and place it beside your disappointing pot. Everyone will think you're a genius and that you planned the whole thing.

and exterior of the saucer. Leave interior portion of saucer unpainted. Set aside to dry.

5. Trace your fruit patterns onto tracing paper and then, using your stylus and transfer paper, place the fruit patterns to the center portions of each pot as follows: Transfer the plum pattern onto the Dioxazine Purple accented pot. Transfer the pear pattern onto the Hauser Medium Green accented pot. Transfer the small apple pattern onto the Yellow Ochre accented pot. Finally, transfer the larger apple pattern onto the Hauser Medium Green accented large pot.

6. To paint the Dioxazine Purple small pot PLUM design, use the #6 or #8 flat brush and basecoat leaf designs with Hauser Light Green. Pick up Deep Teal on the same brush and over-stroke some portions of the leaves. Then with the liner brush, place veins and tendrils as desired. Refer to photo and pattern. Using #12 flat brush, basecoat the plum with Orchid, applying less paint to the front-most portion of the plum so that the Light Buttermilk background shows through. If necessary wipe your brush and blend out more of the Orchid. Using Dioxazine Purple on the same brush, darken the background portion of the plum using long curved strokes to follow the pattern. Add an extra stroke of Dioxazine to the "seam" side of the plum. Set pot aside to dry thoroughly.

7. To paint the Yellow Ochre small pot APPLE design, with #6 or #8 flat brush, stroke in apple leaves with Hauser Light Green. Use small amounts of paint or dilute paint with a touch of water—you want the Light Buttermilk background to show through to act as your highlights. With liner brush and Hauser Medium Green, stroke in leaf veins. Then with Teal and liner, apply tendrils as desired. Refer to photo or

Handy Hint

If you aren't comfortable yet with using a liner brush for tendrils or other little details, substitute a permanent marking pen for portions of the design. Just make sure you spray the areas with matte sealer before you apply a brush-on varnish. Even if a marking pen is labeled "permanent," most marking pen inks will smear when subjected to brush-on varnishes.

pattern. Using #12 flat brush and Burnt Sienna diluted with water, stroke in a baseline behind and under apple shape. Allow to dry. Then with #12 flat brush and Primary Yellow, basecoat the center portion of the apple. While paint is wet, wipe brush and immediately pick up True Red and begin to over-stroke the yellow area, applying less red in the center of the apple. Don't worry at this point if it looks more like a beach ball and less like an apple. Clean brush thoroughly and re-load with True Red. Stroke a "smile line" across the top one-third portion of the apple. Refer to pattern. Load brush with a little Burgundy Wine and stroke downward from the "smile line" with long "c" strokes at both sides of the apple to add a little depth. If you've lost your yellow center above the "smile line", just dab in a bit of Primary Yellow and stroke outward to define what will be the stem area. Using liner and Burnt Sienna, outline stem of apple and, while paint is wet, dip brush into Light Buttermilk and over-paint center and top of stem. With stylus and Burnt Sienna or Teal, add little dots to apple. Set aside to dry.

8. To paint the Hauser Medium Green small pot PEAR design, basecoat pear shape with Lemon Yellow and #12 flat brush. Allow Light Buttermilk background to show through, especially in the center of the fruit. Wipe brush clean and pick up Yellow Ochre. Using long 'c' strokes, darken outer edges of pear. Refer to photo. With liner brush and Burnt Sienna, outline stem and make little strokes at bottom of pear. Pick up a small amount of Light Buttermilk and highlight stem. Then with liner and Teal, apply tendrils on both sides of stem area. Using stylus and Burnt Sienna, apply little dots at edges of pear. Set aside to dry.

9. To paint the Hauser Medium Green large pot APPLE design, dip the 1-inch piece of sponge into True Red and sponge the trim design around the top rim of the pot. You can measure

▼▼▼▼▼▼▼▼▼▼▼▼▼▼▼▼▼▼

Handy Hint

Even though terra cotta
pots have been sealed
and varnished, it is
recommended, if using
live plants in these
pots, that a plastic liner
be inserted into the
pots and saucers first.
Plastic liners are
available for pennies
at home centers and
garden shops along
with the pots. This
simple step will protect
and preserve your
dedicated work for a
generation to come.
Wouldn't it be wonder-
ful if someday a grand-
daughter or a favorite
niece placed your spe-
cially painted pots on
her own windowsill—
just as you did on
yours today?

▲▲▲▲▲▲▲▲▲▲▲▲▲▲▲▲▲▲

increments with a cloth measuring tape and make
little pencil dots for sponge placement—or "just do
it"! Allow the painted trim to dry. As with the small
pot, pick up Primary Yellow on the #12 flat brush
and basecoat in a large portion of the center of
the apple, applying less paint to the center so that
the Light Buttermilk background shows through.
Wipe brush clean and pick up True Red and apply
a "smile line" across upper one-third of the apple.
Then wipe brush slightly and begin to pull down
'c' strokes on each side of apple. Clean brush and
pick up Burgundy Wine and repeat the steps of the
"smile line" and pulling down 'c' strokes. If you've
lost your yellow center in the stem area (refer to
photo) stroke in more Primary Yellow and blend
outward from the stem area. With liner brush and
Burnt Sienna outline stem and make tendrils (or
use a permanent marker). With small flat brush
(#6 or #8) and small amount of Buttermilk, blend
out or highlight stem area. Using a #6 or #8 flat
brush and Hauser Light Green, base in leaves.
Using Teal and liner, apply leaf veins.

10. Finishing. Spray all surfaces inside and out with
    Krylon spray matte sealer. Allow to dry. Using
    1-inch wash brush and satin or gloss varnish of
    choice, apply two or three coats inside and outside,
    allowing to dry between applications.

A Cozy Nest—A Country Home

My sweet grandmother, Muriel Clutter Colle, always had a flock of
chickens and a henhouse. When I was a young girl, sometimes I was

bestowed the dubious honor of going to the henhouse to gather fresh eggs. Usually the hens would be out scratching in the chicken yard so it was easy to tip-toe up and snatch the eggs from their straw-lined wooden boxes. One particular day I encountered what is referred to as a "setting hen." Indeed, in my child's eyes that was one huge hen; and there she sat, waiting for me to dare come a step closer. My grandma came to my rescue, bravely retrieving the booty from under the old biddy. Grandma, this one's for you.

The Cozy Nest project is for the more advanced painter. It incorporates some of the techniques discussed in earlier chapters, such as using a wood-tone acrylic gel stain and rubbing out some of the gel to get a highlighted effect in the center of the tavern sign. Additionally, the instructions for this project were written in a more advanced format to serve as an example of the article structure you may find in publications dedicated to the intermediate to more advanced decorative painter.

Paints (DecoArt Americana Acrylics)

- Oak Gel Stain
- Cadmium Yellow
- Williamsburg Blue
- Antique Gold
- Buttermilk
- Dark Chocolate
- Titanium (Snow) White
- Cranberry Wine
- Brilliant Red
- Lamp (Ebony) Black
- Ice Blue
- Avocado

Brushes

- Langnickel Script Liner 2050, #10/0
- Langnickel Shader Series 2010, #2, 4, 6, 10
- Langnickel Wash Series 2075, 1-inch

Note: Certainly you may use your choice of brushes.
I used these particular ones to paint my project.

A Cozy Nest—A Country Home

Supplies

- Saral or Chacopaper white transfer paper
- Stylus
- Small piece of sponge
- Sandpaper
- Tack cloth or damp towel
- Sawtooth hanger and small nails
- Satin varnish or matte finish of choice

Surface

- 20-inch by 12-inch Wooden Tavern Sign by Walnut Hollow

Preparation

- Lightly sand and tack board. The designer elected not to seal the wood, as a slight roughness adds to the "country look." Stain the interior portion of the board with Oak Gel Stain, rubbing off excess in the centermost portion so it is a bit lighter than the rest of the board. Paint the boards "end caps" with 1-inch wash brush using Williamsburg Blue (two coats). Transfer pattern using white Saral or Chacopaper and stylus.

Painting Instructions

Basecoat Hen

Make a wash of Buttermilk and basecoat in the entire shape of the hen using 1-inch wash brush. Allow some of the oak background to show through.

Nest

Alternating #2 shader and #10/0 liner brushes, "build" the nest with strokes of Antique Gold, Cad Yellow, Dark Chocolate, and Buttermilk.

Hen's Wattle and Comb

With #6 shader, basecoat comb and wattle with Brilliant Red, using two or three coats to cover. Using Cranberry Wine, shade the comb and wattle (see pattern).

Hen's Beak

Basecoat beak with one coat of Antique Gold using #4 shader. Let dry, and apply two coats of Cad Yellow, allowing to dry between applications. With liner and Cranberry Wine, draw the line that separates upper and lower beak. If desired, shade beak with a little Cranberry Wine.

Hen's Feathers

With 1-inch wash brush and Titanium White, lightly stroke from top of head to where detailed feathers begin at base of hen's neck. Keep the strokes curved and unbroken, following the shape of the neck.

Using #10 shader and Titanium White, stroke feathers at wing area and across lower body where hen sits on nest, "overlapping" next grasses just a bit here and there.

Continue with Titanium White and #6 shader and stroke feathers above the wing placement and across lower portion of hen's breast. With a #4 shader, finish the feathers upward to the wattle and base of the neck.

Using #10/0 liner and Titanium White, draw tail feather/quill placement. With either your liner or chisel edge of #4 shader, stroke in all the feather lines upward with diagonal strokes. Make these very random on each side of the quill, sticking out at different lengths at the points where they end.

Hen's Eye and Beak Highlight

Outline the hen's eye with Lamp Black and #10/0 liner. Basecoat the eye with Titanium White; outline the iris with

Lamp Black and paint it Cad Yellow. Paint the pupil Lamp Black. Add a tiny highlight on the iris with Titanium White; also at this time highlight beak with Titanium White.

Chicken Wire

Paint the chicken wire with the #10/0 liner and thinned Ice Blue. Highlight with Titanium White and shade other areas around chicken wire using a bit of Williamsburg Blue.

Sign Lettering

With #4 or #6 shader and Buttermilk, basecoat in lettering (two coats). When dry, highlight letters randomly with Titanium White.

Double load #2 shader with Cranberry Wine and Buttermilk and add small stroke flowers, forming the petals in a circle with tiny "C" strokes. Add the diamond-shaped detail to the letters "C" and "H" with Cranberry Wine. Using #10/0 liner and Avocado, add tiny leaves and vines. Then highlight vines and leaves with touches of Cad Yellow. Use a small piece of sponge and/or tip of stylus to add filler flowers as desired. Cranberry Wine dots may be added to lettering with stylus as an extra touch.

Finishing

- Finish project with two or three coats of Satin Varnish, using 1-inch wash brush, allowing to dry thoroughly between applications. If desired, you may use a matte or satin spray varnish. Add sawtooth hanger to back of project.

Tips

- Don't apply the Titanium White basecoat too heavily; let the oak stain show through to provide natural shadows around feathers.

■ Let your brush strokes do the work for you to gain a dimensional effect; if there are small gaps between your brush strokes, so much the better.

■ The nest detail is best done freehand rather than tracing the pattern completely; real nest material is going to be uneven and not necessarily in true perspective, so don't try too hard.

Pretty Projects Without a Pretty Price

There are wonderful surfaces everywhere that will accept practically plain acrylic paints or the new easy-to-find specialty paints. Whether you need a gift in a hurry or simply want to try something different, the following list is sure to tempt and tease your creative spirit.

■ *Decorator rocks.* Rocks are conveniently available at no cost (go ahead and smile; it's true!). Just wash the rocks, allow to dry, spray with matte sealer. Then paint as desired and varnish. Great gifts as garden stones, desk paperweights and window-sill whimsies.

■ *Small wood birdhouses.* These can be purchased cheep (old pun but still fun) for under a dollar. Just base-coat and freehand small petals and leaves or simply add little dip-dots all over with your stylus. These can be done in quantities for special gifts, place settings, or tree ornaments. You can purchase papier-mâché birdhouses for 50 cents—less if you watch for closeout sales.

Painted Projects for Pennies

Consider painting on:

■ Smooth river rocks

■ Patio stones

■ Plastic switch plate covers

■ Wine bottles

■ Paper bags

■ Card stock

■ Kitchen spoons

■ Egg shells

■ Syrup bottles and pickle jars

■ Discarded shoes and boots

Just for Fun

Consider these surfaces as well:

- *Birdhouses.* Base-coat a dozen papier-mâché birdhouses in assorted colors of choice. Embellish with tiny dip-dot flowers. Varnish birdhouses and let dry. Tie or wire at intervals onto a swag of silk ivy. Place above a window or doorframe, or on the wall above the faucet of your kitchen sink.

- *Terra cotta pots and saucers.* These come in all sizes and are very inexpensive. Paint a pot, pot a plant, and present to your hostess or new neighbor. If you wish to use the pot as an actual planter, seal terra cotta inside and out with several coats of matte sealer before painting. When painting is completed, varnish interior and exterior. Instead of a real plant, choose a silk arrangement; or pack the pot with candy or a bag of muffin mix or a box of teabags. A saucer can be painted as a lid for the pot. For a finishing touch to the lid, glue on a resin bird, frog, or small birdhouse.

- *Stir stick people.* You've met one of them. Paint-stirring sticks are free from home improvement centers. Just base-coat and add simple details. Spray with matte sealer. Create Santas, snowmen, scarecrows, and more. A friend painted a half-dozen stir sticks with vegetable images. She applied several coats of varnish for weather protection and now the sticks grace the rows in her garden.

- *Doorknob hangers.* These are also referred to as "adoorables" (you'll understand why after you create a few). Wood door-knob hangers sell for less than a dollar through catalogs and at craft stores. Sand, wipe, and basecoat. Add a painted design. Include a message with permanent marker. Spray with matte sealer and varnish.

■ *Small seasonal pins.* You can create an unlimited
variety of lapel or sweatshirt pins from birch or other thin
wood cutouts. These are readily available at all craft stores
and through catalogs for 25 to 50 cents. The varieties are
endless (apples, snowmen, cats, leaves, pumpkins) and if
you're gearing up for a bazaar, a couple dozen of each could
be done at once "assembly line" style. Just lightly sand, wipe
clean, and base-coat. Apply design or details of choice, glue
on a pin back, and then varnish.

■ *Laser-cut wood cutouts.* These thin wood shapes are
engraved with a laser cut image or outline. I love
working with laser cutouts, particularly those sup-
plied by West Coast Wood Craft Supplies. Items are
reasonably priced at under a dollar each and the
detailing is incredible. No pattern transfer is required as the image is already on the wood. What
a time-saver! My best sellers at bazaars are usually
wood items from West Coast Wood Craft Supplies,
and because they've done some of the work for
me, I make good profits. So can you. Just seal the
wood cutout and then use either a paint marker designed for wood or paint the cutouts with thinned
acrylic washes. Simply paint within the laser-cut
(engraved) lines; think coloring book. When your
design is complete, spray with matte sealer and varnish
as desired. What could be easier?

> ▼▼▼▼▼▼▼▼▼▼▼▼▼▼▼▼
> ## Handy Hint
> You now can find door-
> knob hangers made of
> very heavy cardboard
> stock, available in craft
> stores. They come in
> packages of ten and re-
> tail for approximately
> two dollars per pack-
> age. Just spray stock
> with matte sealer, base-
> coat, and paint as de-
> sired. Spray again.
> Varnish is optional.
> ▲▲▲▲▲▲▲▲▲▲▲▲▲▲▲▲▲▲

■ *Tiny boxes for stamps, jewelry, trinkets, or treats.* There is a
wide variety of shapes and sizes available in wood or papier-
mâché. The boxes sell for 50 cents to $3, depending on
material and size. If using wood, sand then wipe clean.
Papier-mâché needs no preparation. Basecoat in yummy

shades and add dip-dot flowers in cheerful colors. Personalize if you wish, spray with matte sealer, and varnish.

■ *Garden gloves.* There are wonderful cotton gardening gloves available for under $2 or $3 at home and discount centers. Sometimes I find them in unexpected colors, but the plain chocolate-brown ones can be transformed and are ideal for a masculine theme. Wash gloves and let dry flat. Fabric paints with fine-tip nozzles make it a breeze to inscribe gloves with favorite quotes, make colorful flower doodles, or personalize with the name of your favorite gardener. You can even attach lace trim to the cuffs, by sewing or gluing. Add a couple of buttons or a brass charm if desired. (I almost hate to give away my secret here since these are one of my top sellers!)

Gardener's Love Gloves

Among my favorite things on which to paint, cotton garden gloves rank at the top of the list when it comes to quick, easy, fun, and the delightful responses they generate. I paint two dozen pair at a time for gifting my gardening friends. Some gloves reach their destination by mail. For others, on the first day of spring I sneak to the houses of favorite neighbors at dawn, tie a pair of gloves to their front doors or porch railings—and disappear without being seen. In my heart I'm sure the neighbors smile—but I'm certain it's me who sports the bigger grin. There's more to the story in part 2 of this book.

Recommended Reading for the Painter

This chapter focused on creativity, on keeping inspirational notebooks, on following current markets and what appeals to the customer, on the variety of items to paint and projects you may paint for fun or profit. Hundreds of decorative books on decorative painting and crafts marketing are available through your local bookstores, craft shops, and mail-order catalogs. Refer to the appendices in the back of this book for some helpful titles. Don't forget your local public library and the Internet. I hope you will explore some of the hundreds of publications available and will add some personal choices to your painting library for the purposes of inspiration, creativity, education, technique, and business acumen.

You will want to read the next chapter, which discusses how to develop your painting dreams into reality through setting personal goals. Folklore has it there is a pot of gold at the end of the rainbow. I believe it may well be at the tip of a paintbrush.

Your Crafts Vision

▼▼

NO MATTER WHAT is your current skill level, in the beginning it was enough to just decide to learn to paint. If you are like me, it was the simple vision to picture in my mind's eye that as a novice I could pick up a brush and would feel pleased with my efforts. That concept expanded after my first exhibit on that sunny weekend when I shared a table with my artist friend, and people actually purchased my paintings. I'm reminded of a comment made by Claudia Gentry: "It's exciting to sell something you've created. It's fulfilling to know that someone else likes the item and is happy to buy it."

One of my early marketing undertakings was aimed at the Christmas season. While I was looking through a brochure from a favorite woodcrafter and supplier, Bob Van Horn, who operates Bear With Us, Inc. (see resource section), I spied a birchwood cutout in the shape of a Santa. Of course at that point, without any pattern or paint, I had to stretch my imagination to visualize a Santa. I could have started with something simpler, such as the paint stir-stick project in the previous chapter. Instead I ordered a few dozen wood cutouts from Bob's catalog and convinced myself if I could paint one Santa, I could then develop the design into a numbered series. Once the wood cutouts arrived I was suddenly uptight about picking up my brushes. However, Santa Number One immediately received his plain basecoat then sat on my painter's table in his underwear while I gathered up my creative courage. I know I shouldn't have taken it that seriously, but I did. You see, I already had envisioned selling a series of Santas—not just for pin money, but for a real profit.

Walking by the painting table I suddenly imagined exactly how I would paint Santa. He would indeed be the first in a numbered original series offered for sale. I painted one hundred Santas and sold all but two. I couldn't bear to part with Santa Number One. He has a place of honor on a kitchen wall, my daily reminder that if you can view it you can do it. In addition to retaining Santa Number One, I also kept Santa Number Six because I liked the expression in his eyes.

Nothing but Blue Skies Do I See

In chapter 1 I mentioned a creative friend who now specializes in sponge-painted ceilings. She practiced first in her own house, including the garage. Now she's rejuvenating ceilings in the residences of her friends and doing home decorating in new construction, transforming expanses of boring contractor white into skies of buttermilk clouds floating on tinctures of faded denim blues. Her painting tools consist of a couple of ladders, inexpensive plastic dropcloths, water basins, paint trays, three or four colors of acrylic paints, and a variety of ordinary sponges—one of which was swiped from her husband's car-washing supplies. She told me, "Painting the ceiling of a child's bedroom that measures 10 feet by 10 feet may take me a full day or I may spread the job out over two days, depending on the client's circumstances. I charge by the square foot rather than by the project or by the hour, so the customer knows exactly what the job will cost regardless of how long it takes me. I set my own work schedules."

My friend is just one example of a hobbyist decorative painter turned professional. We met for lunch a few days ago and I asked her how the ceiling painting business was progressing. She smiled and replied: "I've never had so much fun." Apparently she doesn't mind the height of the ladders and mentioned she became more comfortable with that when painting the garage ceiling, which was the last practice project prior to launching her small business. She became so proficient at painting clouds that her husband was heard commenting: "When I pull into the garage and look up, I think I'm still on the driveway."

> **Did you know???**
>
> Centuries ago, the wealthy upper class paid artists handsome prices to paint on their furniture. The peasantry copied the idea, thus creating what we recognize as folk art techniques in almost every country of the world.

Goals, Game Plans, and Calendars

Whether the goal is modest or more earnest, if you are serious about selling your decorative paintings, it's time to develop a strategy. That strategy begins with defining your personal and professional goals. The best way to start the process is to ask yourself some questions: Do I consider painting a hobby purely for personal pleasure? Am I interested only in making occasional pin money? If I were to sell enough items solely to reimburse the cost of supplies, would that satisfy me? Has my full-time job in the corporate world become such a grind that I dream of quitting and making my living selling my projects?

My craft painter and essayist friend, Johnnie Elma Anderson, wrote: "In the beginning, my only goal was to achieve a lovely decorated home. For many years I did not think of making money because I was too absorbed in my children, home, and gardens. Now I do make a bit of money, which is fun; but to be honest, that remains secondary to my current goal: pursuing my creativity and enjoying what I'm doing."

If you're content to paint and sell only part time at seasonal bazaars or to coworkers and neighbors, obviously you can choose to spend as much time—or as little—on your craft as you wish. Linda Maretich of Linda's Ewenique Boutique of Crafts told me her hubby Ivan thought her initial goal was strictly a hobby—until she got serious about craft shows. "I decided I could sell some of our items to get money for more supplies," said Linda. "That is our single goal in selling." If you are a decorative painter determined to make money other than just pocket change, you should try to estimate how many hours a week or month you can dedicate to painting, setting aside blocks of time that will work with other activities. Once you're comfortable with that approach, you can build it into your personal work or family schedule as did one part-time painting friend who is precise concerning her creative calendar. While her immediate goal is not to go into business full time, she does plan for particular inventory for several craft shows annually. She keeps a monthly planner, with notations such as "9:00 to 12:00—Boys' soccer practice; my time to PAINT!"

Susan Nelson of Cats 'n Stuff said that she had hoped within five years to build a craft sales business that might provide viable income (that is, $20,000+ a year to start). She shared, "I am in my third year, and far from my goal." Do not interpret this comment as discouragement. Especially in the early stages of launching our own businesses, many decorative and craft painters must continue working at outside jobs. In addition, most have full-time commitments to home and family. We cannot always devote the hours required to pursue our dreams full time. Realistically one cannot immediately achieve financial goals for a decorative painting business while spending 50 hours a week working for someone else.

I'm not advising you to quit the corporate job until after you've taken time to do serious planning. I'm not recommending that you give up the dream of your own decorative painting business, whether your goal is part-time selling or to ultimately make a total lifestyle change. Rather, recognize you may have to adjust your calendar and modify the long-term goal if necessary. Set a five-year goal if that sounds like a reasonable target. You might just reach it. My goal was to be working from home and earning enough to at least cover all of my studio expenses within three years. It took me closer to six, but I made it. Did I think about giving up on it? Sure. But never for long. Someone expressed it well with the adage: "Quitters never win and winners never quit."

Defining the Dream

There are several avenues for applying your skills and transforming them into making money. It's up to you to decide how many hours you are able to paint and how much money you hope to make by painting. You may want to sell your projects from home through "invitation only" bazaars several times a year. You may wish to design and market pattern packets. You might book only two major craft expositions each year, but in addition you could develop a home show schedule. Your goal might center on owning a private home studio, or on leasing a retail store in a mall. Your objective could evolve into professional publishing, whether submitting one-time designs to magazines or writing an entire book on painting keepsake Christmas ornaments. Your dream may focus on the transition from a boring full-time job to successfully making a living with your paintbrushes.

I'm Not Going to Work Today

I'm not going to work today.
It's totally against my grain.

I must go feed the cat and the birds.
And besides, it's starting to rain.

I'm not going to work today.
I'm developing a pattern packet.

Just got an order for a
three-foot rabbit,
by Easter (if I can hack it!).

I'm not going to work today.
I'm writing a painting column
for "The Globe."

And I've been up doodling
since three o'clock,
in my socks and old bathrobe.

I'm not going to work today.
It no longer is fun for me.

I'll find a way to pay my bills.
My paintbrush has set me free.

I'm not going to work today.
I have my acrylics to thank.

With a bit more luck
and a lot more pluck,
I'll paint my way to the bank.

—*Susan Young*

Planning Your Pathway to Painting Profits

As I close this chapter, I want to touch on its overall theme: "If you can view it, you can do it." While I am a true believer in that simple precept, I must interject emphatically that there is a difference between having a dream and having a goal. Certainly our dreams inspire us, but stars in our eyes and pies in the skies will not become dollars in the depository overnight. The dreams must be transformed into measurable goals, in writing. Assuming that your paintings will sell if you produce them and market them, and that when you do you will start making money is not practical. Convert that supposition into a personal goal and put it on paper: "During this calendar year I will schedule four seasonal shows with enough appropriate inventory to sell at least $500 per show." Now you have a goal kindled by the dream. Now you can determine how many projects you have to paint to exhibit at four shows, what materials you need to purchase, the amount of time required to produce your items, which seasonal themes each show will promote, and how to price your projects in order to meet your written goal.

Where do you want the road to lead? How hard do you want to work? What are your financial goals? Do you want to be a hobbyist and craft painter, or a professional businessperson? Here are some avenues to consider as you plan your personal painting pathway.

- Do home decorating and projects for close friends and family, whether for gifting or selling.

- Paint items for personal use and gifts plus selling to casual friends and to coworkers for pin money.

- Attend two or three shows per year for fun, regardless of profits.

- Exhibit at a few annual shows to recover the cost of supplies.

- Participate in many scheduled annual shows with the intent of earning a living.

- Open a private studio or home bazaar by appointment or invitation to supplement income.

- Teach painting classes through retail chain stores or at home to supplement income.

- Do home decorating (furniture stenciling, wall or ceiling murals) part time or full time for profit.

- Start a mail-order business featuring finished items and custom orders on a limited quantity basis.

- Design and market pattern packets to supplement other painting-related income.

- Publish through magazines, newspapers, and books to supplement income or earn a living.

- Operate a retail business, including selling painting supplies to provide total income.

I am captivated by an expression Johnnie Elma Anderson found engraved on a rubber stamp: "Shoot for the moon. Even if you miss, you'll land among the stars." Thanks Johnnie!

Part Two

For Profit

Profiting from Your Talent

▼▼

DURING MY 25 YEARS of involvement with the wonderful world of decorative painting, I can't recall meeting any fellow painters who started out with the specific goal of painting for profit. Like me they chose to paint, having arrived at a point in their lives when it was time for a new preoccupation, whether it would be a hobby or evolve into something more. Money didn't enter into it except when the time came to splurge on a paint color that wasn't already in the toolbox. For example, one of my painting pals in that first painting class confided that on her weekly grocery day she always wrote the check for $5 over the amount due—which she joyfully spent at the craft store on the way home.

Several within that class collectively agreed that we would as comrades continue to learn to paint for fun once the instructional sessions were over. We did and it was indeed fun. As young wives and mothers we quickly became friends, and during the next year met each Tuesday afternoon to paint together. We clustered around our respective kitchen tables swapping stories about our children or muttering about our husbands' habits as we worked. Most times we painted in the solitude of our individual homes for the simple joy of seeing a project come to life. At times we painted because it was our only respite after a tedious day in a high-tech office or because it was our only retreat after continuous hair-raising hours of hectic parenting. But we all treasured our Tuesday gathering.

As our group became more intimate we learned one of our painting friends was battling breast cancer. Each Tuesday she sat and painted with a smile on her beautiful face and the rest of us never knew. She had never missed a session and never complained. Finally, one afternoon she surprised our little group by simply stating the battle she was waging and her will to survive. But among her infrequent comments, the one I remember most vividly was: "Painting inspires and drives me along life's pathways—even if some are not of my choosing. No matter what I'm facing, it has become my escape from the things that hurt." Sometimes the personal profits of painting are not always measured in dollars.

Part Pastime, Part Profit

A colleague of mine has six children, ages 3 to 17. She paints almost every evening from 10:00 to midnight, after the hyperactive household is finally hushed. With an impish grin, she told me: "My paints and brushes save my sanity and don't cost nearly as much as would seeing a psychiatrist." When her neighborhood hosts twice-a-year community yard sales, she sets up a table of her painted projects and usually sells out, providing her with a fair amount of pin money. Through these community sales, word has spread to her neighbors that she paints so she is now selling painted items out of her kitchen with increasing frequency. What began as a relaxing pastime evolved into an informal part-time business. Right now she still thinks decorative painting serves only as her sanity-saving hobby; but I know she has been bitten by the bug to turn her diversion into dollars. Already looking to the future, she commented not long ago with a twinkle in her eyes: "When that 3-year old starts elementary school (if I survive that long), I'm going to teach decorative painting part-time at two of my local craft stores—and get paid for doing it."

For many years I, too, was strictly a "part hobby, part income" painter. That suited my lifestyle while I juggled the demands of a career, a young family, and all the other aspects of home—such as daily laundry, packing lunches, and rose gardening. While I didn't consider decorative painting as therapy to save my sanity (except on occasion), I did view it as a hobby and as a wonderful means of always having little gifts on hand for friends' birthdays or for a spur-of-the-moment surprise. My friend Betty Hardgrave asked if I would paint coordinating fruit and vegetable designs on her stained pine breadbox, canister set, and paper-towel holder. She would pay me. "Sure," I said. Several mornings found me at Betty's house, brushes in hand and enjoying marathon chats. Despite a friendship spanning 30 years, we still haven't run out of words.

> ## Did you know???
>
> In the 1940s and 1950s, Peter Hung brought decorative painting to public attention in the United States. Hunt's unique style of painting was based on what he had seen in Europe and became extremely popular in the eastern part of this country. Hunt became known for his "transformagic" technique of taking any old discarded item and turning it into an artful and envied home accessory.

One spring day a few years ago, I walked along my street just before dawn and tied a pair of hand-painted gardening gloves to each neighbor's doorknob. Some, of course, knew I was the culprit and responded with delight. Since I didn't leave calling cards, others had no idea where their decorated discoveries had originated. I was a part-time painter then and didn't expect the phone to ring. But it did. Indeed, that very first glove-gifting effort netted me orders for over two dozen custom creations—just in time for Mother's Day. Not bad for a few minutes' jaunt up and down my street. I chose that particular glove-gifting endeavor for my own fun and plan to do it again. Next time I will leave my business card, ribbon-tied to each spring surprise because long ago I

PATRICIA'S STORY

"Never give up hope," says Patricia Rizzo. In her late 50s she lost her job of many years, and a series of unfruitful interviews convinced her that 50-plus candidates weren't appreciated. Having faith in her own abilities, she set up a desktop publishing business.

"Little did I know that path was saturated with people who knew a lot more than I, and they had the equipment to prove it," says Patricia. "In the meantime, funds were low and my sister's birthday loomed. Rather than show up empty-handed and portray how bad things were, I purchased two white ceramic dime store angels. Gosh, they looked boring. They needed flowers in their hands."

Patricia's creativity was fueled when she saw polymer clay on sale. She created tiny roses, painting and gluing them into the angels' hands. "The gift was a big success," recalls Patricia. That started her business of designing and painting jewelry. She became bored with rose pins and earrings and spontaneously began creating angels.

made the commitment to make the transition from painting as a pastime to painting for profit. By offering a complimentary sample of a new creation along with my business card, I'm guaranteed to receive orders for additional pairs of gloves and inquiries about my works. Some times people need only to be informed that you paint. If they like what they see, they'll pursue.

Developing the Dream

When I carted that first basket full of Halloween and fall offerings to display for my office coworkers, it was not without trepidation. But

Patricia researched molding processes, allowing her to design and produce her own molds for hand casting using white resin. Her angels are popular for weddings, showers, birth announcements, and fund raisers. She can now produce them in quantity, but each one is hand painted. During peak demand, Patricia relies on help from family and friends, but "mostly it's me, the angels, and Angel, my cat."

She candidly shares, "Pulling yourself out of a desperate situation requires common sense and sweat equity. It takes faith that no matter how bad things become, you must never give up hope. I wasn't prepared for the way these angels evolved and took off. They truly seem to be in charge and leading me where I must go.

my desire to be perceived as a decorative painter and the prospects of pin money overpowered any real fear. At that improvised (though perhaps not quite appropriate) setting for a "BOO-tique," I unknowingly set the stage for making a lifestyle change—exiting my rat race and entering my painting place. As my colleagues and superiors stopped by during coffee breaks or lunch hours to enjoy my creations, I enjoyed the smiles on their faces. And pocketing their money put a smile on mine. The more I painted, the more I wanted to sell. The more I sold, the more I wanted to paint. The more I painted and sold for profit, the more I wanted to write about it so others might share the joy.

I had been growing increasingly dissatisfied with the daily grind of the corporate world, but didn't have the courage to do anything about it. The more I fought making a decision, the more frustrated I became, and instead of sleeping at night, I was often at my painting table or my computer desk and going to the job bleary-eyed the next day. To make a long story short, within a few months I was being teased at work that my corporate career was just my hobby. I knew I wanted to design and paint; I wanted to write about designing and painting; I wanted to follow the dream. I knew in my heart it was fast becoming time to make the decision and begin the transition, but still I held off. After all, that regular paycheck was dependable and afforded my household lots of extras; and so I kept up the juggling act, knowing it was only a matter of time. Indeed it was.

Timing the Transition

This millennium is an exciting time to launch your own decorative painting business. The technology we enjoy and utilize every day permits retrieving instant information about availability of materials, ordering them online, paying with plastic, and next-day delivery. We can locate decorative painting publications, craft malls, conventions, classes, and fellow painters with a few strokes on the keyboard. However, as exhilarating as is the concept of downloading knowledge in a nanosecond, the continuing expansion of high-tech industry in emerging nations has only spawned more mass-produced inferior merchandise.

In particular because of the tremendous boom that has occurred in the crafting world, imported items pretending to have been hand painted and hand sewn are spilling off shelves and overflowing merchandise bins in discount houses, home improvement centers, and even grocery stores. While the quality of some products appears to be good, it is obvious upon examination that they are stamped out in mass quantity, assembly-line style. Cookie-cutter craft items, including those made to look hand painted, are imported by the millions. They simply do not have the authenticity and craftsmanship of unique pieces individually prepared and finished.

"It can be a real problem to try to compete with imported, mass-produced products that are designed to look like true hand-painted American crafts," Claire Kelly observed. "Sometimes customers honestly think they are buying hand-painted items because a lot of these products look pretty good at first glance." She added: "Now is the perfect time for us to invent ways to promote the unique appeal of our creations and step up to the opportunity of marketing to a better-educated and more-appreciative public."

My experience over the past few years indicates consumers are responding with a new loyalty to and appreciation for the professional artist and craftsman. As they become more desirous of shaping a unique style for their personal environments, they acknowledge the unique creativity that goes into designing and painting a Santa ornament, a tabletop, a desk front, a wall mural—or even a patio stone. Accordingly, the demand for quality one-of-a-kind decoratively painted articles for home decor and gifts has never been greater and should only increase. I truly believe my customers know when they purchase one my creations that as it leaves my studio, a little piece of my heart goes with it. For it does, you know.

Procrastination Postpones Profits

Fear of the unknown probably ranks at the top of the list of reasons we humans procrastinate about making lifestyle changes. During a quarter-century of chasing a professional career as well as preserving a permanent commitment to the subject of decorative painting, I understand the emotions at opposite ends of the anxiety spectrum: fear of failure and fear of success. Either or both can prevent us from making the leap, whether driven by fear or by complete confidence in oneself. Believe it or not, confidence based on previous successes can encourage the fear of failure: "I've never failed yet. What if I fail this time?"

I truly believe life has a way of making decisions for us when we are too stubborn, too frightened, too busy (or just plain too lazy) to pay attention. We can struggle all we want against an intuition that keeps bedeviling us; and while we recognize its continual presence, we still refuse to scratch the itch. One of two things will happen. Either the bug no longer badgers us, or we finally concede we can't put it off any longer and deal with it. I was lucky. At the time I was readying to scratch the itch, life made a decision for me. A management change in my corporation occurred at the same time my desire had peaked to pursue full-time decorative painting. The situation not only fueled the fires always smoldering in me to pursue what I loved, but would ultimately provide proof that I could succeed. There would be no turning back and no regrets.

The Sky Is Not the Limit

What items or surfaces do you envision painting on for producing profits? Do you have certain types of projects in mind you know will lend joy to your painting efforts? Have you thought about specific articles that would appeal to the consumer? How might your painted items be used? Do you want to concentrate on custom home decor, personalized gifts, or seasonal designs and ornaments?

Remember my friend who specializes in buttermilk clouds painted on blue denim skies? She found her niche. The larger scale of the projects appeals to her; she likes the artistic license of creating a sky (after all, no two are the same) and she's making money. She told me in the early days just before she launched her business, "Tiny brushes make me nervous."

A few of the women in my family are experts at quilt making. Their finished projects are truly works of art, deserving of much admiration. Crocheting and cross-stitching are extremely popular crafts, as is knitting. I marvel at the mastery of the creative mind, ingenious in its ability to produce almost overwhelming visual and tactile masterpieces such as the beautiful knitting executed by my friend Elizabeth Kelly and the cross-stitchery done by life-long comrade Donna Hickman. So while there are truly many wonderful crafts available (I've tried most, including paper quilling, floral arranging, rug hooking, and home decor sewing), few offer the practi-

> ## Did you know???
>
> The word *tole* means "tin" or "metal," so in order to actually practice "tole painting," one paints on a metal surface. Today we use the broader term, *decorative painting*, which can be performed on practically every surface.

cally limitless applications of decorative painting. You have seen through the pages of this book only a sampling of its versatility, not only concerning the variety of surfaces you might paint but also the complete freedom to develop your own style. You can be as precise or as loose as you want; it's your project and your brush.

Decorative painting is truly an art form that will lend itself to virtually any surface and technique, especially with the ever-expanding products market. One of my friends executes quilting designs, but her "quilts" will never be used on beds. Instead, her pattern designs, traditional and new, are worked with decoratively painted wood shapes, which are then arranged and glued on wood plaques or tabletops. Her clientele may choose from a half-dozen existing colors and designs, or they may bring in fabric swatches for a custom palette. The finished quilted wood plaque or tavern sign usually finds its place displayed over a fireplace mantel or on a covered front porch—something most of us would not do with a hand-made fabric treasure. The tables make wonderful accents for great rooms, kitchens, or for use as plant stands.

Not long after my painting endeavors assumed a more professional profile, I was presented with the opportunity to work up an outdoor party theme for a local homeowner. The request included designing and painting items to fit an entryway display, as well as the patio luncheon table on the back deck. The client, an avid gardener, had contacted me two weeks prior to her social event and mentioned she wanted a theme focusing around any appropriate seasonal flower. "How much will you charge me for pulling together a motif and how soon may I look at your samples?" she asked me over the phone. As a professional, it was my turn to ask the questions: "Which particular flower would you like to use as a focus? Have you considered the kinds of items you would like to include? Do you have any particular objects in mind that will announce your theme?" Certainly not. That's why she had called me.

We set an appointment for the next afternoon and I presented several display projects incorporating a pansy theme, including terra cotta pots, a pillar candle, and invitations on watercolor cardstock, all of which had been painted with acrylics. I suggested we use the theme "Spring Gardening Gathering." The client loved it. I hand-painted and stenciled an inexpensive sisal floor mat for the front porch, a pair of garden gloves ribbon-tied to the knob of the front door, and decorative terra cotta pots for each of the steps leading up to the porch. That was just for the front entry. The back patio steps sported painted terra cotta pots, a stenciled floor cloth, and on the luncheon table each guest's place setting was marked with a miniature terra cotta pot which, along with their name, included a single hand-painted pansy. The hostess told me later the hit of the garden party was the personalized painted pansy pots that each guest took home as a reminder of a special afternoon. She said, "And can you believe it? Some of the guests asked to buy the large painted pots right off the steps!" Needless to say, it wasn't long until I had more orders for painted pots than I could fill.

The garden-party project should further inspire you about the broad base of products and projects to which decorative painting lends itself. I've painted on wooden pencils, carpet scraps, window shades, desk blotters, wine bottles, kitchen toasters, salt-and-pepper shakers, and lamp shades. One particular Easter even the interior glass of the garage windows was decorated with painted green grasses and a scattering of pastel eggs. The scene was easily visible to passersby. I netted a few customers who wanted their garage windows done, too. Many merchants operating retail stores in strip malls will pay to have their shop windows painted with seasonal designs, particularly for the Christmas season. You can market wherever your imagination leads.

Projecting Your Professional Painting Image

Perhaps until now, you've been giving away most of your projects or selling them at yard sales. The responses from recipients and occasional customers have encouraged you to sell your work. In spite of your hesitation, you've decided you do want to go into business. The next logical question is: How do I let people know I'm serious about earning profits from my paintings? You can achieve this in any of several ways, none of which are difficult or expensive to implement.

Several years ago I read or heard a simple five-word phrase that stuck in my mind: "Image is where it's at." It particularly applies to developing a business reputation. Your demeanor and your dress code make that first important impression when you meet a potential client. Certainly while refinishing, prepping, and painting a drop-lid desk in your home studio or basement, you'll end up covered with smears and spots. Once word gets out about your paintings, a customer may drop by at any time. If you are working from home, always wear laundered, neatly

Handy Hint

Many expert home decor painters always dress in whites. Even when paint-stained, laundered white shirts and trousers appear neat and impart the message: "This is the uniform of a professional." Consistently wearing white work clothes also cuts laundry time.

fitting clothes—paint-stained or not—instead of your husband's sweatsuit two sizes too big and sporting burn holes from his shop welder (personal reminder to myself). Keep an oversized shirt or a denim apron hanging on a peg by the door. I purchased an expensive canvas cobbler's apron and decorated it with chubby teddy bears wielding paintbrushes. I attached my affiliation pins (Society of Decorative Painters and DecoArt Helping Artist) and inscribed the apron "Paint till you Faint." When the doorbell rings unexpectedly, I quickly grab the apron and slip it on over my T-shirt. I'm immediately presentable and it's obvious I am a decorative painter.

If you are displaying at craft shows and bazaars, dress as you wish and make it comfortable and easy on yourself. Jeans and a painted denim shirt or sweat suit (new and bright, not one that's been through the laundry weekly since 1992) sends a message to the passersby that you are a creative artist whether or not your offering is fabric painting. If you are participating in a seasonal show, wear your Santa earrings and a red velvet smock if that's your style. I recall a Christmas bazaar where one of the exhibitors displayed wonderfully painted Santas. He wore jeans and red cotton T-shirt, above which he sported a full beard and Santa hat. When things weren't moving, he'd stand and shout "Ho, Ho, Ho." My kind of businessman! Of course, I always was biased toward a man with a white beard.

Print It Professionally

When you are ready to "go pro," the smallest details can make the biggest impression. Make the most of business cards, brochures, fliers, and other stationery items. There are many specialty catalogs that offer a variety of business-card designs and return-address labels (see resource section). Those of you who have a computer and a basic desktop publishing package can easily design your own. Office-supply chain stores have copy centers with plenty of sample designs available to get you started. You might want to design your own card with a simple sketch and a few lines printed from the computer, which is the way I designed my first business card and flier. Don't forget hangtags for attaching pricing or other information. In the beginning you can make your own (as I did). There are at least a couple of companies who offer wonderful hangtags in many designs (see resource section).

I think the best way to close this chapter is to leave you with two thoughts: "We never get a second chance to make a first impression"; and to paraphrase an expression, "Never underestimate the power of the printed word." Add to your list of personal goals that your first impressions will be impressive; and that your printed materials reflect *your* creativity.

Printed Paraphernalia for Your Professional Painting Profile

- Business Cards
- Return Address Labels
- Hangtags
- Fliers
- Brochures
- General stationery (letterhead and envelopes)
- Specialty items (such as pocket calendar or pencils imprinted with your business name)

Pricing Your Paintings

▼▼▼

WHENEVER I SPEAK to colleagues or read books on marketing decorative paintings and other crafts, I'm struck by a consistent conclusion: Setting the price of merchandise is the most difficult part of showing and selling.

When I began painting for my own enjoyment, profits didn't enter intomy personal equation. But after that first experience in the park, seeing my projects exit in the arms of customers with smiles on their faces, my objective began to evolve from handing the buyer the bagged merchandise to seriously bagging a profit.

I freely admit that even after many years of experience with craft shows, holiday bazaars, and home studios, I've yet to come up with a magic methodology for setting prices. But that doesn't mean we can't figure out our own formulas when it comes to making money. It helps to understand that not every approach works every time for every product. As with most things in our lives, a little insight, business sense, customer communication, and understanding of the market can make all the difference.

It Can Be a Fine Line

How do we find a happy medium? I think the best insight I ever received on the subject of pricing came from the book *Creative Cash* by Barbara Brabec (Prima Publishing). "Knowledge about pricing increases with time and experience," she wrote, "but it is always a challenge, even for professionals who have been selling for years." I'd like to add that it also comes down to a common-sense approach. Surely we know our offerings must be tagged reasonably enough to attract the consumer. But they also have to be priced high enough that we realize a profit, preferably as much as is possible, assuming we're serious about a business approach. None of us will learn the concepts of pricing overnight. I'm still working on it (and I'm not the only one!).

I'm planning on co-exhibiting at an annual fall event with one of my colleagues. We met for lunch to begin our early planning and, as usual, the subject of pricing came up. We've both been painting all summer to get ready for this show. We each also have a couple of boxes of items from last year's event. Do we change the pricetags? Do we lower the prices because the paintings are (to us) leftovers? Should we even attempt to market these dated items? Or do we raise the prices because the economy is strong and people expect to pay $15 for something similar to what they purchased a year ago for $12? Can we put the old stuff in with the new stuff so the tables look really full? Then can't we command better prices because we've got really neat stuff and plenty of it? How is the market running? Oops. We admitted to each other we hadn't been to any shows recently. We should have been out there looking so we would understand current competitive pricing in preparation for the coming event.

Obviously, the discussion was in full swing. Our salads grew soggy in our bowls. "Pricing my paintings is like walking a tightrope," my colleague told me. "I feel if I lean too far one way or the other, it's going to be a disaster either way." Disaster? Thinking she was being a bit melodramatic, I asked my pal what she meant. "Well, you of all people have to understand it as you've surely been there yourself. I can do my best to command a super profit per item and overprice even if I don't mean to. Then I come home with what we were just taking about—leftovers. Or I can try to price items too reasonably in the hopes I'll sell out—but then when I total up everything, my profit money is marginal at best."

Of course, I'd been there myself. I just had to hear it one more time: I am not alone in trying to figure out this pricing game.

Don't Sell Yourself Short

The astonishing fact is most of us consistently underprice our offered items, especially as beginners. We think our projects aren't that good, that no one will want them unless they are dirt cheap, that we'll be laughed at if we price them at what we feel they are worth—or worse, that we won't sell a single piece. This was my thought pattern, especially in the early phases of exhibiting and selling. It was an honest mistake since gratification that customers would actually buy got in the way of my analytical abilities.

There is a definite downside to underpricing items that you think should carry inexpensive pricetags (whatever the reason). Not long ago one of my pricing tactics backfired. In my zeal to tap into a market aimed at real estate firms, I sent out complimentary prototypes of

The Pricing Game

In preparing for a holiday show, I decided I wasn't going to walk into the trap of selling things too cheaply. For one thing, I had just been reading an article on selling and how underpricing was such a pitfall. Besides, I know my work is good, and since my business cards state that I am an artist, I felt I could command high prices. Painted Santas that I knew ordinarily should have sold for no more than $12, I marked up to $20. While I made enough money to cover my expenses at that show, I didn't come out with any profit at all. Instead I packed up and went home with items that were finger-printed, chipped, left in disarray by the non-buying customers—and because I added a date to the pieces when I signed my name, how am I going to sell them at next year's show unless I mark them half-price?

—Anonymous contributor

painted housewarming gifts inscribed with "Congratulations on your New Home." I was quite proud of my ingenuity and thought the samples of inexpensive (read that as cheap) offerings would generate orders for a dozen items at a time because I personally saw them as so affordable. The responses were either nil or chill: "What can you offer in a higher price range?" That question served as a wake up call when it came to pricing.

I once was so green and eager to make a sale that if a customer stopped at my craft booth and asked, "Oh, is $6 the correct price for this item?" I'd blurt out: "You can have it for $5." But as I began to sell in quantity and my confidence increased, I grew brave enough to hold my ground, even when customers wanted to make an offer instead of paying the tagged price. Perhaps the sharing of my early and somewhat embarrassing business history may help you avoid underpricing your work in the hopes of making a sale.

My Time, My Materials, and What Else?

Some painted projects are easier to price than others. Later, we're going to talk about setting higher-than-expected dollar amounts on unique pieces and that sometimes it comes down to where you live and what the local markets will bear. Remember, too, that some of your paintings naturally will command a higher price based on size, surface material, technique, hours invested, or just because of unique appeal.

The success of any pricing formula will depend at least partially on your product line, your geography, how and where you sell, and overhead factors pertaining to individual circumstances. For example, a woodworker specializing in jewelry boxes made from prime woods such as walnut or cherry will have a lot more investment tied up in his wood inventory than a decorative painter who paints a peach on a plain pine plaque. A quilter who places every single stitch by hand will have logged many more hours than a colleague who quilts only by sewing machine applications. Some of us simply have to set our prices accordingly. The only problem is how to arrive at that goal. Once we do that, about all we can do is hope for the best, and if we don't meet our expectations, it's time to rethink.

Finding the Formula

Even though I passed algebra, I never liked it. I didn't get it then. I do now, when it comes to pricing my paintings. It's not a complicated formula and I've been using it for years. I refer to it as "The Rule of Threes." Some craft marketing analysts and authors will tell you the Rule of Threes doesn't work, but it's likely you can become profitable by adding the word "plus" to that formula, as I did. Simply put, it involves multiplying the cost of my material by three and adding an hourly wage for myself; and when I feel it's justified, I may add an additional few cents to the pricetag. So in simple math terminology, the formula for "The Rule of Threes Plus" reads:

**Cost of Materials x 3 + My Hours at My Desired Wage
+ Extras = My Selling Price**

For example, if I spend 50 cents on a wood cutout and multiply that by three, it comes to $1.50. If it takes me one hour to paint and finish the cutout and I think that hour is worth $7 of my time, then the pricetag on that item is $8.50. Depending on the project I may add another 50 cents to help defray the cost of my paints. This may not be a perfect formula but it can serve as a basic starting point while you develop your individual pricing method. I am not the only decorative painter or craftsman who uses the Rule of

▼▼▼

JEAN' STORY

"I grew up surrounded by art," says Jean Fitzgerald, whose parents were schooled in the fine arts. Born and reared in Schenectady, New York, and now living in Lakeland, Florida, Jean is one of many decorative painters whose beliefs and determination resulted in a success story.

"I've had no formal training," Jean told me, "but through the years I felt compelled to express myself in various mediums including watercolor and hand-painted sculptures of my own design. I believe if anyone has the desire to create something, they should try."

Jean worked a regular job for several years and decided to quit and team up with a friend to create and sell hand-painted accessories and soft sculpture. Later a change in geography found Jean back at a regular job, but she continued creating jewelry designs, selling through a retail shop. "The marketing aspect is what hung me up initially," she recalls. "One store was fine, but I wasn't making much money. There were times I became discouraged."

▲▲▲

Threes Plus formula. Said Susan Nelson of Cats 'n Stuff, "I usually figure at least three times what my raw materials cost, and then add my time."

The reasoning behind the Rule of Threes Plus where materials are concerned is it becomes a built-in cycle to assure getting back your initial cost of the base item, enough money to replace the base item, and reimbursement toward other supplies. A further example:

- I spent 50 cents for a wood cutout to paint, which upon customer purchase I will recover my initial expenditure for the wood plus other monies.

Then Jean discovered the Internet. She admits it was a slow start in spite of a 135-page Web site. She expanded into marketing through Internet auction sites and discovered some creations sold at double her retail prices. Jean now works from home at her own pace, spending 10 to 12 hours a day filling orders (including custom requests) and developing new designs. Her income from decorative painting has quadrupled and she's expanding her product lines, many featuring a favorite passion: dogs.

"Whether or not I'm a success in the eyes of the world isn't the most important thing," Jean says. "I'm happy and for me that's what real success is all about."

- If I add another 50 cents, I can replace the wood cutout in my inventory in case I want to market it again or receive a repeat order.

- It's fair to add 50 cents for the cost of paints, varnish, and supplies used to execute the project.

- I may wish to add on a few more dimes toward eventually replacing my brushes or other materials, if I feel the market will allow it for the particular item.

- Then I include a reasonable hourly wage or what I feel is a fair figure for my time.

- The total determines the per-item selling price.

Tracking the Totals

Official record keeping is not my favorite task. It must be done, however, not only for personal tracking but also for business purposes. You will want to evaluate whether you are on the right path when it comes to pricing your paintings for making a profit. There is more to record keeping than storing receipts for paints, brushes, and wood cutouts in a shoebox (although you can do it that way!). In the beginning your record keeping does not have to be sophisticated. If you have a computer and know how to use basic spreadsheet applications, by all means utilize these tools. In particular, if you are launching your own business, keep a paper trail of expenditures and income. As a business operation, you will need this information for tax reporting as well as for your own budgeting and planning purposes. There are several ways to keep records straight.

In particular, when selling out of town or out of state through a mall, consignment shop, or other dealer, I recommend you maintain personal inventory sheets per project, including raw materials cost, item name, and asking price if applicable. When selected items are to be delivered to bazaars or craft malls, it is imperative that you have and provide an inventory list complete with descriptive name, item number, your name or code, and selling price. Label your items so that the information on their hangtag or price sticker matches the inventory sheet description. Lost, misplaced, non-priced, incorrectly priced, or unidentified paintings add up to considerable losses over time. Without comprehensive records, you'll never know if you're making money or dropping dollars; in which case any devised pricing formula isn't going to be much security.

Years ago I kept inventory costs and sales records in a plain spiral notebook. It was cheap, easy, and fun. I still have an early notebook, the entries written in colored inks on lined paper. Back then I didn't think I was getting anywhere with my painting, but the evidence of my success in that handwritten log is indelible. Not only that, I can recall particular craft tables, breezy spring days, and some of the faces of smiling customers as they were handed their painted treasures. Never underestimate the joy and value of keeping records—including writing down ideas about how to set your prices.

Cross-Reference Your Inventory the Easy Way

Keep a list of all items you plan to market before going to an exhibit or show. I've always numbered my pricetags along with the selling price (for example: #152, Red Santa, $12). My inventory list corresponds with exactly what is on each item's hangtag. You can set this up on a spreadsheet or do it in a notebook. When I was selling though a craft mall and boxed up items from my home studio for the first time, I sat on the floor with my notebook and, as I tagged each item, I gave it a corresponding entry line in my book. I still have that notebook—as well some of those items that never sold (even after I read an article on how not to underprice, I plead guilty!).

Hangtags and Pricetags

I like little tags with string ties, though I realize not every item lends itself to those. But self-adhesive stickers can make a real mess, especially during the heat of a summer exhibit. What if a customer tries to remove a sticky sticker, and scratches the paint in so doing? Then she complains: "Look. It's damaged. I don't want it." or "Can

Handy Hint

- Maintain receipts logs and enter every item you sell, including description and total price.

- Keep an inventory log of your painted items, base cost, time invested, and other information.

- Never deliver projects to craft malls or shows without a complete inventory list.

- Always keep a second file copy of all inventory lists in your permanent file.

- Especially on large projects, carefully calculate time and materials.

you give me a discount?" Think through how you want to apply your pricetags. They need to be large enough to contain pertinent information, and possibly ample enough for your stamp or business name and phone number on the reverse side. Several companies offer nice variations of pricetags and hangtags. You can make your own, like I did when I explored my first adventure in a consignment mall (see chapter 7).

Thinking Things Through

Personal experience has shown me that if I don't do a written analysis (especially for a large project), then I will be ineffective at ensuring a fair profit for myself. The past Christmas holiday, a local corporation asked for an estimate to design and produce several painted centerpieces for their annual employee party. I'm an artist and not an accountant; therefore I knew within moments the configuration of the design I would submit. But it took me days to research my supplier base, factor in the cost of raw materials, and work up a prototype for estimating production time. If I had not done my homework on paper, there's a good chance I would have fallen short of my objective, which was to more than triple what I calculated as total investment, including my time. Without a paper trail, I'd never have been able to plan it. Additionally with a written record of my base supply expenditures and estimated hourly wage, there would be no scrambling for documentation to justify my estimate to the client.

What's It Worth?

"Beauty is in the eye of the beholder." That long-used expression indeed applies, not only when pricing your paintings but while observing your customers and overhearing their comments. There is certainly nothing wrong with feeling intense pride and love for your own creations (most of them anyway!). I have a few painted pieces I consider true treasures; it's impossible for me to put dollar values on them. In my eyes, they are worth more than money. If I could convince myself to affix pricetags and display the items for sale, I would drive myself out of the competitive market because of my personal feelings. Potential buyers, instead of purchasing them might offer "That's cute" or "You've got to be kidding!" Keep in mind that you will sometimes hear such comments, regardless of your pricing formula. Also, keep in mind that you shouldn't take it personally (if you figure out how to succeed at this, let me know!).

Intermittently over the years, I've maintained a display of my painted items at a local hair salon. My very talented stylist, Joy Williams, is enthusiastic, supportive, and always willing to do a favor for a friend. During a spring season my exhibit included birdhouses, one of which was personally enchanting so it carried a pretty good pricetag. I was in Joy's salon on a Saturday morning, just a regular client, when I noticed another patron eyeing that particular birdhouse. She picked it up and gushed, "Ohhhh, I like this!" Then she saw the pricetag and said crisply, "I don't like it *that* much!" I kept quiet in spite of my desire to quip: "And I don't want to sell it *that* much!" As with a lot of things, it's a matter of opinion. Claudia Gentry expressed an emotion prevalent among decorative painters: "I love the idea of making money from my creations, but I have mixed feelings about selling them. I think some aren't good enough to give away and others I can't part with."

Public Perceptions

Painters who are new to marketing and selling may never give a thought to an important fact that likely clouds their vision when it comes to setting prices or understanding why some items don't sell. I almost hate to tell you this. The truth of the matter is, the average buyer doesn't care how many hours you've invested in learning your craft, in painting roses on cabinetry, or how much money you've spent on good quality brushes to execute quality work.

I was displaying at a sidewalk fair several years ago, and as I sat at my table I painted small projects to occupy my time between customers and to demonstrate my technique. Most passersby seemed to enjoy taking a moment to watch. Then one observer picked up a kitchen accessory painted in an apple theme. She looked at the pricetag and asked me in front of the crowd: "How can you charge this much? I just saw you paint an apple in three minutes." I gritted my teeth, put a grin on my face and said, "You're right about the three minutes. But it took me three years to perfect the technique."

As my creative friend Eileen Beard told me, bridging the miles from Staffordshire, England, "I hope all things will sell well. But people today forget the time invested by the craftsman, the hours one sits. They want something for peanuts as it were."

Smarter Than the Average Bear

One factor we have to keep in mind, whether we are experienced sellers or novices, is that most buyers already have a bottom line for what they are willing to spend on a particular piece. Not always, of course. Some of my biggest sales were the result of impulse buyers. They didn't plan on finding an irresistible item, but once captured they wanted it so badly the price became irrelevant. So don't overlook the possibility of a surprise sale. Indeed, I think it's smart business to display a few items that you know are attention-getters, both in theme and in price range.

Generally at craft shows or holiday bazaars, you will find that customers are very familiar with the going rate because they browse similar events at every opportunity. Therefore they are educated about competitive pricing. Most likely, they have followed the circuit over several seasons and observed items of similar quality, material, and size. They know what they are willing to pay and what is the average asking price. If the buying public is schooled in its perceptions of the value and pricing of decoratively painted items, then we as artisans must not only develop marketing savvy but also must keep in mind consumer response. Determine the going rate for the types of painted items you will be selling.

"It is almost always a good idea when exhibiting at shows to browse other booths to get a feel for pricing," says Johnnie Elma Anderson. "It's not the best of ideas to undercut the prices of your competition, but instead try to be within the ballpark. You'll sell just as much as if you had not dropped your prices; besides, in dropping prices you sacrifice profits—not to mention damage your rapport with fellow exhibitors."

> ## Tricks of the Trade
>
> "I deliberately plan to show a dozen items that are overpriced and overly glitzy," said a fellow painter. "I put these on one end of my display table with the attitude that I don't care if they sell or not, because I have all other sorts of offerings from $2 to $20. The odd thing about it is the items that portray a top-of-the-line image usually sell out before the end of the show."

Geography and Lifestyles

As decorative painters and craftsmen, we need to develop an awareness that the community, city, state, or region of the country in which we live will affect our pricing strategies regardless of the variety of paintings we offer. Personal experience has shown me that consumers in various parts of the country prefer different themes in home decor and accent pieces. Not only that, they expect to pay different prices. A few years ago I had an unsolicited request from the owner of an out-of-state craft mall who asked if I'd like to participate in a fall show. I shipped a good-sized sampling of decoratively painted Halloween and Thanksgiving items. Not bothering to reevaluate my existing pricetags, the final outcome indicated that prices acceptable in my geography were considered too high for a different locale (in this case a sparsely populated farming community). I figured out that I cleared less than $10 after I paid shipping costs. It pays to do a little homework about regional economics before pricing items or committing to a show.

Painted items focusing on nature and gardening seem to sell successfully nationwide regardless of the season. Some motifs such as the country look and Victoriana remain more popular in the midwestern and southern states, and may not market very well in Hawaii, California, or New York, for example. When exhibiting at craft shows in Oklahoma and Missouri, apples, daisies, and roses were always a hit. The bazaars I hosted in Michigan indicated a preference for wildlife and sailboats. You won't make many sales if you have a booth full of sunflower-painted pots when local residents—not to mention nationally published magazines—prefer pansies, ladybugs, and frogs. Though many traditional items will always remain good sellers, never overlook current and coming trends. Customers respond to fresh ideas.

Commanding Higher Prices

Certainly if you offer exclusive items for which there is no competition, you can and should rely upon your own judgment in setting prices. One-of-a-kind objects, unique in their surfaces or painting techniques, certainly command a higher price. Eye appeal alone (getting back to that impulse buying factor) can close a sale faster than the customer can say, "I'll take it." I remember several years ago when decorative painters would drive for miles in station wagons and pickup trucks, eating dust on a dirt road, looking for old milk cans on which to paint a pastoral scene. It got to a point where every porch in the Midwest had a painted milk can by the front door (I'll admit that mine did, too). Every craft fair at which I exhibited sported rows of prairie-painted milk cans and it didn't take long to saturate the market. Milk cans once priced at $55 at craft shows weren't moving for $12.50. During this era, at one exhibition I noticed a grandmotherly lady selling decorative paintings rendered on old solid wood skateboards (that dates me!) for $25 each. It seemed no one had previously seen paintings done on this type of surface. She sold out and went home early.

Not to be left behind, I later painted one skateboard with a scene of a goose and her single gosling nestled into a straw-filled old bucket. That skateboard has a place of honor on my kitchen wall. No, I can't put a price on it though I have had a couple of offers from people who, until they saw mine, had never seen a decoratively painted skateboard. A frequent comment overheard at craft exhibits and in my studio, as well as from pen pals who subscribe to certain crafting magazines is, "I've already seen it or done it. Is there nothing new?" Learn to develop your own intuition about what grabs a buyer. Offer him something he can't get anywhere else—and don't be afraid to charge him for it.

There is nothing wrong with pricing a few items higher than you feel is competitive or reasonable. You might just sell them. Indeed, sometimes your more exclusive projects may cost you less in materials and time than several "routine" projects combined. Don't let your per-item cost always be a factor in setting prices; instead consider potential customer appeal. When the higher priced items sell, they add to your profit margin and make up the difference for those that netted you less money. Think in terms of getting back your costs the

▼▼▼▼▼▼▼▼▼▼▼▼▼▼▼▼

Handy Hint

- *Be a smart shopper.* Hit every appropriate sale on supplies to save as much money as possible on preferred painting products and accessories. These savings translate into profits down the road.

- *Become a customer.* When you are not exhibiting at shows, browse them so you are aware of competitive marketing and trends. This will help you set your product line and prices at the next event.

- *Practice your skill.* For example, raise your skill level so you can paint an apple in three minutes. Time is money.

continued on next page

▲▲▲▲▲▲▲▲▲▲▲▲▲▲▲▲

best way you can, as long as you feel the customer is happy and you are not being dishonest.

I remember selling one small painting that simple logic told me was overpriced based on the material, project size, and expended effort. However, the customer didn't even flinch when she handed me a $50 bill for a project that cost me $6 in materials and one hour of my time. Old habits are hard to break. I felt guilty momentarily, then thought to myself, "She was smiling and loved the painting so to her it was worth it." She got what she wanted, as did I. That $50, most of which was pure profit, made up for several other sales that barely covered expenses and time invested. Allow yourself the latitude to accept without guilt that greater profits on some items can make up the deficit on others that don't meet your economic expectations.

Johnnie Elma Anderson best expressed the bottom line: "Be fair at all times." Certainly we must be fair to our customers—but also to ourselves.

Handy Hint

- *Set a bottom line for your hourly wage.* Make it what you'd expect if you had an outside job. Never succumb to thoughts such as, "I'd be sitting at home anyway, so my time doesn't mean anything. Besides, I can do the laundry while I paint."

Selling Your Paintings

▼▼

IN THE VOLUMES WRITTEN about launching a business and
the rudiments of selling, you will find some history on how the cus-
toms of selling and trading of goods emerged, including the evolu-
tion of craft fairs and flea markets. Childhood schoolbooks once
included chronicles of simpler times when people bartered services
and goods to meet their needs and to pay their bills. As recently as
75 years ago, depending on geography, it was not unusual for a
small-town physician to be paid for his services in apples or pota-
toes, or with a just-plucked turkey wrapped in a burlap bag. Less
than a century or so ago, farm wives traded fresh eggs for a couple
of yards of gingham. These exchanges were representative of accepted business practices, some of which evolved from bartering
into selling.

In the 1950s, my grandmother sold her farm-fresh eggs to the little country store up the road and was paid in cash. How she enjoyed
having her own "egg money," as she called it. I'm sure she never
thought of herself as a successful seller, but she was. My father always believed that by offering quality products delivered with a personal touch, whether or not their uses were always practical, people
would respond in a positive manner. His principle hasn't really

▼▼▼▼▼▼▼▼▼▼▼▼▼▼▼▼▼▼▼▼▼▼▼▼

Did you know???

Do you know where the term "flea market" originated? Several generations back, it became an accepted social custom to sell or barter used clothing and household articles such as woolen outerwear, blankets, and rugs. In those less cosmopolitan times, it was not uncommon for the consumer to later find that his items of choice were infested with— well, you know.

changed throughout the history of marketing and remains a simple key to successful selling. Find a niche or a need, and fill it.

Scouting Out Selling Sites

Merchandising your painted projects is obviously the only means of making any money from your endeavors. Instead of sitting, you could be selling. Having read to this section of the book, you are now aware of several ways to focus on marketing your decorative painting skills and specialties. After all, there is likely a limit to how many items your friends, neighbors, and coworkers are going to purchase. While giving personally painted gifts makes both you and the recipient happy, sooner or later you will want to expand your horizons.

The different approaches available to you will depend to some degree on your geography and your own lifestyle. If you are employed, you already have a potential market to tap in the forms of coworkers and business contacts. If you live in a close-knit community, once word gets out that you paint and have items on hand, neighbors may beat a path to your door. If you live in a large metropolitan area, you may discover that civic, charity, business, or garden club organizations sponsor a dozen major bazaar events per year. Your own city could be one in which a major craft or consignment mall is an established business. A small community may not even have a craft retail store, let alone be able to offer any annual events at which to exhibit. One circumstance is not particularly better than the other if you're willing to remain open to possibilities. There are advantages and disadvantages to both—and all—selling environments. Large cities may offer more frequent and larger events but can be overwhelming and impersonal. Small towns, where everyone from the school principal to the cook at the local restaurant "knows you're an artist," are wonderful when it comes to acquiring loyal clientele.

Linda Maretich of Linda's Ewenique Boutique of Crafts, told me: "We sell at indoor and outdoor craft shows, out of our home, and take custom orders. I occasionally market at a friend's local restaurant." I got a chuckle when Linda related she sometimes sells items "right off my outfit to people who said they want one of those."

When my son Brit was a small child, we regularly presented our pediatrician with one of my hand-painted items as a Christmas or special "thank you" gift. Upon subsequent visits, we'd find our gifts displayed in the hallway leading to the examining rooms. A favorite painted plaque given to our wonderful doctor included a little verse, written after my child had gone through a few weeks of antibiotic injections:

> MY MOM SAYS I'M LUCKY
> TO HAVE A DOCTOR FRIEND.
> BUT I'D REALLY LIKE TO KNOW
> WHY I ALWAYS GET IT IN THE END!

The project was a gift from the heart, and I was later told it brought smiles to every parent who walked down that pediatrician's hallway—and it also brought me quite a few orders for personalized painted plaques incorporating individualized verse.

Continuing the Course

I think by now you're convinced that "if you can view it, you can do it." The word view has many synonyms including observe, study, or consider. I personally associate view with vision. Do you have a vision as to where you might sell your creations? Why not reserve a page or two in one of your notebooks or journals to write down ideas for selling sites? Not everyone will be attracted to the same potential markets, as personal preferences or individual circumstances differ. Your list of marketing ideas may include some that will be eliminated as you debate the pros and cons of each. Some possibilities might not work for you right now; but they could become ideal avenues in a year or two as personal and family situations change. Never overlook any prospects to promote yourself and your work.

Opportunities Abound

As you may recall from the previous chapter on pricing, I mentioned displaying some of my painted projects at my local hair salon. My stylist, Joy Williams, recently granted a decorative artist the freedom to paint an entire wall mural at her new business location. The artist volunteered her services to Joy at no charge as a means of promoting her decorative painting business. Joy, being the generous person she is, insisted on paying the artist. More important, for the artist, who is serious about going into business in the field of home decorating, that wall mural serves as an exceptional testimony to her talent, which no classified ad would ever capture. So remain alert to such potential opportunities for displaying your work; they may be more numerous than you think.

Cubicle Commissions

I have already shared with you that during my years of pursuing a career I sometimes took my wares to my office, whether it was a sampling of Santas or a group of ghosts. Part of my reason for deciding to sell through this avenue was the almost daily observation of a dozen people in my building continually marketing vitamins, gift wraps, candy, Christmas decorations, collectible baskets, cookbooks, kitchen knickknacks, cosmetic creams, and magical magnets to relieve misery. What did I leave out? Oh, yes—Boy Scout popcorn and Girl Scout cookies. Whew! I certainly did my share of ordering. Observing the employee environment, there seemed to be no problem with anyone earning "cubicle commissions." It was easy to discern no one was selling hand-painted ornaments and customized gifts, and I saw no reason why I couldn't show off—and offer—my individual creative talents. It was a market waiting to be tapped. One particular holiday season I sold $600 worth of painted ornaments and gifts in two days—all from my office cubicle. Never overlook a potential setting for selling.

Another slant on becoming recognized as a decorative painter while keeping a career on track is to be alert to company social events or a promotional to kick off a campaign. Volunteer your creative capabilities. One particular Halloween a corporation for which I was working scheduled a fall breakfast event for its employees. I volunteered to furnish decoratively painted signs and a centerpiece for the coffee bar. The morning of the affair, I was dressed in my hand-painted Halloween garb, and received not only compliments but also orders for "next year." An additional result of that on-site advertising included later being approached with a contract to design 20 custom centerpieces for management's annual Christmas bash, netting me a nice chunk of change. So one never knows when a door is going to open—although sometimes you have to stand ready to turn the knob.

Do Decorative Painters Speak a Unique Language?

I was at a social gathering where, as usual, the men had gravitated to the big screen or to the back deck, leaving most of the women in small groups discussing their own interests. I found myself in a circle with two or three painting friends and a few others whom I had not previously met. During our dialog the topic naturally turned to decorative painting. An acquaintance was extolling the merits of a particular brush she had just ordered. I said, "That reminds me: I need a new stylus." One of the gals in the group who had not offered a single word during our painting discussion eagerly piped up: "Oh, honey. Let me give you the name of my hairdresser! She is really good!"

"One of my first shows was on the Court House Square in Kermit, Texas," says Johnnie Elma Anderson. "It was open invitation so my daughter Deanna, who was about nine at the time, and I set up a table. We went home only $16.50 richer, but I was pleased. During that same show a visitor from Houston had stopped at our table and asked for my address in case she wanted to order some items for Christmas. She did, and that was my first of hundreds of subsequent mail-order sales." So what started out as a small craft show ended up being the catalyst that set Johnnie on a lucrative and enjoyable expedition.

Finding the Fairs

If statistics are correct, there are approximately 10,000 major arts and craft events held in this country each year. So how do you find out about them? Where do you look for shows and how do you determine which ones are right for your particular product? As a decorative painter, your interests may have taken you to some local exhibitions so you know a little of what is available in your area. I encourage you to subscribe to periodicals dedicated to selling where you will consistently find announcements of conventions and fairs in the classified section as well as full- or half-page spreads within the pages.

Call your local craft shops that carry painting supplies or otherwise cater to the decorative painter and ask whether they know of any scheduled shows. Contact your chamber of commerce and request information on civic or community events. A schedule may be available, including whom to contact so you can inquire whether the events will offer exhibit space for arts and crafts. If you want to start out locally, which I recommend for beginners, your Sunday newspaper is a good place to watch for arts and crafts shows. These are likely advertised in the Living or Entertainment sections of the paper, but you might find them in the classified section as well.

"Craft shows are listed in the classifieds of our local newspaper," Linda Maretich told me. "For out-of-town events, fellow painters and crafters often recommend certain shows and will give you the information and a contact number. We all help out each other that way." She's right. Artisans and crafters who follow the show circuit can generally offer advice and insight based on their actual experience, and they're nearly always ready to share. So get to know your fellow exhibitors!

Susan Nelson also relies on local advertising and on territorial publications specializing in listing and promoting regional exhibition events. For example, a newsletter or magazine may concentrate on scheduled art fairs to be held within a five-state area. In addition to general publications, Susan makes use of magazines geared to her particular interests that sometimes provide advertising about theme shows. "Because my specific focus is cats, I've learned of vendor opportunities from national publications such as *Cats* and *Cat Fancy*," said Susan.

> **Handy Hint**
>
> Here is a unique way to display the prices of items during a show: Just paint the price on decoratively painted wood blocks and place them among the appropriate offerings.

Practically every magazine available to the decorative and craft painter includes advertisements for major exhibitions or conventions, and these publications are an excellent source for obtaining event information. In addition to magazines dedicated to painting or other specific topics that are of interest, you can find periodicals or show guides that list arts and crafts events for an entire calendar year. Information is often categorized regionally and includes dates, fees, contacts, and entry deadlines so you can plan for events in a specific part of the country.

These show guides also carry major advertisements for show supplies such as portable booths, tents, pricetags, and shopping bags. Specific publications you might look for at newsstands include *Sunshine Artist*, *Crafts Fare*, *Arts 'n Crafts Showguide*, *The Crafts Report*, and *The ABC Directory of Arts and Crafts Events*. If your business is directed toward the wholesale market, and more of you are exploring this option, look for product dealers, shows, and events listings in specialty trade reviews such as *craftrends*. Additional publications of interest to the retail and wholesale painter include magazines that accept paid advertising of your finished crafts for sale, such as *Country Marketplace* and *Folk Art Treasures*. Contact information for these sources is listed in the back of the book.

The Society of Decorative Painters (SDP) hosts an annual painting exhibition; display space is available to members by advance reservation. The society's magazine, available only through membership in the organization, contains information about this huge event, as well as details on many private seminars and major suppliers of painting accessories. If you are interested in membership and a schedule of events, contact the SDP.

The Las Vegas Creative Painting Convention is another large exhibition requiring submitting a reservation application in advance. The show is advertised in most major craft and painting magazines, or you may contact the promotional staff at *Creative Painting*. Check the resource section at the end of the book for addresses or points of contact concerning these two national painting events.

Major Decorative Painting Conventions

(See resource section for information.)

- Creative Painting Convention
- Extrav—Painting Exposition
- IFFA (International Faux Finishers Association)
- Kaswood Expositions (Canada)
- Society of Decorative Painters
- Stencil Artisans League, Inc.
- Western Regional Decorative Painting Conference

Holiday Happenings

Every November our local community center is the site of a huge Christmas arts and crafts show. It's a full three-day affair, and the exhibitors number in the hundreds. On Saturday and Sunday afternoons, browsers can barely walk through the aisles. It's quite "the event," and is so popular that some of my working friends schedule a day's vacation from the office on the first day of the show (Friday) so they can be first in line for new Christmas decorations and gifts. Booth spaces go fast, with many artists reserving next year's spot before the current show has even closed. "Seasonal or holiday shows that have become highly attended events demand planning ahead if you want to get in," according to Johnnie Elma Anderson. "As a current show ended, I paid in advance for my next year's booth rent. This way I had my choice space and no one else could rent it. I did this at particular shows for at least five years and it worked out great."

In some communities, civic groups may sponsor holiday open houses in the Historical District or in 'landmark' homes to serve as sites for a public arts and crafts show. The event usually serves as an annual fundraiser, but it also provides exposure for new artists. The sponsoring group exacts a small entry fee and may also take a commission on sales, as well as charging public admission. Generally the sponsors handle all the promoting so the exhibitors have no expense for advertising and these events are always well attended and well publicized via the news media.

Check with your Chamber of Commerce or the Historical Preservation Society to see if your town has such an event. If not, you might just get something started by making an inquiry. You might even consider heading up the committee to promote artistic events and holiday fundraisers. The role likely will be strictly volunteer, but what an opportunity to achieve local publicity as a decorative artist—one who is involved in community functions.

Craft Malls— and What's a Craft, Anyway?

The concept of selling through a craft mall is appealing because generally all the craft or decorative painter has to do is make a local delivery or else ship finished projects out of town or state. If the mall is local, plan on doing your own maintenance; if maintenance is provided, you're likely to pay higher sales commissions to the proprietor to make up for their service. If shipping to an out-of-state-mall, the mall operator generally does the rest. If you decide to explore this route, be sure to ask up front what is involved. Keep in mind that some malls may carry far more "cutesy" crafts than decoratively painted items, so the consumer looking for the latter may not consider shopping at what is described as a craft mall. Certainly you can display your work through craft outlets, as decorative painting seems to have become classified as a craft. A few decorative painters who take their work seriously will argue that point based on what the word "craft" implies. More than one colleague has commented that most crafts are just crafts, while true decorative painting is an art form. Sometimes misconceptions result from having too little knowledge of particular art forms, their histories, and their respective objectives.

Judy Higgins of Ruskin, Florida, is a certified instructor for the World Organization of China Painters. Judy executes beautiful florals on porcelain surfaces, a technique also referred to as china painting. "China painting is considered a fine art and not a craft," she explained. "Our organization is an international community with members in Brazil, Japan, Australia, and several European countries, and our skill is a recognized art form that has existed for generations." Judy reinforced that as artisans and craftsmen, our learning process is ongoing. Consider the basic topics of heritage, individual style, and skill level; add to that the variety of surfaces our forerunners have experimented with, utilized, and shared. Every artisan deserves to treasure, honor, and preserve the history of his chosen medium and technique as well as his finished projects. Judy presented me with a beautifully painted porcelain plate that occupies a place of honor in our entryway, a reminder of a long-treasured friendship and of her remarkable talent.

The descriptive terms craft and crafting are frequently used interchangeably with those of art, technique, mastery, and skill. "As far as I am concerned," Claire Kelly recently related, "anything made by hand is art. Maybe it's time to throw the terms crafts and crafter out the window for good." Regardless of which side of the fence you're on when it comes to the definitions of art and craft, there's no reason to eliminate "craft malls" as potential selling sites—as long as you do a little homework.

Wrong Track, Missed Train

I pride myself in having good common sense, but I'll admit that one of the routes I pursued was off the main track. Logic told me I was loitering on the wrong platform, but I decided to stand there and wait anyway. I rented display space in a large mall that advertised "ANTIQUES AND COLLECTIBLES." After all, decoratively painted items are surely considered collectibles. Besides the rent was right and the sales commission was reasonable. I signed a six-month contract, which was straightforward, so I can't say I didn't know the rules. During that situation I never came away with enough sales to make the effort and investment worthwhile. I recall an old saying: "Experience is a great teacher, but the tuition is sure expensive." In brief:

- My earlier intuition that I was in the wrong marketing area had been on target. The sign over the building announcing "Antiques and Collectibles" would mainly draw in antique hunters and collectors of memorabilia. The consumers frequenting this mall were not looking for art, whether folk or fine. Most months I did sell enough to cover my rent and sales commissions. That's not making a profit; that's not even breaking even because I was still out the cost of my inventory and supplies plus car expenses; and it seemed there were always incidentals required to keep the display fresh.

SUCCESS SELLING ORIGINAL DESIGNS

- Make the commitment to become a business. You may choose to start small or part-time, but understand that the goal of business is to grow and make a profit.

- Put it all in writing. Write a business plan and keep it with your business records. If you don't know what a business plan is, read a book on starting a business. Your plan should include short- and long-term goals.

- Know your talents and skills. Know your assets and liabilities. The way to succeed is to show off your best. Stay in focus.

- Know your markets. Investigate. Place your best work in the markets that will make your work shine.

- Educate yourself, not only in the business of design, but also in the business of anything on the consumer's or manufacturer's mind. Always trust your own instincts.

- My rental fee paid only for a share of bare concrete floor. I had to provide all my own shelving, tables, and any other display units of my choice. By the time I bought shelf units, a carpet remnant for my space, table and shelf coverings, and a few embellishments, I'd spent more than I wanted to spend. I could have invested some of that money in my favorite line of paintbrushes (Expressions by Robert Simmons).

- Even though the mall was within a reasonable commuting distance, driving into town every few days for the sole purpose of checking on my display space was soon (after about the third steaming trip during the month of July) viewed as an unnecessary hassle.

- Keep an updated résumé and portfolio. Don't assume others know who you are or what you do. A business card in your pocket could mean a job.

- Grow in your talents and your craft. Experiment and have fun every once in awhile. Change is part of the business. You are not the same person today as you were five years ago, trust me.

- Share your talents in your community. Volunteer. Network with your industry. Once or twice a year, give your craft away for free.

- Believe in yourself and your abilities. If you don't believe in yourself, no one else will. Self-promotion is not bragging.

- Enjoy your work. Rest often. Daydream every day. And go for it!

- I discovered I am not a "mall maintenance" person. At that operation, the staff didn't busy themselves with any arranging or tidying. Each exhibitor was responsible for devising and setting up her own vignettes. Vacuuming, dusting, rearranging, and restocking would usually involve an entire day's work—and I didn't even own the floor space. I quickly realized I'm not cut out to be a renter.

- Trying to keep up with (and allow for) vandalism, theft, and misplaced items annoyed me. In a mall with several hundred displays, expect that a customer who picks up a Santa at Booth 52 will decide by the time she gets to Booth 300 that she no longer wants Santa. He is abandoned at Booth 300, where he sits forlornly while Christmas comes and goes. I saw red one afternoon when I checked on my display. Someone's sticky-fingered darling had deposited a half-eaten lime-green lollipop into the three-dimensional silk-ribbon beard of my favorite fabric-painted Saint Nick.

So when the contract was up, I got out. Even if the most positive thing I can share about that experience is that I learned more than I earned, it wasn't a total derailment. I certainly became better educated about selecting selling sites.

Location and Other Logistics

While connecting with various contributors to this book, I received several observations concerning craft mall selling that I construed as potential red flags. "I have just removed some things from a craft mall where they were not getting much traffic," says Vada Dolph of Cramalot Inn. "Location of the mall is vital."

Then Lea Skaggs's emphatic commentary arrived by mail: "I pursued all avenues, and I lost money and was ripped off in some craft malls." Be sure to ask plenty of questions of the owner or manager, especially when dealing with a small or new operation, such as:

- Do you have a brochure describing the business?

- What products do you handle?

- Do you have a published map available showing your location?

- What amount of traffic do you receive?

- Can I ship my painted projects or do I have to deliver in person?

- What style of pricetags are permitted, or does the store use its own?

- Do I supply a price list?

- What commission is charged on sales?

- Will I be charged handling fees on credit card sales to consumers?

- Is there a minimum number of items I must provide?

- How much display space (square feet) do I have to fill?

- How often do I need to restock, or may I do that on my own timetable?

- Will I be reimbursed for theft or damaged items, or am I at my own risk?

- Are my items insured along with your tangible business, or am I at my own risk?

- How will I be paid, and on what schedule?

- Do I have to sign a contract for a certain time frame or can I get out any time I want?

- If I have any questions or concerns, who is my contact person or representative?

In spite of some unknowns, certainly a well-operated credible craft mall can offer diversified markets for your painted projects, and that is beneficial from a profit perspective. If you are a prolific painter who continually seems to have excess inventory on hand, you're going to want to branch out in every conceivable means. After all, finished items sitting on shelves or bundled in boxes aren't delivering any dollars. Craft malls can serve you well in addition to alternative marketing methods, whether those are small home bazaars or large out-of-state exhibits. One of my painting friends keeps so many projects going that she's never short on merchandise.

She utilizes a well-publicized craft mall more for the function of off-loading what she calls her "excess inventory" than for the actual purpose of selling. I don't know what the secret to her productivity is, but if I find out I'll share it with you in my next book.

For me personally, the downside to craft mall selling is a combination of these two issues:

1. **How do I ensure making a profit once I allow for rent, commissions, and shipping?**
2. **How do I compensate for lack of personal presence concerning my merchandise?**

Further questions surface concerning my merchandise: Is it displayed to its best advantage? Is it dusty? Who's going to answer the customer's question about whether the paint is non-toxic? If a staff member sets up my booth, will she notice whether Easter rabbits are mixed in with the Santas?

If this marketing method appeals to you, give it a try. You can always change strategies later. The larger reputable malls are definitely worth your consideration if this selling approach fits into your profit plan. There are at least two or three major craft malls that seem to have earned excellent professional reputations and have practically become household words among crafters and decorative painters. Consider as examples Crafters Showcase, Country Sampler Store, and Coomers Craft Mall (refer to the back of the book for contact information). Obviously the major craft malls must be doing something right, for not only are they still in business but are apparently expanding, including to the Internet. Going with an established entity is probably good advice.

Consignment Cons and Pros

I chose the unorthodox sequence of those words deliberately, based on the feedback I've received from decorative artists who have tried the consignment route, in particular those who have dealt with an out-of-state operation. The foremost word of caution concerning consignment is "Know with whom you are dealing." I would never put my paintings in a consignment setting without seeing the operation firsthand; or failing that, viewing a series of good clear photographs of the setup. As when dealing with craft malls, you must ask questions based on your observations, directing them to the proprietor. Here are just a few to consider.

- Is the store neat, tidy, dusted, bright, light, and cheerful?

- How much is the sales commission?

- How often will I get paid—monthly, or only when items sell?

- Is the business insured for fire, theft, and water damage? Are consignment items covered?

- May I retrieve or add particular items as I wish, or do guidelines exist for updating displays?

- Do you have a consignment business contract? May I have a copy to review?

Claire Kelly recently related, "My husband Shaun and I sell wholesale to stores and through consignment, in addition to setting up booths at large and small shows in Southern California and Arizona." Claire added a perspective that reinforces why show events could be more favorable to the artist rather than selling by consignment or through other types of stores. "Store sales generally are quite small compared to what we net at shows," she said. "Stores involve the middleman and I think the public enjoys dealing directly with the actual artist at shows. Also, shows are temporary events lasting only a few days. People feel that with a store, they can always go back and buy. But at a show, they know they'd better grab an item before it's gone." Good point, one I've heard expressed many times by other artisans.

You need to be aware that consignment store commissions can run 30 percent to 70 percent. I called one store and was told that their commission is (are you sitting down?) 67 percent. I have seen these types of commission fees in print in classified ads so I know this kind of arrangement can be a reality if one gives in to it. How can a decorative painter—or any craftsperson—hope to make a profit in a competitive market?

I certainly understand most shop owners have hefty overhead and that it takes money to keep a business operational. I've seen consignment shops close their doors due to lack of profits. Realize that proprietors have to pay their bills just like the rest of us. Don't assume shop owners are grinning with glee as they fix their fees. Many consignment shop owners are certainly reputable, and I've had experiences that were extremely pleasant and profitable. On the other hand, I've had at least one experience over which I'm still seething. As I said early on: Determine with whom you are dealing and this will help ensure a positive—if not the most lucrative—selling experience. Keep in mind that you have other options, and don't overlook other avenues. There are several ways of doing business and it's as simple as keeping your options open. Read on.

Gift Shops

Several times over the years I've packed a basket of painted samples, walked into a small gift shop, and asked to see the manager or stock buyer, with the intent of showing my wares and getting a wholesale order on the spot. There is certainly no harm in trying. It's actually worked for me a few times. The probability of success is increased if you're dealing with a privately owned small business rather than a retailer associated with a large chain of stores. Chain stores often have constraints concerning the types and sources of the merchandise they carry.

An independent retailer or his store manager has free rein to decide whether he wants to stock a collection of unique items by a local artist. A gift shop owner or manager may place an order for a quantity of items to be delivered on a certain date, with payment granted upon delivery. Get it in writing. Set your acceptable whole-sale price in advance. As a businessperson, you don't want to be standing there thinking "duh" when the shop manager asks you to quote his per item cost.

Be wary of proprietors who say, "Leave your goods, and as they sell, I'll pay you." Even if each of you have in hand an inven-tory sheet and an agreed-upon price schedule, this is risky. I got into one situation, complicated by a personal friendship, where I agreed to leave my painted items in a gift shop with the assurance that "when they sold I'd get paid." I wasn't worried about getting paid, although it soon registered that I was hearing nothing from the gift shop. Finally I drove into town to take a look.

The shop owner had priced my items way beyond competitive range. No wonder they weren't selling! Not only that, what hadn't been overpriced hadn't been priced at all. Everything was covered with a thin layer of dust. Well, since I had not been paid a wholesale price up front, the merchandise still belonged to me so I hastily but tactfully retrieved it. Nothing earned, but a lesson learned. Now when I sell wholesale, the retailer receives my painted payload and I collect his currency. Whether the merchandise sells, or when, and how dusty it becomes in the meantime is the retailers' responsibility.

Home Mail-Order Business

I read an article indicating that over one hundred million con-sumers in this country spend over $50 billion annually on catalog, mail, and phone orders, and that nearly two-thirds of the population orders something by mail at least once a year. If you are looking for alternative means to expand sales of your painted items, consider producing your own mail-order brochure or catalog that features a selection of your unique items. Today most of us have access to a computer and a basic desktop publishing package. Those who don't usually have friends or colleagues who are willing to help. A two-sided tri-fold color brochure may take only a couple of hours to produce using simple graphics software.

I've also seen some very nice literature reproduced from originals that were done "the old-fashioned way": simple black ink sketches and brief written descriptions. One of my first studio fliers advertising my mail-order items was carefully sketched and casually penned. I included a little comment in one corner that stated, "Yes, I have a fancy computer, but isn't it fun to see what can be created by hand?" Don't let the lack of high-tech equipment keep you from getting out the word—whether it's a flier for a home bazaar or for a mail-order business.

You can start a small home-based mail-order business quite easily. Here are some basics to consider if you are interested in this type of marketing.

- Assuming you've tested the waters and have some items that sell well locally, do you feel they'd sell just as well through the mail?

- How many items do you want to offer? You can start with as few as a half-dozen or offer as much variety as you think you can produce.

- Do you have a means of designing, printing, or getting copies of your brochure or flier? You don't need to print a thousand; start with a hundred.

- What kinds of items will you market, and what will it take to package and ship them? Obviously 1/4-inch-thick birchwood

Developing a Mailing List

Start with those you know:

- Personal friends

- Neighbors

- Relatives

- Local business contacts

- Previous show and bazaar attendees

- Coworkers

To expand your mailing list, ask close friends or relatives whether those in their circle of acquaintances would mind receiving one of your free brochures or catalogs. If three of your contacts each provide 10 names, you've just found 30 potential customers.

Santas won't be much of a problem. But what about hand-painted plant stands or terra cotta pots?

- Do you have a head start on inventory if orders start coming in, or can you produce on the spot to fill orders as they are received?

- Do you have or can you develop a mailing list?

- How is the customer going to pay—in advance? by check, money order, or credit card?

Is mail order for everyone? Probably not, unless either you have enough capital and inventory to launch in a big way or are willing to start small and test the waters. I began a mail-order operation about three years ago in conjunction with other marketing methods. Has it made me rich? No, but I'm not using it as a full-time selling tool, either. Three or four times a year I send out a little brochure to 25 or 30 people. I receive adequate orders to make it worthwhile. It does provide enough pleasure and profit that I'm going to continue the process.

> ## Handy Hint
> The Federal Trade Commission (FTC) requires mail orders to be filled within 30 days unless you include a disclaimer in your brochure or catalog. My brochures include the words: "Because these items are hand painted and custom ordered, please allow a minimum of six weeks for delivery."

Selling Through "Show" Magazines

Several major magazines on the market provide avenues for the artist to sell hand-painted items and other crafts directly to the consumer. These include publications such as *Country Marketplace, Country Folk Art, Country Sampler, Better Homes and Gardens Crafts Showcase,* and *Folk Art Treasures.* The artist or craftsman simply reserves and pays for the size of display ad desired and arranges to ship the items to be marketed. The publisher will set up the advertisement that includes attractive copy layout and professional photography of the projects. With broad national distribution and large numbers of subscribers, this kind of exposure certainly supports the theory that hundreds of potential customers will see your items and your name. An additional benefit is that within your ad, you may mention that a brochure or catalog is available for a dollar or two. Sometimes the eventual number of requests for your brochure will cover the cost of your advertisement.

If you become serious about running a retail ad in a "show" magazine, keep in mind that generally the costs aren't exactly inexpensive for the beginning artist. Consider also that running a one-time advertisement won't get the job done. Be prepared to run at least a three-ad campaign (an ad in three consecutive issues) if you're ardent about getting profitable results. Many mail-order consumers procrastinate. Unless something really grabs them with overwhelming impulse, armchair shoppers tend to sit on their credit cards until they just happen to reread a magazine ad—or they receive the next issue and remember they wanted the product. When advertising in magazines or catalogs, think tenacity.

Based on personal experience (and not necessarily true with show magazines), among the biggest mistakes mail-order sellers make is overestimating demand. It's a lesson we only need to learn once. I had the opportunity to market a pattern packet, which I just knew would fly off the pages of the magazine. In my zeal I ordered 1,000 reproductions of the packet, including top-quality photographs. I would have been wiser to begin with an order of 100. Two-thirds of the packets, complete with color pictures, remain in a box in the closet, fighting for space with my shoes. The shoes are winning.

The Internet—The Ultimate Mall?

Even today not quite everyone owns a computer. When I began writing this book, a number of contributors sud-

Lots 'n Lots of Terra Cotta Pots

Stir Up a Santa

A Cozy Nest—A Country Home
and Classrom Angel

denly decided to acquire computers, or accessed one either through their jobs or through a friend or relative. A few of those I asked to share their thoughts for inclusion within the book responded quickly by e-mail rather than returning handwritten information in the SASE (self-addressed stamped envelope) I'd sent them. It seemed to be an overnight transition for a particular few.

Computers! I can remember few things in history that have changed the way human beings live, think, and view their world— other than perhaps the emergence of the automobile, the invention of television, and the marvel of space exploration. As I mentioned earlier, not everyone owns a computer. Likewise, not everyone is comfortable yet with the concept of Internet selling. One day selling via the Internet seemed a faddish concept; the next day it was an accepted and expected practice. It didn't just appear to have caught on so quickly. It did catch on, and is here to stay from all indications.

"Virtual malls are proliferating in cyberspace," said my web master Shirley Thomas at CRAFTMALL-WEB (www.craftmallweb.com) when I asked her for some thoughts about selling via the Internet. The numbers of people who advertise and who shop on the Internet continue to increase by leaps and bounds. Vada Dolph, who operates her Web site business "Cramalot Inn Crafts," tells me she receives an average of 1,200 hits (visitors) a month. "Some months might only generate 10 orders," she says. "But the feedback it brings is so encouraging. Customers love the character of my offerings as well as the feel of the Web site itself. I think the key phrase here is 'Share the fun!'"

Some Internet sites focusing on decorative painting average as many as 40,000 visitors per day, and those sites are usually linked to other crafting and painting sites as well. If you decide to sell your paintings online, for maximum benefit spend a little time researching those sites that link to many other sites as well. The following Web sites have been recommended by several of my fellow painters and craftsmen:

- Artfully Crafted at www.artfully-crafted.com
- Craftmall-USA at www.craftmallusa.com
- Craft Mark at www.craftmark.com
- Tolenet at www.tolenet.com

The process of setting up one's own Web site seems to become less complicated by the hour. Just last night I was reading an article that claims once you become a member of a particular site and decide to sell finished products, you only have to upload digital images of the products through an easy-to-use online web form. No, old dog that I am, I haven't tried this yet. But I promise you I'm going to check it out—with some caution.

Shirley Thomas observes: "Do-it-yourself Web sites run the gamut from very well done to 'what were you thinking!' A Web site is your little shop in cyberspace and will reflect upon your business just as does a concrete store front. As always, "First impressions are lasting." Does that sound familiar? I know somewhere within these pages I've shared a long favorite motto: Image is where it's at.

"The better cybermalls are juried, just as are top craft shows," Shirley told me. "However, if your works are top quality, it's easy to get in because virtual malls don't have the space limitations of shows. Customers can shop juried cyber craft malls in confidence, knowing each site they click to will feature quality items by reliable craftsmen." A juried mall will ask for photos or to see your products before accepting them.

Before we all become too excited about getting rich overnight through Internet selling, note that a few of my e-mail responders to this topic indicate they aren't yet making enough profits to retire to a private island. "We tried selling finished crafts via the Internet with no success and finally gave up our site," reported Linda Maretich. "It was fun seeing our crafts on the net, but it just wasn't profitable." I have since learned Linda has decided to try it again, and plans to experiment with a line of original pattern packets presented exclusively through her Web site.

Another contributor who prefers to be quoted anonymously offered this opinion: "Word of mouth tells me this is not the way to go. Ninety-nine percent of the visitors to a craft type Web site are only looking to see what their competition is doing, and since they are in the same business, you sure aren't going to get any orders from that segment of traffic." But the same day my e-mail brought that negative feedback, I received this wistful response via "snail mail" from my creative pal Eileen Beard in Staffordshire, England. I had asked if she was marketing via Internet. "No," she lamented, "I wouldn't know how to start. Artisans in the United States are so lucky to have so many outlets for marketing."

I don't know how many of us have been—or still are—holdouts when it comes to using e-mail and the Internet for communicating and advertising, nor do I know the reasons why. We each had or have our own. "We have resisted getting involved with selling on the Internet," Claire Kelly responded when I asked whether she and husband Shaun were using it as a marketing tool for their business, the Village Craft Gallery. "We prefer face-to-face contact with other people whenever possible." Then she added, "We know we can't hold out forever. Eventually we may have to erect a Web site if we hope to expand and grow our businesses on a larger and wider scale."

When Internet technology first flooded the news media and the markets, I scoffed at it. I told my husband Dennis, "You won't catch me using e-mail." He smirked knowingly but didn't say anything. I got away with my attitude for awhile, even during a temporary management contract. Everyone in the department was either dog-paddling or doing the backstroke in the pools of corporate communications, which soon overflowed with wave after wave of outgoing and incoming electronic epistles—except me. I don't need this, I huffily articulated more than once. Now as I'm working, Dennis sometimes sticks his head into the home office and exclaims, "It's the Internet lady." Oh, by the way, my studio Web site address is: www.craftmallweb.com/peachkitty—and you can e-mail me at dgyshy@aol.com.

Where to Peddle Your Paintings:

- Garage and yard sales
- Local businesses
- Place of employment
- School, church, and civic events
- Craft malls
- Consignment stores
- Gift shops
- Home mail order
- Show magazines or catalogs
- Internet
- Regional shows and fairs
- Home bazaars

Planning on the Profits

You've decided you're ready to attempt some serious selling—whether through a Web site, a holiday boutique, an out-of-town annual fair, a private home bazaar, or a combination of markets. The next big question is, what steps might you take to ensure making a profit?

There are no guarantees. If I could offer one, this book would sell ten million copies today. There are as many theories on how to make money as there are painting patterns—well, maybe not quite. But if you ask 100 different exhibitors for their thoughts, you'll probably receive 100 different answers. Let's take a look at some insights that may well add to your success stories.

As you have gathered by now, there is a big difference between pin money and serious profits. My experience tells me the method arrived at for pricing your paintings (refer back to chapter 7) is at the top of the list when it comes to developing a profit plan. Remember the Rule of Threes Plus? I'm convinced you can't go too far wrong by simply factoring in your per item cost (which includes restocking inventory and accessory items), adding in your labor, then multiplying by three. You absolutely have to consider that kind of calculation regardless of how you personally decide to formulate it. But that's only part of the picture if you are serious about making money, and there is more than one way to arrive at a formula for financial success.

At an out-of-town show, I found myself exhibiting next to another decorative painter. To pass the time, we began talking in general about different events, selling, and making money. At one point she expressed: "Oh, I just price my paintings to cover the cost of the raw surface with an estimate of how much paint I think I used up, and add a couple of bucks for myself," she said. "I always go home with some money so I don't think about it." I'm positive she hadn't a clue whether she was realizing a profit. Likely she was not; she was merely covering the cost of her raw materials. It seemed apparent she hadn't factored in the cost of replacing inventory and other supplies. That's not all she hadn't factored in, either. When it comes to realizing profits, there's more to the equation than just replacing your inventory and adding a couple of dollars. Read on.

In addition to setting a profitable price on a per-item basis, consider that where you choose to show and sell will also affect the bottom line. If you are selling out of your kitchen, an established home studio, or from your garage, obviously you have relatively little in the way of overhead expenses. In these selling environments, you're going to be primarily concerned with getting a lucrative price per item so that collectively the total sales will more than cover your inventory costs and labor plus provide a good profit. If you're hosting a bazaar at your home, again your overhead won't be a major factor—unless you decide to offer refreshments and buy additional decorations to enhance the setting. This is a good example of what can be easily overlooked. When you're planning on profits, don't forget to tally the costs for a new set of twinkling lights, a couple of gallons of fresh apple cider, and ingredients for the snickerdoodles.

Betting on the Bottom Line

Without a selling plan and without records of what actually sells, there is no sure way to track the history of your success. How do you ascertain whether you're actually making a profit? I recommend working up a simple hard-copy proposal or balance sheet for every bazaar, fair, or show at which you plan to exhibit. This can be set up in a computerized spreadsheet format, or you can make notations by hand in a notebook.

I mentioned earlier in this book that I discovered old records I'd kept, written by hand in colored inks. At the time I made those notebook entries, I didn't feel I was actually getting ahead; but reviewing the detail proved otherwise. It's important to have a tracking system in place. It can be as simple or as complicated as you wish.

For one of my home shows, I simply sat down with a sheet of plain paper. At the top of the page I wrote a title, added the date, and made the following entries:

SUSAN'S EASTER BAZAAR   April 4, 1998

Total Sales If I Sell Out (Potential Income)	$1,800
Estimated Cost of Raw Materials	$200
Postage, Fliers, and Printing	$38
New Tablecloth and Fresh Flowers	$65
Baking Expenses for Cookies	$8
Apple Cider	$11
Carpet Cleaning after the Show	$50
Total Expenses	$372
My Profit If I Sell Out (Potential Income minus Total Expenses)	$1,428

If you do a little basic math, you can see that my proposal or balance sheet testifies to The Rule of Threes Plus. My expenses totaled $372 and if I multiply that times three, it comes to $1,116. If I subtract that figure from $1,428, that amounts to my "plus" of $312 to cover my labor, to buy a couple of new brushes, or allow for what I may have overlooked when doing my accounting. In this case I didn't just multiply the cost of my materials times three. Instead I multiplied my total expenses by three to give me a serious projection of sales results.

On the Road Again

Remember the lady who remarked about selling and profits, "I don't think about it"? Hitting the highway proposes even more of a challenge in assessing the bottom line. Planning ahead becomes crucial. You need to figure all travel expenses and overnight lodging, entry fees, and any other overhead (including phone calls home) in order to assess what is required to make enough profit to justify the effort. Yes, shows and fairs can be a ton of fun. However, the driving, unpacking, and setting up is a ton of toil, and who wants to work for nothing? And besides, the last time I filled up my little red car, I noticed gasoline prices have climbed.

Let's take a quick look at a similar example of a projection for a weekend road show.

Total Sales If I Sell Out (Potential Income)	$3,000
Raw Materials Cost	$325
Entry Fees (may be zero)	$100
Gasoline/Car (varies, depending on location)	$40
Meals, Motel	$250
Phone Calls (collect to home or on charge card)	$10
Miscellaneous (I might want to buy from a fellow painter)	$50
Total Expenses	$775
My Profit If I Sell Out (Potential Income minus Total Expenses)	$2,225

If you do the math, in this example I didn't exactly meet The Rule of Threes Plus. Multiplying my expenses of $775 times three comes up $2,325. So in this case, I didn't make enough for the Plus factor. But, a profit is a profit, and it's still a good one.

I don't know about you, but I'm about ready to hit the road—as soon as I give you a little more homework.

Setting Up for a Successful Show

Have you noticed at large craft fairs some booths or tables are practically thronged and others barely have a single browser? I have seen this in a variety of settings, whether it was an indoor craft show at a major shopping mall or at an outdoor event in the city park. Why do some painters practically sell out, and others end up packing everything back into the minivan?

Several aspects come into play, some more pivotal than others. Paying heed to the more important points will help compensate for overlooking smaller details, especially in the beginning. My personal experience with craft shows, both as a participant and as an observer, has me convinced that the way you set up your display can literally make you or break you when it comes to attracting a crowd.

Let's imagine you've booked a spot for a spring show. You've paid your entry fee and received confirmation. If you're dealing with a promoter (in particular a professional one), you may have received a tip sheet on how to set up your space or what you may expect to find at the location. Don't count on it—especially if the show is part of a small civic event or a promotional for a shopping mall. Likely you're on your own in such situations. Planning your first few exhibitions can be confusing, frustrating, and fatiguing without some preliminary organizing, particularly if you are a beginner and have no groundwork information about the physical layout of the show. How can you prepare yourself ahead of time to ensure a less stressful and more successful setup?

Getting a Head Start

If the travel distance to the event site is not prohibitive, I strongly recommend you check out the location a few days in advance. Even if you don't know exactly which is your space, you'll see whether there are shade trees, no trees, water faucets, and electrical outlets within a reasonable distance. What about restroom facilities and parking space? If you are unable to make a preliminary visit to the location and will be totally unfamiliar with it upon arrival, communicate ahead of time with the show promoter or coordinator and request information concerning the site (if it's not provided after your query or with your reservation confirmation). There is an easy way to obtain the necessary details through simple methods.

For several years I've kept a file folder of general information about bazaars and craft shows that includes hints and how-to's and any notes I've taken about past experiences (good and bad). Stapled right inside the front cover of the folder is what I call my Twenty Questions list, with loose copies in the back of the file. When necessary I can easily mail a copy to the promoter or coordinator with my query or reservation fee, or I can ask the questions by phone. Having the list right in front of me has saved making a follow-up phone call (or three!) because I've forgotten something the first time. Following are the questions on my personal list; you may think of others and decide that some of mine do not apply to you. With experience, and also by modifying some questions to fit your own circumstance, you can make your own list.

Twenty Questions

1. Is the event publicized by the media and how do you advertise?
2. How many seasons or years has the event taken place?
3. How many exhibitors can be accommodated? How many are expected?
4. Is there a layout plan showing where each crafter is to set up, or is it first come, first choice?
5. Can I unload my vehicle close to the exhibit area? How far away is the parking area?

6. Are there shaded areas available for setup, or is the site completely open to the sun?

7. In the event of bad weather, is shelter available (such as a gazebo, canvas tents, or awnings)?

8. Will there be food vendors participating in the event or fast-food operations close by?

9. Are there drinking fountains and bathroom facilities near the exhibit area?

10. If I'm driving a long distance, how close are motels? Can you recommend any for the event?

11. Will electricity/outlets be within reach for extension cords? Are extension cords permitted?

12. If I should need to call home, is a phone available, or how far away are pay phones? (Not all of us utilize car phones or cell phones even in this new millennium.)

13. Will there be a security officer or local police on site? Should I or a customer have a medical emergency, is assistance available?

14. Do I need to bring my own display tables and chairs? What is my space allotment?

15. Are portable booths or overhead canopies permitted? Are there size constraints?

16. Are certain props disallowed (such as decorated Christmas trees, lighted votive candles, lamps)?

17. If this is an outdoor event, are small pets welcome if carefully confined or controlled?

18. Are there existing backdrop walls (for example, against a store front or brick wall as in a strip mall)?

19. Are the exhibit grounds on a paved parking lot, a concrete sidewalk, a park meadow, or other setting?

20. If I'm out of state, are sales tax reporting forms available or do I need to obtain my own?

Before you think it's too much trouble to consider so many details, I can assure you it isn't. Remember the little painted plaques or pin-on buttons inscribed with the words "PLAN AHEAD," on which the lettering got smaller until the last letter dropped to the next line. I think every painter, craftsman, and exhibitor should mount that expression over his or her workbench or painting table, or stencil it on the truck bumper sticker. Receiving answers to your questions ahead of time eliminates so many unpleasant surprises and frees your mind to concentrate on pigeonholing, pricing, packing up your painted pieces—and other preparations prior to traveling to a show.

Almost Ready

Now that you have a Twenty Questions list, whether mine or your personal version, let's follow-up by taking a few of those questions one step further. Earlier in this chapter I mentioned that no single answer explains why some exhibits are mostly mobbed and others are virtually vacant; and that paying attention to the crucial details can make up for less important shortfalls.

> ## Handy Hint
>
> It never hurts to add a touch of professional courtesy to any business dealing. When mailing queries or questions to a show promoter or coordinator, include a self-addressed stamped envelope (SASE). It's a nice gesture and helps to insure a prompt response.

Once you arrive at the exhibit site, the physical setting up begins the moment you find your space. You may find that the promoter provided tables. More likely you had to bring your own furnishings, about which you wisely inquired and therefore came prepared. Years ago at a large outdoor show I provided an extra folding table and folding chair to a young painter who was participating in his first exhibit. From the looks of his truck, he'd packed everything he owned, including his dog—except a table and chair. To be able to help in that small way (small to me; not to him) set for both of us a positive tone; we became comfortable friends, if only for the duration of the event.

Seven Tips for Setting Up

1. *Consider your backdrop.* If you're going rent or otherwise obtain a portable booth or tent, opt for off-white or beige. Dark colors (unless natural wood) or bold stripes may overpower your exhibit and compete with your merchandise and can make your display look dismal on a cloudy day. Some indoor events allow the hanging of fabric backdrops. Plain white sheets work well; they're easy to pack, store, and launder.

2. *Make full use of display space.* Plan for as many tables or shelves as possible. The more merchandise you have available, the better chance for larger profits and any extra space allows room for adding a personal touch such as seasonal decorations.

3. *Use table covers and shelf liners.* Again, white or plain pastel sheets work nicely and are large enough to drape a big surface plus allow for overhang. Table covers provide a uniform background for your painted pieces; and by letting the covers extend to the floor or ground, you can stow your packing boxes and supplies under display tables. Stashing empty boxes and extra merchandise gives you the added edge of appearing organized and ready for business.

4. *Set up early.* If you are unpacking your paintings as the customers begin to appear, you have already lost sales. Arrive as early as is permissible and immediately arrange your tables or shelves. Some larger indoor events allow exhibitors to set up the night before a big show. Ask ahead.

5. *Make your display unique and easy to find.* Have business signs available to display in more than one size and material, to accommodate different show lay-

Handy Hint

Look for plain white or pastel sheets at discount stores or as 'seconds' in the bedding section of major retailers. They are very inexpensive for the amount of material. Check out neighborhood yard sales. Sheets in good condition can often be purchased for a dollar or two.

outs. You may want a plywood panel, a canvas or vinyl banner, and several poster-board placards. If you use a particular design on your business cards, incorporate the same one on your advertising signs. Utilize one great prop, even if it takes a bit of table space. Whether a 3-foot plastic rabbit or a table-top Christmas tree, place it within your display—the taller the better. Customers who wander past will take notice immediately and those who wish to "come back later" can spot you more easily. If the promoter allows, place several small lamps among your paintings. These could be battery operated if electricity is not allowed or not available. Soft lighting helps show off painted surfaces to best advantage, especially on a cloudy or drizzly day.

6. *Don't display multiples of identical items.* Though many of your more expensive pieces are likely to be one of a kind, there is a benefit to painting multiples of smaller items when it comes to shows and bazaars. Put out only two or three of each even if you brought six dozen. Some passing customers, seeing volume, will think you have plenty of merchandise and that they have plenty of time to come back later. Chances are they will not, for in the meantime they'll have made other purchases or are too tired to backtrack. It is more tempting to the buyer to make an impulse purchase if he thinks you only have one or two of a particular painted item. As projects sell, reach under the table into your packing box and restock.

7. *Make sure every painting or painted item has a pricetag.* For reasons I've never figured out, people hesitate to inquire, "How much is this?" Many times an item missing a pricetag will be passed over, no matter how appealing. Also if prices are easily visible, projects will be handled less, which saves wear, tear, and fingerprints on your paintings.

Susan Nelson of Cats 'n Stuff offers her main goals in setting up for a successful show and they are right on target with the message of this chapter. "My number one goal is good visibility of products," she said. "Then I strive for an attractive display, and often one that incorporates a theme. I also plan for safety and security from theft." Good points to remember, don't you agree? Are you feeling less anxiety now about getting ready for your first show? Or just better prepared for your next one?

Handy Hint

If vehicle space permits, take along an extra folding table and chair regardless of the information you received about accommodations. You may find you have more room than anticipated and can use the extra furniture. Also, a fellow crafter may come up short, expecting to find tables provided and there are none.

Successful Selling

Johnnie Elma Anderson has enjoyed a long relationship with successful exhibiting and selling since that first show in Kermit, Texas. She participated in public shows for at least 20 years. "With my daughters (and partners) Fern, Frances, and Deanna, we could easily sell $500 to $800 at one event," she recently told me. "Those were the days!" She also contributed one of my favorite tips: "Keep all of your extra projects under your tables hidden by nice cloths that hang to the floor." Johnnie is one of several who eventually shifted to selling from home rather than packing up and traveling the show circuit. We're going to address hosting home bazaars and the secrets to their success at a bit later in this chapter.

It's been expressed for generations that there is no form of education more lasting than actual life experience. That holds true even when setting up for a show. It only took one episode of being caught unprotected in the rain to make sure it didn't happen to me again. I learned another good lesson as a crafter, prior to taking up decorative painting, when I participated in my very first crafts bazaar. It was held on the sidewalk in front of a mini-mall. I showed up with only a bare card table to use as my display surface. All of the other exhibitors had table covers. One lady actually had a white lace table cover under her offered items. I felt like a wart. Fortunately, the show was local so I called my husband and asked him to grab a sheet out of the linen closet and rush it to me. How much difference did it actually make in my sales? I'll never know for sure, but it certainly made a difference in my self-confidence. Confidence in your presentation helps sell.

Just Plain Attracting Attention

Elizabeth Bishop operates her home studio business, Seams Sew Creative Patterns. She told me, "You need to be just as creative in calling attention to your business or product as you were in developing and launching it. Some exhibits just naturally draw a crowd. If yours does not, you need to create a splashy extravagance that relates to your specialty."

Linda Maretich of Linda's Ewenique Boutique of Crafts prefers a straightforward approach to setting up for a show. "Keep it simple, neatly arranging things at various height levels using plain-colored table coverings, step-shelves, and a peg rack for hanging some items," she says. "Consider using latticework sections hinged together to flank your table and set it apart."

As with most things in life, rules are rarely cast in stone, and even those that are seem to have exceptions, particularly when it comes to being creative. While plain table coverings are adequate, functional, and simple to use, take into account the flavor of your painted works, your geography, and the location of the exhibit. Will you be exhibiting a garden theme complete with painted terra cotta pots, plant markers, welcome signs, and watering cans? Consider a table covering of denim, striped ticking, or burlap. One enterprising exhibitor who was selling paintings of gardening scenes and old farm tractors had covered his show tables with black landscape cloth purchased from his local garden center. He had interspersed his offerings with old hand tools and empty seed packets. What an interesting display!

If your wares focus on portraits of ladies in Victorian hats or birdhouses painted with a variety of old garden roses, consider the approach taken by Claire and Shaun Kelly of the Village Craft Gallery. "We put doilies under most of our projects to create displays and to highlight certain items," related Claire. "All of our tables are covered with pretty country or Victorian-look cloths and we cover some of the shelves on our display units with fancy linen laces." I have seen photographs of the displays arranged by this creative couple, and the meticulous attention to detail is quite striking—not only in their many floral-themed projects, but also in the continuity of their presentation to the buying public.

Hints for Hitting the Road

When it came to hitting the road for my first two or three shows, I hate to admit I was primarily concerned with packing my paintings into the back of the car with my folding table, chair, and cash box. After all, what else did I need?

As I mentioned earlier, experience is the ultimate teacher. Weather-wise, luck had been with me until about my fifth exhibit (all had been outdoor events). Before the end of that show, I was scrambling to pack my paintings and rush to a nearby covered picnic pavilion along with a few others who were equally unprepared for a sudden shower. "At our yearly local show," related my pal Eileen Beard in Staffordshire, England, "the weather was fine when we started out. The very moment the booth was set up, down came the rain! We grabbed our plastic sheeting and covered our booth so thoroughly that no one could see what we were selling; but we stayed dry and had a good laugh." Here are some suggestions triggered by the account of Eileen's good planning.

It's easier to "have a good laugh" (to quote Eileen Beard) if you are physically comfortable, and your happy attitude will help increase your sales.

Selling at a Show

This chapter is already cram-packed with all sorts of methodology on selling in general so I'm not going to make this a homework section with a string of self-proposed questions. (Did I just hear a sigh of relief?) Let's just cover some basics.

Most of us already know that successful sales hinge on good customer relations. Once you've captivated the customer with your display, it doesn't mean you'll get his money. Though your perfectly executed exhibit will attract attention, the browser may still walk away with pursed lips and a padlocked purse. Did I mention somewhere that "image is where it's at"?

Coexisting and Conversation

Johnnie Elma Anderson is adamant about presenting a professional selling stance. "Never eat while waiting on customers," she says. "Don't be pushy, but by all means greet each browser. If you have been sitting down, stand up and offer your help. Sometimes it's best to be quiet and let the customer look." Knowing how much information to volunteer can be difficult depending on the customer. Sometimes you have to sell your work if it's not selling

▼▼▼▼▼▼▼▼▼▼▼▼▼▼▼▼▼▼

Handy Hint

Outfit a duffel bag with extras. Include a pair of shoes, socks, and a T-shirt or two, as well as disposable wipes, paper towels, and tissues; a major credit card and your phone calling card; and some additional single bills and rolls of coins. Make sure you pack a jacket, sweater, or windbreaker with a hood. Depending on the geography or the calendar, a sunny September Saturday can quickly become a drizzly, windy 45 degree afternoon.

▲▲▲▲▲▲▲▲▲▲▲▲▲▲▲▲▲▲

itself. As Johnnie added, "When a customer seems interested in an item but is hesitating, mention that the piece is available in custom color choices and that mail-order delivery is available upon request."

I agree with that idea. One might also suggest ways in which a painted project may be displayed within the home, or mention to the customer that hand-painted items are perfect all-occasion gifts. Whether browsers buy or keep walking, Johnnie says, "Always thank them for stopping by your table and hand out a business card." That's a successful closure even if no money changes hands. If the browsers don't find what they're looking for at other exhibits, they may pass your way again.

If there's one rule at the top of my personal list for successful selling at a show, it's this: No matter how tempting it might be to alleviate your own boredom during a slow show, don't sit behind your display table with your nose in a book. You will appear uninterested—not only in selling, but also in your potential customers. Depending on geography, not saying "hello" is an omission and is considered rude. Worse, you are sending a message that you have no interest in your own works of art. If you have no interest in what you are selling, why would anyone else? When I pass a craftsman's table and see the seller hunkered in his canvas chair with his nose buried in a book—not even bothering to glance up, let alone speak— I will take my dollars to another display.

While some conversation with the buying public is good business (and I encourage you to be accommodating and friendly), I do understand the exchange can be frustrating. After about seven hours straight of hearing customers say, "I painted those years ago" or "My mother-in-law sells exactly the same birdhouses," I've bitten not only my tongue but through my bottom lip. Difficult

Handy Hint

Take along some refreshments. You'll appreciate a small, insulated cooler with sodas and a couple of sandwiches, or a thermos of hot soup or tea. Include some nibbles such as packaged crackers and snack spreads in pop-top cans. Don't forget plastic knives and forks and a small trash bag. Even if there are food vendors at the event, there may be times when you can't leave your exhibit to get refreshments.

as it can be, it is important to maintain a sense of humor, especially when the commentary is complimentary but the profits are pitiful.

Hosting a Home Bazaar

"For the most part, I resist paying rent to sell my items, when they can be displayed for free in my own house," said Vada Dolph of Cramalot Inn Crafts. "I have one or two home shows before Christmas each year that are quite successful."

Several years ago I completely gave up hitting the exhibition highway. The idea of following the craft show circuit was just too much to juggle with a career and an extended and blended family that totaled four teenagers at one point (maybe painting can save one's sanity after all). Then there were the flowerbeds and 14 loads of laundry a week—and kitty. Weekend traveling for the purpose of peddling my paintings seemed out of the question at that stage of my life. This also was during the period prior to building (gratefully) my own studio that has since solved the problem of where to display and store my works.

> **Handy Hint**
>
> Smile, smile, smile! Greet every browser as though each was going to spend $100. For all you know, a few of them will!

In the meantime, I became one of many who are enjoying the fun and success associated with hosting home bazaars. As with most everything else, I'm a firm believer in planning ahead, and that's important when considering hosting a home bazaar. Three things that come to mind immediately are:

1. Do you have plenty of merchandise to make a home show worthwhile? If not, include two or three artist friends and make the event a fun joint effort.
2. When do you want to hold the event? There are no rules. You are your own boss here.
3. Can you work around existing furniture to provide an attractive and plentiful display space?

I am an enthusiastic advocate of these types of events. You may decide to give home bazaars a try. Warning: It may be habit-forming.

"Christmas in August"

A theme chosen by Susan Nelson of Cats 'n Stuff in Rochester, Minnesota, for a summer showing is "Christmas in August." It has become an annual event. I participated in her third show, albeit by long distance; and from all reports I regret missing the actual scene. Everyone had a great time and all exhibitors came away with a jingle in their jeans (mine was in the form of a mailed check).

The popularity of buying for Christmas has almost escalated to a year-round activity. Like it or not, by Labor Day the major department stores in shopping malls start putting out Santa-embroidered hand towels and snowman-patterned dinnerware. I've seen Christmas trees being assembled in the aisles of discount stores before the Halloween displays are completed. If the retailers can do it, so can we.

Aside from that, I am well aware that several of my acquaintances appreciate having lots of time to order a custom gift, or finding an unexpected painted trinket box just perfect for a secret pal. So they buy when the opportunity presents itself, even if it's spring. Several regular customers at the studio call me as soon as the children return to school in August; they want to start their Christmas shopping. Why not get the jump on the season by hosting a "Christmas in August" home bazaar? Start small if you feel more comfortable that way and invite only a few people; but with a good game plan, you can expand the event as large as you wish.

Artist Ruby Tobey has for many years operated a small business, Scribbles and Sketches Studio, from her home in Wichita, Kansas. Ruby's offerings include painted china plates, mugs, and jewelry in addition to watercolor works and ink sketches. "I use my living room for double duty," she told me. "Often people will call and need a gift, or a friend may have a visitor who wishes to see my work. Some of my painted items are always on display in my living room, and I utilize open bookshelves as well. One unit has a drop-down shelf that becomes a desk, and another has a hidden bin that holds my change box, business cards, and sales tax schedules. Once the customer leaves, I put things away and have a normal living room."

With Ruby's system, one might say her business is always open. Additionally, twice a year she sends out invitations for a Weekend Open House to show and sell her painted pieces. Ruby added, "Those are the times I set up extra folding tables to achieve maximum display space at home."

Home Bazaar How-To's

1. *Pick the date.* A weekend in late July or August is not too soon to host a holiday bazaar. You'll be way ahead of local groups who advertise their annual craft shows in October and November. Once you've chosen a tentative weekend, make sure your family's schedule won't present conflicts. Can someone else in the household (or a neighbor) cover events like soccer practice carpooling? Is there a toddler who will need a babysitter? Do you have an indoor pet that will need to be secluded or boarded? Will teenagers be in their rooms or at friends' houses if they—or you—prefer that alternative?

   As soon as you have a firm date in mind, make any arrangements now for household help. Then alert the family members of the event and when it will take place. Post it on the refrigerator and on calendars, so the night before the event you don't have to hear: "But I didn't know it was this weekend!" If family members will be in the house during the bazaar and have not been enlisted to help, warn them in advance that unless the house is on fire, you will not respond to anyone screaming "MOM!"

2. *Check your inventory.* Do you have enough items for a one-person showing? If you're uncertain, call on painting and crafting friends and ask if they'd like to participate in a home bazaar. Require each one to provide an inventory sheet of items they'll be placing on display and to tag all items with prices and their initials or a number for identification prior to delivery.

3. *Evaluate your space.* Is there room for additional folding tables if needed? Can you remove personal objects from existing bookcase units and tables to use as display areas? Consider traffic patterns so people can walk without bumping into things. You might want to relocate huge recliners to another room that can be closed off during the bazaar.

4. *Announce the event.* If your bazaar is a small showing, you may prefer the "invitation only" approach and send personal invitations to close friends, coworkers, and neighbors. If you're attempting a larger scale event, an effective way to advertise is by using fliers. These can be printed on your home computer, or if you don't have access to one, likely a neighbor or fellow painter does. Mail the fliers to as many friends and business acquaintances as you feel you can accommodate. If you have plenty of space and are not worried about attracting a crowd, post fliers at work and on public bulletin boards at neighborhood supermarkets and banks.

I do not have space for a casual crowd in my small house, and I'm also toiling toward a golf course turf lawn so I decline the bulletin board approach. But one of my painting friends lives out in the country on five acres and even has a couple of cows in her front yard. She hosts her annual "Barnyard

Handy Hint

Even if advertising for a late summer bazaar includes the word "Christmas," you should plan to display a table of Halloween and Thanksgiving decorative projects. The availability of these items will provide extra impulse sales as buyers begin to look toward fall.

Christmas" in the renovated barn (hence the name of her event) and doesn't care how many people park in the yard as long as the cows don't escape the gate at the end of the driveway.

5. *Set your hours.* A 'sneak preview' offered on a Thursday evening (from 6:00 to 7:30, for example) can generate early traffic and help spread the crowd. You might offer an incentive of 10 percent off for the Thursday showing only. For the main showing, consider Friday evening from 5:00 to 9:00 and the Saturday event from 10:00 to 5:00. These hours should not be overly taxing to your household, to your participants, or to yourself; and yet they will encourage attendance by providing a broad window to accommodate your customers work and personal schedules.

6. *Provide a place to sign in.* Place a guest book at an entry table. This is an easy way to update and increase your mailing list for future invitations. It also gives you an accurate count of how many people attended.

7. *Divide up the hosting duties.* If fellow painters are displaying along with you, they likely have volunteered to help during the event. One friend may act as a greeter at the door, ensuring the guest book is signed; another might handle the cash box and write down each item that sells (and check off items on exhibitors' inventory lists as they sell).

8. *Serve refreshments.* This is optional depending on your floor space, traffic pattern, and personal tolerance for crumbs and spills. A fresh batch of cookies and a pot of cider (even if it is August) imparts the spirit of Christmas. Instead of refreshments, you might hand out individually wrapped cookies to guests as they leave. Attach a tag to the cookies: "Thank you for attending Christmas in August. Hope to see you at the next event!"

9. *Clean up.* Plan a full day to put your house back in order. This might involve steam-cleaning carpets and repositioning furniture. Box up remaining bazaar items and arrange for participants to pick up any unsold paintings—and their profits.

10. *Plan the next bazaar.* While the event is a fresh memory, start or update a notebook or computer file to record which items were best-sellers, observations about traffic flow, parking problems, and customer requests or suggestions. Update your mailing list from the guest book so everyone receives an invitation to your next bazaar.

Selecting What Sells

This is a concept communicated and shared by many decorative painters and craftsmen. The public's fascination with home decorating never loses its momentum even in weaker economic times; and there are no category constraints. People clamor for the unique, for a signature piece, or something that they feel expresses their interests, personalities, memories, and dreams.

Painted items may speak to the customer of the present millennium through air-brushed modernistic mouse pads. They may serve to recall the previous century by portraying a collection of hand-painted Victorian ladies complete with flowered hats and flowing dresses. They might bring to life the memory of a favorite pet. Or perhaps they foster a vision of someday seeing the creatures of the rain forests or the big cats of Africa before they disappear from the face of our wonderful earth.

So stop and consider for a moment what your paintbrushes can give to others. "One reason I thought about selling my decoratively painted items is because I loved them so much I wanted to share them in other people's homes," expressed Claudia Gentry. "I think everyone needs beautiful decorative items in their surroundings." Certainly, home dec will never go out of style as long as consumers desire and can obtain items that add pleasure to their lives. If they can't create their own accessories (and most people today do not have the time, even if they have the inspiration), they'll be looking to buy them from you. I have fond memories of spending a particular day with my long-time pal, Martha Dover. She had the idea of transforming the atmosphere of her kitchen from typical ranch style to an Oriental garden. "Can you come over here?" she asked. "I'll bet you can do this in one day." She was right.

> **Handy Hint**
>
> If you wish to discourage strollers and sticky-fingered darlings, just include within your invitation or flier a line or two: "Due to small spaces and many breakables, for safety reasons strollers are not permitted. Unattended toddlers will be traded in for paints and brushes." It gets the point across with a bit of a grin.

Many years ago as a young housewife, though money was extremely tight, I wanted to add a new accent color to my kitchen. With my few dollars, I went to a discount store and bought a couple of cans of spray enamel. Lining my patio with newspapers, I spray painted a pair of ordinary bricks to use as bookends for my recipe album collection. I sprayed my old salt and pepper shakers, the base of a lamp, a hand-me-down canister set, and a couple of thrift-store picture frames. Every neighbor who visited my kitchen wanted to know where I found my perfectly color coordinated accessories. Home dec is a permanent trend. Just browse any home improvement center, discount store, or magazine—and see for yourself.

Little Things Mean a Lot

Remember Eileen Beard who lives in England? "I tried all sorts of avenues but it didn't seem successful," she said. "But I finally hit on decorative florals on ordinary wooden kitchen spoons, and hooray.

Victory!" Some of her creations have made their way to the United States as well as to Ireland. Incidentally, Eileen donates dozens of her decorative spoons to her church and a local rehabilitative organization for their fund-raising events. She recently told me, "Now I can hardly keep up with the orders coming to me through friends at the club and the church." Not bad for someone who once said, "It didn't seem successful."

Copyright Laws

The laser cutouts I purchase from West Coast Wood Craft Supplies (WCWCS) are copyrighted by the supplier and the actual designs may not be reproduced by any means without permission. However, artisans and crafters may purchase, paint, and sell as many cutouts as they wish for personal profit, and with permission may incorporate them within original designs. If you have any questions as to legal limitations or buying in bulk quantities, contact WCWCS.

Several of my favorite quick and easy items to sell for profit are based on small laser wood cutouts from West Coast Wood Craft Supplies. Since the designs are already engraved on the wood, it's a simple matter of sealing the items and painting with acrylic washes or detailing with brush-tip markers. Then I just finish with a spray sealer and apply glitter accents or gloss varnish of my choice. The cutouts may be hole-drilled for Christmas ornaments or package ties, or fitted with pin backs for attaching to a hat, shirt, jacket, or bookbag. These make great gifts and bazaar sellers because they work up so quickly.

Some of my biggest profit margins regardless of where or how I'm marketing have been realized through utilizing laser-cut wood designs. My preparation time is virtually nil, which is an important factor when it comes to profit margins; and the costs are quite reasonable for the unfinished pieces. The cutouts easily lend themselves to an "assembly line" process, and with very little practice, I'm able to produce a dozen finished projects in under two hours. These are the kinds of bazaar or show items that quickly build your profits and help to make up time and expense demanded by your more labor-intensive, larger, and uniquely painted offerings.

Assessing Your Audience

When displaying at the average civic event or local small show, keep in mind you will always have many browsers who want to spend 50 cents to $3; and if you don't have anything in those price ranges, those customers will keep walking. Consider that children and teens might be looking for a friendship gift or a Christmas present for Mom and have limited funds. Set up a couple of large baskets or trays of inexpensively painted paperweights, small herb pots for the kitchen, windowsill and shelf decorations, lapel pins, desk ornaments, or bookmarks for under a dollar or two. You will be surprised how quickly those displays empty. Claudia Gentry recalls a memory from childhood days when she went to weekend shows with her artist parents: "I remember going to shows and looking very thoroughly at everything before choosing to buy a painted pot or jewelry."

Your decisions about where you choose to market will dictate to some degree your customer base. If you've booked a Christmas event, you can assume the crowd expects to buy decoratively painted holiday ornaments and gifts. If you're exhibiting at a Spring Fling, you should be able to turn a profit by concentrating your display on Easter, floral, and gardening themes.

When it comes to other selling environments, consider that a customer visiting your studio may be agreeable to spending $1,200 on a one-of-a-kind hand-painted drop-leaf desk. A browser at an August sidewalk exhibit may want to purchase a $5 painted terra cotta pot—and will ask if you'll take less. Even if you prefer to concentrate on exclusive specialty items, you can't go wrong by having additional items in many price ranges. And don't forget my father's theory: Find a niche or a need and fill it.

Profitable Peddling—You Can Start Small

You may recall my story about the traveling peddler, By Golly, who traded my mother a charcoal rendering of me for a dollar. Many years later I first heard the word entrepreneur and understood what it meant. "By Golly" had figured out a way to earn a living sufficient for his needs, whether he received a half-dollar for a decoratively painted dented teakettle—or a plate of beans bartered for his breakfast. By Golly was an entrepreneur—and a successful salesman if ever there was one.

Looking back, I can see I had an early interest in the delight of luring the public to a display of delicacies. In recent years, I've come to realize my father had innocently passed the entrepreneurial bug to me without recognizing how serious was its bite. Dad had a woodworking shop in the small nearby town to which he went each day to build, paint, and sell what today would be described as decorative woodcrafts. One day after school my first-grade pal Mary Ann Harp Ellis and I walked down to the shop. We soon became bored and wheedled a couple of nickels out of Daddy. Running next door to Mrs. Higgins' General Store we bought penny candy, whispering between ourselves how we could get the most pieces for the price. Then we went to sit on the splintery wooden porch of Dad's shop to watch the passing cars. Suddenly we had an idea.

We sneaked an empty nail keg from the back of the shop. It became a table on the porch. We divided up our booty into as many small servings as possible, cutting sticks of gum into halves and quartering mint patties into little pie shapes. Using crayons and sheets of lined paper from our Big Chief school tablets, we made our signs and held them up: "PENNY CANDY. STOP HERE." Cars actually braked. Morsels and monies were exchanged through rolled-down windows. We were a success! That is, until Daddy detected the difference in the flow of highway traffic and stuck his head out of the shop door. Once he determined we had not been abducted by aliens, he decided we were hoodwinking the public. We each got a smack on our sit-downs. (Back then, parents weren't penalized for dispensing "parental guidance.")

A Final Note—Financial Matters

I'm keeping this subject brief because there are so many wonderful books dedicated to addressing the important issues of operating a home-based business, in particular those authored by Barbara Brabec. Barbara's books have become my personal and professional business doctrines, and her information has been invaluable over the years. I would never have had the courage to launch my own retail businesses or my publishing endeavors without Barbara's business acumen and marketing insights. Be sure to check the Resource Guide in the back of this book for titles that are a must-have for your decorative painting business library.

We have already touched base on dealing with craft mall and consignment selling, as well as shows and fairs and the many how-to's of painting for profits and marketing for money—and what to do if you're not making any. About all I can add to this chapter is a bit of advice about keeping accurate records, no matter your chosen method. You must do this not only for your own profit tracking, but also in the event you declare your decorative painting activity a small business operation. The IRS won't be too happy with haphazard hearsay should you ever need to prove points concerning the profitability of painting. A few final tips close this chapter:

- Keep all receipts of expenses, whether gasoline for a road show or for a new paintbrush.

- Maintain a travel log of all shows with dates, mileage, and notes about the events.

- Log in every sale for your own progress tracking and to insure a profitable pricing plan.

- If you have legally registered as a small business, don't succumb to the temptation to "forget" to enter cash sales in your ledger. Amounts of sales taxes collected and paid aren't significant enough to justify being a crook. Besides, you'll sleep better at night.

■ If you accept custom orders, ask for at least 50% of the fee in advance if not the entire amount. My friends pay on delivery; strangers at shows pay in full when they place an order.

■ Before considering going wholesale or selling in bulk, make sure you can deliver the goods on time in the quantity specified. Get the requirements and specifications in writing, including delivery date, the total amount you will be paid, and the terms of payment (up front, in installments, or upon delivery).

Believe it or not, we've barely scratched the surface when it comes to painting for profit. Additional avenues remain to be explored but there are only so many pages in this book. Don't overlook the many helpful information sources available (see Resource Guide). Creative people often follow personally determined directions. Often upon reaching a particular point, they may stop and decide to carve out a new course.

My painting pathway diverged and presented me with the additional opportunity to realize my lifelong dream of publishing. One sign over my computer desk says PLAN AHEAD. I've added a second one: JUST DO IT!

Marketing Your Paintings

▼▼

YOU HAVE NOW BEEN EXPOSED to a variety of ways by which you can publicize your abilities as a decorative painter. Most methods are not complicated; practically all are inexpensive. Some require no financial investment other than samples of your painted projects, which speak for themselves.

I launched my local reputation as a decorative painter the moment I transported that first basket of seasonal goodies to my office. We've already touched upon giving little gifts to friends, coworkers, and relatives when the opportunities arise. Do you recall the fun I had leaving painted gardening gloves on neighbors' doorknobs and then running? Next year I think I'll place a small painted pot, patio stone, or papier-mâché bag on front porches. The surfaces are inexpensive, easy to paint, and make great gift items. People respond almost immediately to the tangible and the touchable. There is no better way to promote your work than by showcasing and displaying at every opportunity, no matter what your product line.

Word Gets Around

Certainly, there are many avenues for advertising your abilities. Be aware that the most basic procedures for achieving publicity can often provide the most lucrative results. One spring when my office workspace demanded a new look, I placed a couple of hand-painted pots and a coordinating birdhouse on my desk purely for personal enjoyment. I was immediately bombarded with requests for Mother's Day gifts though I hadn't expressed that I was taking orders. Once my coworkers noticed my handiwork, word traveled fast.

Remember Linda Maretich, who sometimes sells her decoratively painted items "right off my outfit"? I recently asked whether she utilized any method of formal advertising. She replied: "My advertising mainly consists of my own mouth and word of mouth by others. Since I often wear clothing, hair ornaments, and jewelry of my own creation, people continually ask where I found these things; that's my opportunity to advertise what I do." Linda is one of several who shared how valuable word-of-mouth advertising can be, particularly when one lives in a close-knit or artistic community.

Having grown up in the small artist-dwelling town of Eureka Springs, Arkansas, I could readily relate to a wonderfully expressed comment from Pama Colle. "Great word of mouth is a good fortune abounding in this part of the world," she said. "Cooperation among a variety of organizations within several small communities in our mountain valley has led to tremendous support for all the arts. There are many opportunities for artists. Word gets around."

In chapter 7 we covered some basics on utilizing printed materials such as business cards and hangtags as promotional materials.

Getting Noticed

"I travel with one of my life-sized Granny dolls when I have to drive any distance by myself," Elizabeth Bishop told me. "I was on my way to teach an out-of-town class on a hot July day when I stopped at a fast-food restaurant and dashed in for a soda to go. When I came out, a lady was standing by my car, red-faced and furious: "Don't you know your grandmother could die in this heat with the windows rolled up?" she fumed. I was in a big hurry and knew if I explained about Granny, the lady would ooh and aah for a long time. So I just said, "Aw, she's tough; she can take it." Then I got in the car and drove away while the lady stood there waving her arms and yelling. The rest of the drive, I half-expected a patrolman to pull up behind me, ready to arrest me for abusing the elderly."

These inexpensive items not only do your advertising legwork for you but also help shift your image from hobbyist to professional. Those tools become increasingly valuable as your advertising instruments, especially once you become earnest about earnings. Other printed materials such as postcards, bookmarks, and shopping bags serve dual purposes, enabling maximum mileage from a small investment.

Terrific Tiny Tools

The simple business card is probably the most elementary form of advertising, other than word of mouth. Yet it sometimes is the most overlooked. I wrote a column for an area newspaper on the subject of business cards, referring to them as "terrific tiny tools." The power they can wield in proportion to size and cost is nothing short of remarkable. Yet a few of my colleagues, despite asserting that they are serious about decorative painting as a professional venture, have never utilized business cards. Quite frankly, I am surprised. Considering that each card costs them mere pennies (in relation to quantity received), artists can be generous in handing them out and leaving small stacks at every appropriate opportunity. Whether or not you invest in a full line of business stationery is your individual choice, but decorative painters or craftsmen who do not take advantage of this one simple tool—the business card—are shooting themselves in the foot. My conviction is shared by the average customer, particularly at shows and fairs, who regularly ask for my card.

I recently read a trade publication that included an article focusing on mistakes made by exhibitors. Near the top of the list was failing to have a supply of business cards. Even if you feel business cards aren't personally necessary or believe that they have no serious bearing on sales, consider this scenario: You've been working for six months to build enough inventory for a three-day event. You've spent good money on a canopy to shelter your exhibit, and this year you even set up the display with new tablecloths and lighting. You're not only hoping to make a good showing, but to sell out. As the event progresses, browsers and buyers ask you for a business card to take with them. You have no choice but to respond: "I don't have any" or "I'm all out at the moment." Fellow craftsmen may interpret the attitude as unprofessional, and you can bet the buying public is likely to as well.

While exhibiting at a large event one summer, I overheard a browser mumble as she left the adjacent exhibit and walked toward my booth: "I don't get it! No business cards, no brochures, and he didn't even offer to write down his phone number!" She may have been talking to herself, but I got the message. Well, she didn't buy anything at my exhibit either, but I put on my best grin and gave her a dozen business cards and a homemade brochure about my studio.

A few months later the woman called, introduced herself, and continued: "My girlfriends and I are going to be traveling through your area next month and want to know if we can stop and see your work." I told her that would be fine with me and added, "Please call first to make sure I'm here." I forgot about the conversation until she called one afternoon. I gave her directions and quickly tidied my displays. The travelers pulled up, spotted my studio, snatched up their selections, and bundled their booty into the trunk of the car. I watched out the window as they pulled away. Then I filled out a bank deposit slip for $327, all because I'd handed a handful of business cards to one baffled browser.

Notes About Newspapers

When I asked several painters how they advertised, only Susan Nelson of Cats 'n Stuff mentioned newspaper ads. She stated: "I've only used newspaper ads when hosting a show at my home."

When it comes to general newspaper advertising, consider which avenues have a chance to succeed and which are sure to fail. Classified ads don't do much if anything to promote home shows. Though your ad may read "Art Sale" or "Craft Bazaar," likely you'll see it published in the garage sale or miscellaneous columns. Be aware the public is usually looking specifically for garage or yard sales and will bypass your ad. Those few curiosity seekers who do find your ad in the garage sale section and decide to stop expect 50-cent and $2 prices, and they won't spend any more. You might consider combining a yard sale with a craft show if you expect to generate worthwhile traffic. Personal experience, however, indicates the profits don't compensate the preparation required to host a dual event unless you have plenty of help.

If you're serious about advertising a seasonal bazaar or home show in a newspaper, consider running a small display ad in the Living or Entertainment section. You can design your own ad (it can be as small as a business card) or let the section editor work from your basic information. Display advertising targets a different audience and presents a professional approach. It costs several dollars, but if you and a few fellow painters collaborate, you can split the expense to make the cost reasonable for each participant.

You aren't limited to classified or display ads when it comes to newspapers. How about seeking free publicity? With a little advance footwork, you could find yourself and your paintings spread over an entire page. Newspapers are always looking for human interest stories about local residents who present a unique lifestyle.

"When I moved to this area," said Elizabeth Bishop, "I volunteered my life-sized doll creation Minerva to sit at the town library in the reading section. The local newspaper came to photograph her and interview me, 'the new entrepreneur on the block.'" Obviously, Elizabeth is on to something we all should be taking advantage of, whether our art form is handmade dolls or decorative painting.

A few years ago I sent a cover letter to an area paper and included a self-written press release about my decorative painting endeavors and a recent achievement. Within days I received a phone call from the staff photographer. We set up an appointment for a photo shoot and an interview to be conducted in my backyard studio. Guess who made the Sunday Edition? Many excellent books available on the market describe in detail how to write your own classified ads and press releases that can result in free community-wide publicity. Explicit information on these subjects may be found in the book *Homemade Money,* authored by craft marketing authority Barbara Brabec (see Resource Guide).

More Than One Medium

There are additional tools that not only will set you apart as a professional craftsman, but are likely to become your most effective ways to achieve attention at several levels. Let's explore some other advertising methods, at least two of which should generate publicity for your business, reaching beyond your own community backyard. You would be surprised at the coverage you can get at virtually no cost.

Radio, TV, and Film

You may be thinking that unless you're already a media star, the broad category of radio, TV, and film have nothing to do with advertising decorative painting. If you have an established business that you want to advertise over the airwaves, it's a simple matter of calling your local radio or television stations and asking for advertising pricing. Many small businesses rely on what is referred to as 30- to 60-second spots to keep their name literally within hearing distance of the general public. Particularly in small communities, rates may be quite reasonable.

In my video library relative to decorative painting and crafting in general, I have four programming tapes, compliments of the television show *Aleene's Creative Living*. Over the course of several months, I contributed articles or essays related to the creative spirit (I could have submitted decoratively painted items instead). When a particular broadcast including one of my contributions was aired on national television networks, *Aleene's* sent me a taped copy of that episode. I'm not advising you to send an unsolicited project to just any television production, magazine, or newspaper. Neither am I suggesting that by so doing you will suddenly find yourself in the public spotlight. In deference to the media in general, which is probably overrun with those of us who want our 15 minutes of fame, I'm sure the production studios and publishing houses have bulging warehouses. However, the media is available and surely they expect us to take advantage. Just use a little discretion, be courteous and professional in your dealings, and give it your best shot.

The World Wide Web

"The theory 'Build it and they will come' may work for baseball diamonds, but not in cyberspace, where each shop is barely a pinpoint in the universe," said Shirley Thomas, the web master who maintains my site at www.craftmallusa.com/peachkitty. "Promotion is the key. An obvious method of promotion often missed is omitting your Web site address on business cards and other stationery items. Include it even on your

Web Site Advertising Tips

The following tips come from Web master Shirley Thomas, of CRAFTMALLUSA

- Even if you are in a cybermall, you still need to promote your site yourself. Local promoting is extremely productive and may be an area the cybermall web master never reaches.

- Register your site within search engines, which is simply a matter of visiting the search engine site, clicking on the Add Site icon, and entering your site address.

- Be sure to post on bulletin boards (that is, by answering questions, not by sending unsolicited information, also known as "spamming") and sign guest books, always using a signature line that includes your Web site address.

▼▼▼▼▼▼▼▼▼▼▼▼▼▼▼▼▼▼

Getting Out the Word

You can promote your business in many ways without spending much money. Some methods won't cost you a penny. Here are some suggestions:

- Word of mouth
- Community events and fund raisers
- Business cards with complete contact information
- Fliers and brochures to announce special sales or shows
- Press releases, newspaper and magazine articles or columns
- Radio and television productions
- Membership in professional organizations
- Hangtags, rubber stamps
- Printed calendars, pens, photo postcards
- Letterhead and invoices
- Return address and mailing labels
- Memo pads and thank-you notes

▲▲▲▲▲▲▲▲▲▲▲▲▲▲▲▲▲▲

answering machine and voice mail messages. Don't miss a single opportunity to tell the world about your site."

Networking Works

Everyone with whom you come in contact is a potential customer, client, or mentor. Expand your personal and professional circle at every opportunity. This doesn't mean you have to accept every order or attend every craft show from coast to coast. But you want to maintain your mailing lists, your index of primary customers, and your directory of business colleagues.

Membership in professional societies is the ultimate networking privilege. I recommend the Society of Decorative Painters and the Society of Craft Designers (see Resource Guide for contacts). These organizations have their fingers on the pulse of the decorative painting industry as a whole and on virtually every related product, manufacturing, marketing, and economic aspect of the general field. In addition to gaining access to invaluable information, you will find your name listed among the ranks of professionals who are world famous and nationally known. Avenues are wide open for exhibiting your skills, evaluating products for manufacturers, and working with your fellow artisans. These societies are wonderful pathways that lead serious decorative painters to inspiring visions and likely financial rewards.

What Goes Around Comes Around

Formal advertising is certainly beneficial, but there are other ways to promote not only your business but also to expand your creative spirit. Without personal growth the vision can lose its focus. So think about ways to reinforce the positive influences in your painting endeavors, not just for yourself but for others in your business and personal circles.

Volunteering for a community service event may establish you as the artist in residence, netting you a paid commission to design a billboard for the spring garden club event. It may also show others that they, too, can step forward and commit to helping a local organization. Most civic groups are grateful for any type of assistance—especially within the arts and humanities. After Elizabeth Bishop volunteered Minerva's presence at the local library, I can't help but wonder how many citizens visited the reading section. Perhaps your local children's clinic could use a hallway facelift in the form of a wall mural sporting life-sized images of Noah, the animals, and a sherbet rainbow.

Contributing a well-thought-out idea to a painter's magazine might result in a personal phone call from the editor asking whether you'd be willing to author a feature story. I published my first major article for *Tole World* magazine on painting at home for profit because I took the time to write a few lines on a postcard. Share your questions, suggestions, and solutions. Keep the information flowing, and what better source than from your own personal painting experiences? Take the time to be a contributor.

Balance your hard work through maintaining a sense of humor. I am reminded of Linda Maretich and her Canned Lady, a light-hearted representation of pursed-lipped, tight-pursed customers who offer up nothing more than "Oh, how cute!" Browsers who stop to look at the Canned Lady may well end up buying one of Linda's craftily painted creations, because her spirit of fun captured their attention. As Pama Collé expressed in two short words: "Humor sells."

Remember Johnnie Elma Anderson's practice of keeping a Gratitude Attitude journal? Many things in life, including projecting a positive attitude, become part of a never-ending process of renewal—unless we neglect to nurture them. Nurturing a goal will include making conscious choices. Recently I found myself agonizing over whether to focus less on retailing decorative paintings and more on writing about the subject. Shortly after I reached my conclusion to shift more energy to writing, I was "feeling a bit at loose ends," as my English pal Eileen Beard would say. Every night before falling asleep, my Gratitude Attitude thoughts included these words: "I am grateful for the vision of a different painting pathway, and for the freedom to explore a new opportunity."

I'll say it one last time: If you can view it, you can do it. In your hands you are holding the results of a personal vision.

Now, where's your jar of paintbrushes?

A Mini-Course in Crafts-Business Basics

by Barbara Brabec

▼▼

THIS SECTION OF THE BOOK will familiarize you with important areas of legal and financial concern and enable you to ask the
right questions if and when it is necessary to consult with an attorney, accountant, or other business adviser. Although the tax and
legal information included here has been carefully researched by
the author and is accurate to the best of her knowledge, it is not the
business of either the author or publisher to render professional services in the area of business law, taxes, or accounting. Readers
should therefore use their own good judgment in determining when
the services of a lawyer or other professional would be appropriate
to their needs.

Information presented applies specifically to businesses in the
United States. However, because many U.S. and Canadian laws are
similar, Canadian readers can certainly use the following information as a start-up business plan and guide to questions they need to
ask their own local, provincial, or federal authorities.

Contents

7. **Insurance Tips**

   Homeowner's or Renter's Insurance
   Liability Insurance
   Insurance on Crafts Merchandise
   Auto Insurance

8. **Important Regulations Affecting Artists and Craftspeople**

   Consumer Safety Laws
   Labels Required by Law
   The Bedding and Upholstered Furniture Law
   FTC Rule for Mail-Order Sellers

9. **Protecting Your Intellectual Property**

   Perspective on Patents
   What a Trademark Protects
   What Copyrights Protect
   Copyright Registration Tips
   Respecting the Copyrights of Others
   Using Commercial Patterns and Designs

10. **To Keep Growing, Keep Learning**

   Motivational Tips

   A "Things to Do" Checklist with Related Resources
   Business Start-Up Checklist
   Government Agencies
   Crafts and Home-Business Organizations
   Recommended Craft Business Periodicals
   Other Services and Suppliers
   Recommended Business Books
   Helpful Library Directories

1. Starting Right

In preceding chapters of this book, you learned the techniques of a particular art or craft and realized its potential for profit. You learned what kind of products are likely to sell, how to price them, and how and where you might sell them.

Now that you've seen how much fun a crafts business can be (and how profitable it might be if you were to get serious about selling what you make!) you need to learn about some of the "nitty-gritty stuff" that goes hand-in-hand with even the smallest business based at home. It's easy to start selling what you make and it's satisfying when you earn enough money to make your hobby self-supporting. Many crafters go this far and no further, which is fine. But even a hobby seller must be concerned about taxes and local, state, and federal laws. And if your goal is to build a part- or full-time business at home, you must pay even greater attention to the topics discussed in this section of the book.

Everyone loves to make money . . . but actually starting a business frightens some people because they don't understand what's involved. It's easy to come up with excuses for why we don't do certain things in life; close inspection of those excuses usually boils down to fear of the unknown. We get the shivers when we step out of our comfort zone and try something we've never done before. The simple solution to this problem lies in having the right information at the right time. As someone once said, "Knowledge is the antidote to fear."

The quickest and surest way to dispel fear is to inform yourself about the topics that frighten you. With knowledge comes a sense of power, and that power enables you to move. Whether your goal is merely to earn extra income from your crafts hobby or launch a genuine home-based business, reading the following information will help you get started on the right legal foot, avoid financial pitfalls, and move forward with confidence.

When you're ready to learn more about art or crafts marketing or the operation of a home-based crafts business, a visit to your library or bookstore will turn up many interesting titles. In addition to the special resources listed by this book's author, you will find my list of recommended business books, organizations, periodicals, and other helpful resources in section 10 of this chapter. This information is arranged in a checklist you can use as a plan to get your business up and running.

Before you read my "Mini-Course in Crafts-Business Basics," be assured that I understand where you're coming from because I was once there myself.

For a while I sold my craft work, and this experience led me to write my first book, *Creative Cash*. Now, twenty years later, this crafts-business classic ("my baby") has reached its 6th edition. Few of those who are totally involved in a crafts business today started out with a business in mind. Like me, most began as hobbyists looking for something interesting to do in their spare time, and one thing naturally led to another. I never imagined those many years

Social Security Taxes

When your craft business earnings are more than $400 (net), you must file a Self Employment Tax form (Schedule SE) and pay into your personal Social Security account. This could be quite beneficial for individuals who have some previous work experience but have been out of the workplace for a while. Your re-entry into the business world as a self-employed worker, and the additional contributions to your Social Security account, could result in increased benefits upon retirement.

Because so many senior citizens are starting home-based businesses these days, it should be noted that there is a limit on the amount you can earn before losing Social Security benefits. The good news is that this dollar limit increases every year, and once you are past the age of 70, you can earn any amount of income and still receive full benefits. For more information, contact your nearest Social Security office.

ago when I got serious about my crafts hobby that I was putting my-self on the road to a full-time career as a crafts writer, publisher, author, and speaker. Since I and thousands of others have progressed from hobbyists to professionals, I won't be at all surprised if some-day you, too, have a similar adventure.

2. Taxes and Record Keeping

"Ambition in America is still rewarded . . . with high taxes," the comics quip. Don't you long for the good old days when Uncle Sam lived within his income and without most of yours?

Seriously, taxes are one of the first things you must be concerned about as a new business owner, no matter how small your endeavor. This section offers a brief overview of your tax responsibilities as a sole proprietor.

Is Your Activity a "Hobby" or a "Business?"

Whether you are selling what you make only to get the cost of your supplies back, or actually trying to build a profitable business, you need to understand the legal difference between a profitable hobby and a business, and how each is related to your annual tax return.

The IRS defines a hobby as "an activity engaged in primarily for pleasure, not for profit." Making a profit from a hobby does not auto-matically place you "in business" in the eyes of the Internal Revenue Service, but the activity will be *presumed* to have been engaged in for profit if it results in a profit in at least three years out of five. Or, to put it another way, a "hobby business" automatically becomes a "real business" in the eyes of the IRS at the point where you can state that you are (1) trying to make a profit, (2) making regular business transactions, and (3) have made a profit three years out of five.

As you know, all income must be reported on your annual tax return. How it's reported, however, has everything to do with the amount of taxes you must pay on this income. If hobby income is under $400, it must be entered on the 1040 tax form, with taxes payable accordingly. If the amount is greater than this, you must file a Schedule C form with your 1040 tax form. This is to your advantage, however, since taxes are due only on your *net profit*. Since you can deduct expenses up to the amount of your hobby income, there may be little or no tax at all on your hobby income.

Self-Employment Taxes

Whereas a hobby cannot show a loss on a Schedule C form, a business can. Business owners must pay not only state and federal income taxes on their profits, but self-employment taxes as well. (See sidebar, "Social Security Taxes" page 223.) Because self-employed people pay Social Security taxes at twice the level of regular, salaried workers, you should strive to lower your annual gross profit figure on the Schedule C form through every legal means possible. One way to do this is through careful record keeping of all expenses related to the operation of your business. To quote IRS publications, expenses are deductible if they are "ordinary, necessary, and somehow connected with the operation and potential profit of your business." In addition to being able to deduct all expenses related to the making and selling of their products, business owners can also depreciate the cost of tools and equipment, deduct the overhead costs of operating a home-based office or studio (called the Home Office Deduction), and hire their spouse or children.

Given the complexity of our tax laws and the fact that they are changing all the time, a detailed discussion of all the tax deductions currently available to small business owners cannot be included in a book of this nature. Learning, however, is as easy as reading a book such as *Small Time Operator* by Bernard Kamoroff (my favorite tax and accounting guide), visiting the IRS Web site, or consulting your regular tax adviser.

You can also get answers to specific tax questions twenty-four hours a day by calling the National Association of Enrolled Agents (NAEA). Enrolled agents (EAs) are licensed by the Treasury Department to represent taxpayers before the IRS. Their rates for doing tax returns are often less than what you would pay for an accountant or CPA. (See my checklist for NAEA's toll-free number you can call to ask for a referral to an EA in your area.)

An important concept to remember is that even the smallest business is entitled to deduct expenses related to its business, and the same tax-saving strategies used by "the big guys" can be used by small business owners. Your business may be small now or still in the dreaming stage, but it could be larger next year and surprisingly profitable a few years from now. Therefore it is in your best interest always to prepare for growth, profit, and taxes by learning all you

Keeping Tax Records

Once you're in business, you must keep accurate records of all income and expenses, but the IRS does not require any special kind of bookkeeping system. Its primary concern is that you use a system that clearly and accurately shows true income and expenses. For the sole proprietor, a simple system consisting of a checkbook, a cash receipts journal, a cash disbursements ledger, and a petty cash fund is quite adequate. Post expenses and income regularly to avoid year-end pile-up and panic.

If you plan to keep manual records, check your local office supply store or catalogs for the *Dome* series of record-keeping books, or use the handy ledger sheets and worksheets included in *Small Time Operator*. (This classic tax and accounting guide by CPA Bernard Kamoroff includes details on how to keep good records and prepare financial reports.) If you have a computer, there are a number of accounting software programs available, such as Intuit Quicken, MYOB (Mind Your Own Business) Accounting, and Intuit Quick-

can about the tax laws and deductions applicable to your business. (See also sidebar, "Keeping Tax Records.")

Sales Tax Is Serious Business

If you live in a state that has a sales tax (all but five states do), and sell products directly to consumers, you are required by law to register with your state's Department of Revenue (Sales Tax division) for a resale tax number. The fee for this in most states ranges from $5 to $25, with some states requiring a bond or deposit of up to $150.

Depending on where you live, this tax number may also be called a Retailer's Occupation Tax Registration Number, resale license, or use tax permit. Also, depending on where you live, the place you must call to obtain this number will have different names. In California, for example, you would contact the State Board of Equalization; in Texas, it's called the State Comptroller's Office.

Books, the latter of which is one of the most popular and best bookkeeping systems for small businesses. The great advantage of computerized accounting is that financial statements can be created at the press of a key after accounting entries have been made.

Regardless which system you use, always get a receipt for everything and file receipts in a monthly envelope. If you don't want to establish a petty cash fund, spindle all of your cash receipts, tally them at month's end, and reimburse your personal outlay of cash with a check written on your business account. On your checkbook stub, document the individual purchases covered by this check.

At year's end, bundle your monthly tax receipt envelopes and file them for future reference, if needed. Since the IRS can audit a return for up to three years after a tax return has been filed, all accounting and tax records should be kept at least this long, but six years is better. Personally, I believe you should keep all your tax returns, journals, and ledgers throughout the life of your business.

Within your state's revenue department, the tax division may have a name such as Sales and Use Tax Division or Department of Taxation and Finance. Generally speaking, if you check your telephone book under "Government," and look for whatever listing comes closest to "Revenue," you can find the right office.

If your state has no sales tax, you will still need a reseller's permit or tax exemption certificate to buy supplies and materials at wholesale prices from manufacturers, wholesalers, or distributors. Note that this tax number is only for supplies and materials used to make your products, not for things purchased at the retail level or for general office supplies.

Once registered with the state, you will begin to collect and remit sales and use tax (monthly, quarterly, or annually, as determined by your state) on all *taxable sales*. This does not mean *all* of your gross income. Different states tax different things. Some states put a sales tax on certain services, but generally you will never have to pay sales tax on income from articles sold to magazines, on teaching or consulting fees, or subscription income (if you happen to publish a newsletter). In addition, sales taxes are not applicable to:

- **items sold on consignment through a charitable organization, shop, or other retail outlet, including craft malls and rent-a-space shops (because the party who sells directly to the consumer is the one who must collect and pay sales tax.)**

- **products you wholesale to others who will be reselling them to consumers. (Be sure to get their tax-exemption ID number for your own files, however, in case you are ever questioned as to why you did not collect taxes on those sales.)**

As you sell throughout the year, your record-keeping system must be set up so you can tell which income is taxable and which is tax-exempt for reporting on your sales tax return.

Collecting Sales Tax at Craft Shows

States are getting very aggressive about collecting sales tax, and agents are showing up everywhere these day, especially at the larger craft fairs, festivals, and small business conferences. As I was writing this chapter, a post on the Internet stated that in New Jersey the sales tax department is routinely contacting show promoters about a month before the show date to get the names and addresses of exhibitors. It is expected that other states will soon be following suit. For this reason, you should always take your resale or tax collection certificate with you to shows.

Although you must always collect sales tax at a show when you sell in a state that has a sales tax, how and when the tax is paid to the state can vary. When selling at shows in other states, you may find that the show promoter has obtained an umbrella sales tax certificate, in which case vendors would be asked to give management a check for sales tax at the end of the show for turning over to a tax agent. Or you may have to obtain a temporary sales tax certificate for a show, as advised by the show promoter. Some sellers who regularly do shows in two or three states say it's easier to get a tax ID number from each state and file an annual return instead of doing taxes on a show-by-show basis. (See sidebar, "Including Tax in the Retail Price, page 230.")

Collecting Sales Tax at a Holiday Boutique

If you're involved in a holiday boutique where several sellers are offering goods to the public, each individual seller will be responsible for collecting and remitting his or her own sales tax. (This means someone has to keep very good records during the sale so each seller receives a record of the sale and the amount of tax on that sale.) A reader who regularly has home boutiques told me that in her community she must also post a sign at her "cash station" stating that sales tax is being collected on all sales, just as craft fair sellers must do in some states. Again, it's important that you get complete details from your own state about its sales tax policies.

Collecting Tax on Internet Sales

Anything you sell that is taxable in your state is also taxable on the Internet. This is simply another method of selling, like craft fairs or mail-order sales. You don't have to break out Internet sales separately; simply include them in your total taxable sales.

3. The Legal Forms of Business

Every business must take one of four legal forms:

Sole Proprietorship
Partnership
LLC (Limited Liability Company)
Corporation

Including Tax in the Retail Price

Is it okay to incorporate the amount of sales tax into the retail price of items being sold directly to consumers? I don't know for sure because each state's sales tax law is different.

Crafters like to use round-figure prices at fairs because this encourages cash sales and eliminates the need for taking coins to make change. Some crafters tell their customers that sales tax has been included in their rounded-off prices, but you should not do this until you check with your state. In some states, this is illegal; in others, you may find that you are required to inform your customers, by means of a sign, that sales tax has been included in your price. Your may also have to print this information on customer receipts as well.

If you make such a statement and collect taxes on cash sales, be sure to report those cash sales as taxable income and remit the tax money to the state accordingly. Failure

As a hobby seller, you automatically become a sole proprietor when you start selling what you make. Although most professional crafters remain sole proprietors throughout the life of their business, some do form craft partnerships or corporations when their business begins to generate serious money, or if it happens to involve other members of their family. You don't need a lawyer to start a sole proprietorship, but it would be folly to enter into a partnership, corporation, or LLC without legal guidance. Here is a brief look at the main advantages and disadvantages of each type of legal business structure.

Sole Proprietorship

No legal formalities are involved in starting or ending a sole proprietorship. You're your own boss here, and the business starts when you say it does and ends automatically when you stop running it. As discussed earlier, income is reported annually on a Schedule C form

to do this would be a violation of the law, and it's easy to get caught these days when sales tax agents are showing up at craft fairs across the country.

Even if rounding off the price and including the tax within that figure turns out to be legal in your state, it will definitely complicate your bookkeeping. For example, if you normally sell an item for $5 or some other round figure, you must have a firm retail price on which to calculate sales tax to begin with. Adding tax to a round figure makes it uneven. Then you must either raise it or lower the price, and if you lower it, what you're really doing is paying the sales tax for your customer out of your profits. This is no way to do business.

I suggest that you set your retail prices based on the pricing formulas given in this book, calculate the sales tax accordingly, and give your customers change if they pay in cash. You will be perceived as a professional when you operate this way, whereas crafters who insist always on "cash only" sales are sending signals to buyers that they don't intend to report this income to tax authorities.

and taxed at the personal level. The sole proprietor is fully liable for all business debts and actions. In the event of a lawsuit, personal assets are not protected.

Partnership

There are two kinds of partnerships: General and Limited

A *General Partnership* is easy to start, with no federal requirements involved. Income is taxed at the personal level and the partnership ends as soon as either partner withdraws from the business. Liability is unlimited. The most financially dangerous thing about a partnership is that the debts incurred by one partner must be assumed by all other partners. Before signing a partnership agreement, make sure the tax obligations of your partner are current.

In a *Limited Partnership,* the business is run by general partners and financed by silent (limited) partners who have no liability beyond an investment of money in the business. This kind of partnership is more complicated to establish, has special tax withholding regulations, and requires the filing of a legal contract with the state.

LLC (Limited Liability Company)

This legal form of business reportedly combines the best attributes of other small business forms while offering a better tax advantage than a limited partnership. It also affords personal liability protection similar to that of a corporation. To date, few craft businesses appear to be using this business form.

Corporation

A corporation is the most complicated and expensive legal form of business and not recommended for any business whose earnings are less than $25,000 a year. If and when your business reaches this point, you should study some books on this topic to fully understand the pros and cons of a corporation. Also consult an accountant or attorney for guidance on the type of corporation you should select—a "C" (general corporation) or an "S" (subchapter S corporation). One book that offers good perspective on this topic is *INC Yourself—How to Profit by Setting Up Your Own Corporation.*

The main disadvantage of incorporation for the small business owner is that profits are taxed twice: first as corporate income and again when they are distributed to the owner-shareholders as dividends. For this reason, many small businesses elect to incorporate as subchapter S corporations, which allows profits to be taxed at owners' regular individual rates. (See sidebar, "The Limited Legal Protection of a Corporation, below.")

The Limited Legal Protection of a Corporation

Business novices often think that by incorporating their business they can protect their personal assets in the event of a lawsuit. This is true if you have employees who do something wrong and cause your business to be sued. As the business owner, however, if you personally do something wrong and are sued as a result, you might in some cases be held legally responsible, and the "corporation door" will offer no legal protection for your personal assets.

Or, as CPA Bernard Kamoroff explains in *Small Time Operator,* "A corporation will not shield you from personal liability that you normally should be responsible for, such as not having car insurance or acting with gross negligence. If you plan to incorporate solely or primarily with the intention of limiting your legal liability, I suggest you find out first exactly how limited the liability really is for your particular venture. Hire a knowledgeable lawyer to give you a written opinion." (See section 7, "Insurance Tips.")

4. Local and State Laws and Regulations

This section will acquaint you with laws and regulations that affect the average art or crafts business based at home. If you've unknowingly broken one of these laws, don't panic. It may not be as bad as you think. It is often possible to get back on the straight and narrow merely by filling out a required form or by paying a small fee of some kind. What's important is that you take steps now to comply with the laws that pertain to your particular business. Often, the fear of being caught when you're breaking a law is often much worse than doing whatever needs to be done to set the matter straight. In the end, it's usually what you don't know that is most likely to cause legal or financial problems, so never hesitate to ask questions about things you don't understand.

Even when you think you know the answers, it can pay to "act dumb." It is said that Napoleon used to attend meetings and pretend to know nothing about a topic, asking many probing questions. By feigning ignorance, he was able to draw valuable information and insight out of everyone around him. This strategy is often used by today's small business owners, too.

Business Name Registration

If you're a sole proprietor doing business under any name other than your own full name, you are required by law to register it on both the local and state level. In this case, you are said to be using an "assumed," "fictitious," or "trade" name. What registration does is enable authorities to connect an assumed name to an individual who can be held responsible for the actions of a business. If you're doing business under your own name, such as Kay Jones, you don't have to register your business name on either the local or state level. If your name is part of a longer name, however (for example, Kay Jones Designs), you should check to see if your county or state requires registration.

Local Registration

To register your name, contact your city or county clerk, who will explain what you need to do to officially register your business on the local level. At the same time, ask if you need any special municipal or county licenses or permits to operate within the law. (See next section, "Licenses and Permits.") This office can also tell you how and where to write to register your name at the state level. If you've been operating under an assumed name for a while and are worried because you didn't register the name earlier, just register it now, as if the business were new.

Registration involves filling out a simple form and paying a small fee, usually around $10 to $25. At the time you register, you will get details about a classified ad you must run in a general-circulation newspaper in your county. This will notify the public at large that you are now operating a business under an assumed name. (If you don't want your neighbors to know what you're doing, simply run the ad in a newspaper somewhere else in the county.) After publication of this ad, you will receive a Fictitious Name Statement that you must send to the County Clerk, who in turn will file it with your registration form to make your business completely legitimate. This name statement or certificate may also be referred to as your DBA ("doing business as") form. In some areas, you cannot open a business checking account if you don't have this form to show your bank.

State Registration

Once you've registered locally, contact your Secretary of State to register your business name with the state. This will prevent its use by a corporate entity. At the same time, find out if you must

Picking a Good Business Name

If you haven't done it already, think up a great name for your new business. You want something that will be memorable—catchy, but not too cute. Many crafters select a simple name that is attached to their first name, such as "Mary's Quilts" or "Tom's Woodcrafts." This is fine for a hobby business, but if your goal is to build a full-time business at home, you may wish to choose a more professional-sounding name that omits your personal name. If a name sounds like a hobby business, you may have difficulty getting wholesale suppliers to take you seriously. A more professional name may also enable you to get higher prices for your products. For example, the above names might be changed to "Quilted Treasures" or "Wooden Wonders."

Don't print business cards or stationery until you find out if someone else is already using the name you've chosen. To find out if the name has already been registered, you

obtain any kind of state license. Generally, home-based craft businesses will not need a license from the state, but there are always exceptions. An artist who built an open-to-the-public art studio on his property reported that the fine in his state for operating this kind of business without a license was $50 a day. In short, it always pays to ask questions to make sure you're operating legally and safely.

Federal Registration

The only way to protect a name on the federal level is with a trademark, discussed in section 8.

Licenses and Permits

A "license" is a certificate granted by a municipal or county agency that gives you permission to engage in a business occupation. A "permit" is similar, except that it is granted by local authorities. Until recently, few craft businesses had to have a license or permit

▼▼▼

can perform a trademark search through a search company or hire an attorney who specializes in trademak law to conduct the search for you. And if you are planning to eventually set up a Web site, you might want to do a search to see if that domain name is still available on the Internet. Go to www.networksolutions.com to do this search. Business names have to be registered on the Internet, too, and they can be "parked" for a fee until you're ready to design your Web site.

It's great if your business name and Web site name can be the same, but this is not always possible. A crafter told me recently she had to come up with 25 names before she found a domain name that hadn't already been taken. (Web entrepreneurs are grabbing every good name they can find. Imagine my surprise when I did a search and found that two different individuals had set up Web sites using the titles of my two best-known books, *Creative Cash* and *Homemade Money*.)

▲▲

of any kind, but a growing number of communities now have new laws on their books that require home-based business owners to obtain a "home occupation permit." Annual fees for such permits may range from $15 to $200 a year. For details about the law in your particular community or county, call your city or country clerk (depending on whether you live within or outside city limits).

Use of Personal Phone for Business

Although every business writer stresses the importance of having a business telephone number, craftspeople generally ignore this advice and do business on their home telephone. While it's okay to use a home phone to make outgoing business calls, you cannot advertise a home telephone number as your business phone number without being in violation of local telephone regulations. That means you cannot legally put your home telephone number on a business card or business stationery or advertise it on your Web site.

That said, let me also state that most craftspeople totally ignore this law and do it anyway. (I don't know what the penalty for breaking this law is in your state; you'll have to call your telephone company for that information and decide if this is something you want to do.) Some phone companies might give you a slap on the wrist and tell you to stop, while others might start charging you business line telephone rates if they discover you are advertising your personal phone number.

The primary reason to have a separate phone line for your business is that it enables you to freely advertise your telephone number to solicit new business and invite credit card sales, custom order inquiries, and the like. Further, you can deduct 100 percent of the costs of a business telephone line on your Schedule C tax form, while deductions for the business use of a home phone are severely limited. (Discuss this with your accountant.)

If you plan to connect to the Internet or install a fax machine, you will definitely need a second line to handle the load, but most crafters simply add an additional personal line instead of a business line. Once on the Internet, you may have even less need for a business phone than before since you can simply invite contact from buyers by advertising your e-mail address. (Always include your e-mail and Internet address on your business cards and stationery.)

If your primary selling methods are going to be consignment shops, craft fairs, or craft malls, a business phone number would be necessary only if you are inviting orders by phone. If you present a holiday boutique or open house once or twice a year, there should be no problem with putting your home phone number on promotional fliers because you are, in fact, inviting people to your home and not your business (similar to running a classified ad for a garage sale).

If and when you decide a separate line for your business is necessary, you may find it is not as costly as you think. Telephone companies today are very aware of the number of people who are working at home, and they have come up with a variety of affordable packages and second-line options, any one of which might be perfect for your craft business needs. Give your telephone company a call and see what's available.

Zoning Regulations

Before you start any kind of home-based business, check your home's zoning regulations. You can find a copy at your library or at city hall. Find out what zone you're in and then read the information under "home occupations." Be sure to read the fine print and note the penalty for violating a zoning ordinance. In most cases, someone who is caught violating zoning laws will be asked to cease and desist and a penalty is incurred only if this order is ignored. In other cases, however, willful violation could incur a hefty fine.

Zoning laws differ from one community to another, with some of them being terribly outdated (actually written back in horse-and-buggy days). In some communities, zoning officials simply "look the other way" where zoning violations are concerned because it's easier to do this than change the law. In other places, however, zoning regulations have recently been revised in light of the growing number of individuals working at home, and these changes have not always been to the benefit of home-based workers or self-employed individuals. Often there are restrictions as to (1) the amount of space in one's home a business may occupy (impossible to enforce, in my opinion), (2) the number of people (customers, students) who can come to your home each day, (3) the use of non-family employees, and so on. If you find you cannot advertise your home as a place of business, this problem can be easily solved by renting a P.O. box or using a commercial mailbox service as your business address.

Although I'm not suggesting that you violate your zoning law, I will tell you that many individuals who have found zoning to be a problem do ignore this law, particularly when they have a quiet business that is unlikely to create problems in their community.

Zoning officials don't go around checking for people who are violating the law; rather, they tend to act on complaints they have received about a certain activity that is creating problems for others. Thus, the best way to avoid zoning problems is to keep a low profile by not broadcasting your home-based business to neighbors. More important, never annoy them with activities that emit fumes or odors, create parking problems, or make noise of any kind.

While neighbors may grudgingly put up with a noisy hobby activity (such as sawing in the garage), they are not likely to tolerate the same noise or disturbance if they know it's related to a home-based business. Likewise, they won't mind if you have a garage sale every year, but if people are constantly coming to your home to buy from your home shop, open house, home parties, or holiday boutiques every year, you could be asking for trouble if the zoning laws don't favor this kind of activity.

5. General Business and Financial Information

This section offers introductory guidelines on essential business basics for beginners. Once your business is up and running, however, you need to read other craft-business books to get detailed information on the following topics and many others related to the successful growth and development of a home-based art or crafts business.

Making a Simple Business Plan

As baseball star Yogi Berra once said, "If you don't know where you are going, you might not get there." That's why you need a plan.

Like a road map, a business plan helps you get from here to there. It doesn't have to be fancy, but it does have to be in written form. A good business plan will save you time and money while helping you stay focused and on track to meet your goals. The kind of business plan a craftsperson makes will naturally be less complicated than the business plan of a major manufacturing company, but the elements are basically the same and should include:

- *History*—how and why you started your business
- *Business description*—what you do, what products you make, why they are special
- *Management information*—your business background or experience and the legal form your business will take
- *Manufacturing and production*—how and where products will be produced and who will make them; how and where supplies and materials will be obtained, and their estimated costs; labor costs (yours or other helpers); and overhead costs involved in the making of products
- *Financial plan*—estimated sales and expense figures for one year
- *Market research findings*—a description of your market (fairs, shops, mail order, Internet, etc.), your customers, and your competition
- *Marketing plan*—how you are going to sell your products and the anticipated cost of your marketing (commissions, advertising, craft fair displays, etc.)

If this all seems a bit much for a small crafts business, start managing your time by using a daily calendar/planner and start a notebook you can fill with your creative and marketing ideas, plans, and business goals. In it, write a simple mission statement that answers the following questions:

- What is my primary mission or goal in starting a business?
- What is my financial goal for this year?
- What am I going to do to get the sales I need this year to meet my financial goal?

The most important thing is that you start putting your dreams, goals, and business plans on paper so you can review them regularly.

It's always easier to see where you're going if you know where you've been.

When You Need an Attorney

Many business beginners think they have to hire a lawyer the minute they start a business, but that would be a terrible waste of money if you're just starting a simple art or crafts business at home, operating as a sole proprietor. Sure, a lawyer will be delighted to hold your hand and give you the same advice I'm giving you here (while charging you $150 an hour or more for his or her time). With this book in hand, you can easily take care of all the "legal details" of small business start-up. The day may come, however, when you do need legal counsel, such as when you:

Form a Partnership or Corporation

As stated earlier, an attorney's guidance is necessary in the formation of a partnership. Although many people have incorporated without a lawyer using a good how-to book on the topic, I wouldn't recommend doing this because there are so many details involved here, not to mention different types of corporate entities.

Defend an Infringement of a Copyright or Trademark

You don't need an attorney to get a simple copyright, but if someone infringes on one of your copyrights, you will probably need legal help to stop the infringer from profiting from your creativity. You can file your own trademark application (if you are exceedingly careful about following instructions), but it would be difficult to protect your trademark without legal help if someone tries to steal it. In both cases, you would need an attorney who specializes in copyright, patent, and trademark law. (If you ever need a good attorney who understands the plight of artists and crafters, contact me by e-mail at barbara@crafter.com and I'll refer you to

Get a Safety Deposit Box

The longer you are in business, the more important it will be to safeguard your most valuable business records. When you work at home, there is always the possibility of fire or damage from some natural disaster, be it tornado, earthquake, hurricane, or flood. You will worry less if you keep your most valuable business papers, records, computer disks, and so forth off-premises, along with other items that would be difficult or impossible to replace. Some particulars I have always kept in my business safety deposit box include master software disks and computer back-up tapes; original copies of my designs and patterns, business contracts, copyrights, insurance policies, and a photographic record of all items insured on our homeowner's policy. Remember: Insurance is worthless if you cannot prove what you owned in the first place.

the attorney who has been helpful to me in protecting my common-law trademark to *Homemade Money*, my home-business classic. The 6th edition of this book includes the details of my trademark infringement story.)

Negotiate a Contract

Many craft hobbyists of my acquaintance have gone on to write books and sell their original designs to manufacturers, suddenly finding themselves with a contract in hand that contains a lot of confusing legal jargon. When hiring an attorney to check any kind of contract, make sure he or she has experience in the particular field involved. For example, a lawyer specializing in real estate isn't going to know a thing about the inner workings of a book publishing company and how the omission or inclusion of a particular clause or phrase might impact the author's royalties or make it difficult to get publishing rights back when the book goes out of print. Although I have no experience in the licensing industry, I presume the same thing holds true here. What I do know for sure is that the problem with most contracts is not so much what's *in* them, as what *isn't.* Thus you need to be sure the attorney you hire for specialized contract work has done this kind of work for other clients.

Hire Independent Contractors

If you ever grow your business to the point where you need to hire workers and are wondering whether you have to hire employees or can use independent contractors instead, I suggest you to seek counsel from an attorney who specializes in labor law. This topic is very complex and beyond the scope of this beginner's guide, but I do want you to know that the IRS has been on a campaign for the past several years to abolish independent contractors altogether. Many small businesses have suffered great financial loss in back taxes and penalties because they followed the advice of an accountant or regular attorney who didn't fully understand the technicalities of this matter.

If and when you do need a lawyer for general business purposes, ask friends for a reference, and check with your bank, too, since it will probably know most of the attorneys with private practices in your area. Note that membership in some small business organizations will also give you access to affordable prepaid legal services. If you ever need serious legal help but have no funds to pay for it, contact the Volunteer Lawyers for the Arts (see resources in section 10).

Why You Need a Business Checking Account

Many business beginners use their personal checking account to conduct the transactions of their business, *but you must not do this* because the IRS does not allow co-mingling of business and personal income. If you are operating as a business, reporting income on a Schedule C form and taking deductions accordingly, the lack of a separate checking account for your business would surely result in an IRS ruling that your endeavor was a hobby and not a business. That, in turn, would cost you all the deductions previously taken on earlier tax returns and you'd end up with a very large tax bill. Don't you agree that the cost of a separate checking account is a small price to pay to protect all your tax deductions?

You do not necessarily need one of the more expensive business checking accounts; just a *separate account* through which you run all business income and expenditures. Your business name does not have to be on these checks so long as only your name (not your spouse's) is listed as account holder. You can save money on your checking account by first calling several banks and savings and loan institutions and comparing the charges they set for imprinted checks, deposits, checks written, bounced checks, and other services. Before you open your account, be sure to ask if the bank can set you up to take credit cards (merchant account) at some point in the future.

Accepting Credit Cards

Most of us today take credit cards for granted and expect to be able to use them for most everything we buy. It's nice to be able to offer credit card services to your craft fair customers, but it is costly and thus not recommended for beginning craft sellers. If you get into selling at craft fairs on a regular basis, however, at some point you may find you are losing sales because you don't have "merchant status" (the ability to accept credit cards as payment).

Some craftspeople have reported a considerable jump in sales once they started taking credit cards. That's because some people who buy with plastic may buy two or three items instead of one, or are willing to pay a higher price for something if they can charge it. Thus, the higher your prices, the more likely you are to lose sales if you can't accept credit cards. As one jewelry maker told me, "I always seem to get the customers who have run out of cash and left their checkbook at home. But even when they have a check, I feel uncomfortable taking a check for $100 or more."

A list follows of the various routes you can travel to get merchant status. You will have to do considerable research to find out which method is best for you. All will be costly, and you must have sufficient sales, or the expectation of increased sales, to consider taking credit cards in the first place. Understand, too, that taking credit cards in person (called face-to-face transactions where you have the card in front of you) is different from accepting credit cards by phone, by mail, or through a Web site (called non–face-to-face transactions). Each method of selling is treated differently by bankcard providers.

Merchant Status from Your Bank

When you're ready to accept credit cards, start with the bank where you have your business checking account. Where you bank, and where you live, has everything to do with whether you can get merchant status from your bank or not. Home-business owners in small towns often have less trouble than do those in large cities. One crafter told me Bank of America gave her merchant status with no problem, but some banks simply refuse to deal with anyone who doesn't operate out of a storefront. Most banks now insist that credit card sales be transmitted electronically, but a few still offer manual printers and allow merchants to send in their sales slips by mail. You will be given details about this at the time you apply for merchant status. All banks will require proof that you have a going business and will want to see your financial statements.

Merchant Status through a Crafts Organization

If you are refused by your bank because your business is home based or just too new, getting bankcard services through a crafts or home-business organization is the next best way to go. Because such organizations have a large membership, they have some negotiating power with the credit card companies and often get special deals for their members. As a member of such an organization, the chances are about 95 percent that you will automatically be accepted into an its bankcard program, even if you are a brand new business owner.

One organization I can recommend to beginning sellers is the National Craft Association. Managing Director Barbara Arena tells me that 60 percent of all new NCA members now take the MasterCard/VISA services offered by her organization. "Crafters who are unsure about whether they want to take credit cards over a long period of time have the option of renting equipment," says Barbara. "This enables them to get out of the program with a month's notice. NCA members can operate on a software basis through their personal computer (taking their laptop computer to shows and calling in sales on their cell phone), or use a swipe machine. Under NCA's program, crafters can also accept credit card sales on their Internet site."

For more information from NCA and other organizations offering merchant services, see "Craft and Home-Business Organizations" on page 288.

Merchant Status from Credit Card Companies

If you've been in business for a while, you may find you can get merchant status directly from American Express or Novus Services, Inc., the umbrella company that handles the Discover, Bravo, and Private Issue credit cards. American Express says that in some cases it can grant merchant status immediately upon receipt of some key information given on the phone. As for Novus, many crafters have told me how easy it was to get merchant status from this company. Novus says it only needs your Social Security number and information to check your credit rating. If Novus accepts you, it can also get you set up to take VISA and MasterCard as well if you meet the special acceptance qualifications of these two credit card companies. (Usually, they require you to be in business for at least two years.)

Merchant Status from an Independent Service Organization Provider (ISO)

ISOs act as agents for banks that authorize credit cards, promoting their services by direct mail, through magazine advertising, telemarketing, and on the Internet. Most of these bankcard providers are operating under a network marketing program (one agent representing one agent representing another, and so on). They are everywhere on the Internet, sending unsolicited e-mail messages to Web site owners. In addition to offering the merchant account service itself, many are also trying to get other Web site owners to promote the same service in exchange for some kind of referral fee. I do not recommend that you get merchant status through an ISO because I've heard too many horror stories about them. If you want to explore this option on the Internet, however, use your browser's search button and type "credit cards + merchant" to get a list of such sellers.

In general, ISOs may offer a low discount rate but will sock it to you with inflated equipment costs, a high application fee, and extra fees for installation, programming, and site inspection. You will also have to sign an unbreakable three- or four-year lease for the electronic equipment.

As you can see, you must really do your homework where bankcard services are concerned. In checking out the services offered by any of the providers noted here, ask plenty of questions. Make up a chart that lets you compare what each one charges for application and service fees, monthly charges, equipment costs, software, discount rates, and transaction fees.

Transaction fees can range from 20 to 80 cents per ticket, with discount rates running anywhere from 1.67 percent to 5 percent. Higher rates are usually attached to non–face-to-face credit card transactions, paper transaction systems, or a low volume of sales. Any rate higher than 5 percent should be a danger signal since you could be dealing with an unscrupulous seller or some kind of illegal third-party processing program.

I'm told that a good credit card processor today may cost around $800, yet some card service providers are charging two or three times that amount in their leasing arrangements. I once got a quote from a major ISO and found it would have cost me $40 a month to lease the terminal—$1,920 over a period of four years—or I could buy it for just $1,000. In checking with my bank, I learned I could get the same equipment and the software to run it for just $350!

In summary, if you're a nervous beginner, the safest way to break into taking credit cards is to work with a bank or organization that offers equipment on a month-by-month rental arrangement. Once you've had some experience in taking credit card payments, you can review your situation and decide whether you want to move into a leasing arrangement or buy equipment outright.

6. Minimizing the Financial Risks of Selling

This book contains a good chapter on how and where to sell your crafts, but I thought it would be helpful for you to have added perspective on the business management end of selling through various outlets, and some things you can do to protect yourself from financial loss and legal hassles.

First you must accept the fact that all businesses occasionally suffer financial losses of one kind or another. That's simply the nature of business. Selling automatically carries a certain degree of risk in that we can never be absolutely sure that we're going to be paid for anything until we actually have payment in hand. Checks may bounce, wholesale buyers may refuse to pay their invoices, and consignment shops can close unexpectedly without returning merchandise to crafters. In the past few years, a surprising number

State Consignment Laws

Technically, consigned goods remain the property of the seller until they are sold. When a shop goes out of business, however, consigned merchandise may be seized by creditors in spite of what your consignment agreement may state. You may have some legal protection here, however, if you live in a state that has a consignment law designed to protect artists and craftspeople in such instances. I believe such laws exist in the states of CA, CO, CT, IL, IA, KY, MA, NH, NM, NY, OR, TX, WA, and WI. Call your Secretary of State to confirm this or, if your state isn't listed here, ask whether this law is now on the books. Be sure to get full details about the kind of protection afforded by this law because some states have different definitions for what constitutes "art" or "crafts."

of craft mall owners have stolen out of town in the middle of the night, taking with them all the money due their vendors, and sometimes the vendors' merchandise as well. (This topic is beyond the scope of this book, but if you'd like more information on it, see my *Creative Cash* book and back issues of my *Craftsbiz Chat* newsletter on the Internet at www.crafter.com/brabec).

Now I don't want you to feel uneasy about selling or suspicious of every buyer who comes your way, because that would take all the fun out of selling. But I *do* want you to know that bad things sometimes happen to good craftspeople who have not done their homework (by reading this book, you are doing *your* homework). If you will follow the cautionary guidelines that follow, you can avoid some common selling pitfalls and minimize your financial risk to the point where it will be negligible.

Selling to Consignment Shops

Never consign more merchandise to one shop than you can afford to lose, and do not send new items to a shop until you see that pay-

ments are being made regularly according to your written consignment agreement. It should cover the topics of:

- insurance (see "Insurance Tips," section 7).
- pricing (make sure the shop cannot raise or lower your
  retail price without your permission).
- sales commission (40 percent is standard; don't work with
  shop owners who ask for more than this. It makes more
  sense to wholesale products at 50 percent and get payment
  in 30 days).
- payment dates.
- display of merchandise.
- return of unsold merchandise (some shops have a clause
  stating that if unsold merchandise is not claimed within
  30 to 60 days after a notice has been sent, the shop can
  dispose of it any way it wishes).

Above all, make sure your agreement includes the name and
phone number of the shop's owner (not just the manager). If a shop
fails and you decide to take legal action, you want to be sure your
lawyer can track down the owner. (See sidebar, "State Consignment
Laws," page 250.)

Selling to Craft Malls

Shortly after the craft mall concept was introduced to the crafts
community in 1988 by Rufus Coomer, entrepreneurs who understood the profit potential of such a business began to open malls all
over the country. But there were no guidebooks and everyone was
flying by the seat of his or her pants, making up operating rules
along the way. Many mall owners, inexperienced in retailing, have
since gone out of business, often leaving crafters holding the bag.
The risks of selling through such well-known chain stores as Coomers
or American Craft Malls are minimal, and many independently
owned malls have also established excellent reputations in the

industry. What you need to be especially concerned about here are new malls opened by individuals who have no track record in this industry.

I'm not telling you *not* to set up a booth in a new mall in your area—it might prove to be a terrific outlet for you—but I am cautioning you to keep a sharp eye on the mall and how it's being operated. Warning signs of a mall in trouble include:

- **less than 75 percent occupancy**
- **little or no ongoing advertising**
- **not many shoppers**
- **crafters pulling out (usually a sign of too few sales)**
- **poor accounting of sales**
- **late payments**

If a mall is in trouble, it stands to reason that the logical time for it to close is right after the biggest selling season of the year, namely Christmas. Interestingly, this is when most of the shady mall owners have stolen out of town with crafters' Christmas sales in their pockets. As stated in my *Creative Cash* book:

> If it's nearing Christmas time, and you're getting uncomfortable vibes about the financial condition of a mall you're in, it might be smart to remove the bulk of your merchandise— especially expensive items—just before it closes for the holidays. You can always restock after the first of the year if everything looks rosy.

Avoiding Bad Checks

At a crafts fair or other event where you're selling directly to the public, if the buyer doesn't have cash and you don't accept credit cards, your only option is to accept a check. Few crafters have bad check problems for sales held in the home (holiday boutique, open house, party plan, and such), but bad checks at craft fairs are always possible. Here are several things you can do to avoid accepting a bad check:

- Always ask to see a driver's license and look carefully at the picture on it. Write the license number on the check.

- If the sale is a for a large amount, you can ask to see a credit card for added identification, but writing down the number will do no good because you cannot legally cover a bad check with a customer's credit card. (The customer has a legal right to refuse to let you copy the number as well.)

- Look closely at the check itself. Is there a name and address printed on it? If not, ask the customer to write in this information by hand, along with his or her phone number.

- Look at the sides of the check. If at least one side is not perforated, it could be a phony check.

- Look at the check number in the upper right-hand corner. Most banks who issue personalized checks begin the numbering system with 101 when a customer reorders new checks. The Small Business Administration says to be more cautious with low sequence numbers because there seems to be a higher number of these checks that are returned.

- Check the routing number in the lower left-hand corner and note the ink. If it looks shiny, wet your finger and see if the ink rubs off. That's a sure sign of a phony check because good checks are printed with magnetic ink that does not reflect light.

Collecting on a Bad Check

No matter how careful you are, sooner or later, you will get stuck with a bad check. It may bounce for three reasons:

> nonsufficient funds (NSF)
> account closed
> no account (evidence of fraud)

I've accepted tens of thousands of checks from mail-order buyers through the years and have rarely had a bad check I couldn't collect with a simple phone call asking the party to honor his or her obligation to me. People often move and close out accounts before all checks have cleared, or they add or subtract wrong, causing their account to be overdrawn. Typically, they are embarrassed to have caused a problem like this.

When the problem is more difficult than this, your bank can help. Check to learn its policy regarding bounced checks. Some automatically put checks through a second time. If a check bounces at this point, you may ask the bank to collect the check for you. The check needs to be substantial, however, since the bank fee may be $15 or more if they are successful in collecting the money.

If you have accepted a check for a substantial amount of money and believe there is evidence of fraud, you may wish to do one of the following:

- notify your district attorney's office
- contact your sheriff or police department (since it is a crime to write a bad check)
- try to collect through small claims court

For more detailed information on all of these topics, see *The Crafts Business Answer Book*.

7. Insurance Tips

As soon as you start even the smallest business at home, you need to give special attention to insurance. This section offers an introductory overview of insurance concerns of primary interest to crafts-business owners.

Homeowner's or Renter's Insurance

Anything in the home being used to generate income is considered to be business-related and thus exempt from coverage on a personal policy. Thus your homeowner's or renter's insurance policy will not cover business equipment, office furniture, supplies, or inventory of finished goods unless you obtain a special rider. Such riders, called a "Business Pursuits Endorsement" by some companies, are inexpensive and offer considerable protection. Your insurance agent will be happy to give you details.

As your business grows and you have an ever-larger inventory of supplies, materials, tools, and finished merchandise, you may find it necessary to buy a special in-home business policy that offers broader protection. Such policies may be purchased directly from insurance companies or through craft and home-business organizations that offer special insurance programs to their members.

Liability Insurance

There are two kinds of liability insurance. *Product* liability insurance protects you against lawsuits by consumers who have been injured while using one of your products. *Personal* liability insurance protects you against claims made by individuals who have suffered bodily injury while on your premises (either your home or the place where you are doing business, such as in your booth at a crafts fair).

Your homeowner's or renter's insurance policy will include some personal liability protection, but if someone were to suffer bodily injury while on your premises for *business* reasons, that coverage might not apply. Your need for personal liability insurance will be greater if you plan to regularly present home parties, holiday boutiques, or open house sales in your home where many people might be coming and going throughout the year. If you sell at craft fairs, you would also be liable for damages if someone were to fall and be injured in your booth or if something in your booth falls and injures another person. For this reason, some craft fair promoters now require all vendors to have personal liability insurance.

As for product liability insurance, whether you need it or not depends largely on the type of products you make for sale, how careful you are to make sure those products are safe, and how and where you sell them. Examples of some crafts that have caused injury to consumers and resulted in court claims in the past are stuffed toys with wire or pins that children have swallowed; items made of yarn or fiber that burned rapidly; handmade furniture that collapsed when someone put an ordinary amount of weight on them; jewelry with sharp points or other features that cut the wearer, and so on. Clearly, the best way to avoid injury to consumers is to make certain your products have no health hazards and are safe to use. (See discussion of consumer safety laws in section 8.)

Few artists and craftspeople who sell on a part-time basis feel they can afford product liability insurance, but many full-time craft professionals, particularly those who sell their work wholesale, find it a necessary expense. In fact, many wholesale buyers refuse to buy from suppliers that do not carry product liability insurance.

I believe the least expensive way to obtain both personal and product liability insurance is with one of the comprehensive in-home or craft business policies offered by a craft or home-business organization. Such policies generally offer a million dollars of both personal and product liability coverage. (See "Things to Do" Checklist on page 283 and Resources for some organizations you can contact for more information. Also check with your insurance agent about the benefits of an umbrella policy for extra liability insurance.)

Insurance on Crafts Merchandise

As a seller of art or crafts merchandise, you are responsible for insuring your own products against loss. If you plan to sell at craft fairs, in craft malls, rent-a-space shops, or consignment shops, you may want to buy an insurance policy that protects your merchandise both at home or away. Note that while craft shops and malls generally have fire insurance covering the building and its fixtures, this coverage cannot be extended to merchandise offered for sale because it is not the property of the shop owner. (Exception: Shops and malls in shopping centers are mandated by law to buy fire insurance on their contents whether they own the merchandise or not.)

This kind of insurance is usually part of the home-business/crafts-business insurance policies mentioned earlier.

Auto Insurance

Be sure to talk to the agent who handles your car insurance and explain that you may occasionally use your car for business purposes. Normally, a policy issued for a car that's used only for pleasure or driving to and from work may not provide complete coverage for an accident that occurs during business use of the car, particularly if the insured is to blame for the accident. For example, if you were delivering a load of crafts to a shop or on your way to a crafts fair and had an accident, would your business destination and the "commercial merchandise" in your car negate your coverage in any

Insuring Your Art or Crafts Collection

The replacement cost insurance you may have on your personal household possessions does not extend to "fine art," which includes such things as paintings, antiques, pictures, tapestries, statuary, and other articles that cannot be replaced with new articles. If you have a large collection of art, crafts, memorabilia, or collector's items, and its value is more than $1,500, you may wish to have your collection appraised so it can be protected with a separate all-risk endorsement to your homeowner's policy called a "fine arts floater."

way? Where insurance is concerned, the more questions you ask, the better you'll feel about the policies you have.

8. Important Regulations Affecting Artists and Craftspeople

Government agencies have a number of regulations that artists and craftspeople must know about. Generally, they relate to consumer safety, the labeling of certain products and trade practices. Following are regulations of primary interest to readers of books in the For Fun & Profit series. If you find a law or regulation related to your particular art or craft interest, be sure to request additional information from the government agency named there.

Consumer Safety Laws

All product sellers must pay attention to the Consumer Product Safety Act, which protects the public against unreasonable risks of injury associated with consumer products. The Consumer Product Safety Commission (CPSC) is particularly active in the area of toys and consumer goods designed for children. All sellers of handmade products must be doubly careful about the materials they use for children's products since consumer lawsuits are common where products for children are concerned. To avoid this problem, simply comply with the consumer safety laws applicable to your specific art or craft.

Toy Safety Concerns

To meet CPSC's guidelines for safety, make sure any toys you make for sale are:

- too large to be swallowed
- not apt to break easily or leave jagged edges

- free of sharp edges or points
- not put together with easily exposed pins, wires, or nails
- nontoxic, nonflammable, and nonpoisonous

The Use of Paints, Varnishes, and Other Finishes

Since all paint sold for household use must meet the Consumer Product Safety Act's requirement for minimum amounts of lead, these paints are deemed to be safe for use on products made for children, such as toys and furniture. Always check, however, to make sure the label bears a nontoxic notation. Specialty paints must carry a warning on the label about lead count, but "artist's paints" are curiously exempt from CPS's lead-in-paint ban and are not required to bear a warning label of any kind. Thus you should *never* use such paints on products intended for use by children unless the label specifically states they are *nontoxic* (lead-free). Acrylics and other water-based paints, of course, are nontoxic and completely safe for use on toys and other products made for children. If you plan to use a finishing coat, make sure it is nontoxic as well.

Fabric Flammability Concerns

The Flammable Fabrics Act is applicable only to those who sell products made of fabric, particularly products for children. It prohibits the movement in interstate commerce of articles of wearing apparel and fabrics that are so highly flammable as to be dangerous when worn by individuals, and for other purposes. Most fabrics comply with the above act, but if you plan to sell children's clothes or toys, you may wish to take an extra step to be doubly sure the fabric you are using is safe. This is particularly important if you plan to wholesale your products. What you should do is ask your fabric supplier for a *guarantee of compliance with the Flammability Act*. This guarantee is generally passed along to the buyer by a statement on the invoice that reads "continuing guaranty under the Flammable Fabrics Act." If you do not find such a statement on your invoice, you should ask the fabric manufacturer, wholesaler, or distributor to furnish you with their "statement of compliance" with the flammability standards. The CPSC can also tell you if a particular manufacturer has filed a continuing guarantee under The Flammable Fabrics Act.

Labels Required by Law

The following information applies only to crafters who use textiles, fabrics, fibers, or yarn products to make wearing apparel, decorative accessories, household furnishings, soft toys, or any product made of wool.

Different governmental agencies require the attachment of certain tags or labels to products sold in the consumer marketplace, whether manufactured in quantity or handmade for limited sale. You don't have to be too concerned about these laws if you sell only at local fairs, church bazaars, and home boutiques. As soon as you get out into the general consumer marketplace, however—doing large craft fairs, selling through consignment shops, craft malls, or wholesaling to shops—it would be wise to comply with all the federal labeling laws. Actually, these laws are quite easy to comply with because the required labels are readily available at inexpensive prices, and you can even make your own if you wish. Here is what the federal government wants you to tell your buyers in a tag or label:

- **What's in a product, and who has made it.** The Textile Fiber Products Identification Act (monitored both by the Bureau of Consumer Protection and the Federal Trade Commission) requires that a special label or hangtag be attached to all textile wearing apparel and household furnishings, with the exception of wall hangings. "Textiles" include products made of any fiber, yarn, or fabric, including garments and decorative accessories, quilts, pillows, place mats, stuffed toys, rugs, etc. The tag or label must include

(1) the name of the manufacturer and (2) the generic names and percentages of all fibers in the product in amounts of 5 percent or more, listed in order of predominance by weight.

- How to take care of products. Care Labeling Laws are part of the Textile Fiber Products Identification Act, details about which are available from the FTC. If you make wearing apparel or household furnishings of any kind using textiles, suede, or leather, you must attach a permanent label that explains how to take care of the item. This label must indicate whether the item is to be dry-cleaned or washed. If it is washable, you must indicate whether in hot or cold water, whether bleach may or may not be used, and the temperature at which it may be ironed. (See sample labels in sidebar)

- Details about products made of wool. If a product contains wool, the FTC requires additional identification under a separate law known as the Wool Products Labeling Act of 1939. FTC rules require that the labels of all wool or textile products clearly indicate when imported ingredients are used. Thus, the label for a skirt knitted in the U.S. from wool yarn imported from England would read, "Made in the USA from imported products" or similar wordage. If the wool yarn was spun in the U.S., a product made from that yarn would simply need a tag or label stating it was "Made in the USA" or "Crafted in USA" or some similarly clear terminology.

The Bedding and Upholstered Furniture Law

This is a peculiar state labeling law that affects sellers of items that have a concealed filling. It requires the purchase of a license, and products must have a tag that bears the manufacturer's registry number.

Bedding laws have long been a thorn in the side of crafters because they make no distinction between the large manufacturing company that makes mattresses and pillows, and the individual crafts producer who sells only handmade items. "Concealed filling" items include not just bedding and upholstery, but handmade pillows and quilts. In some states, dolls, teddy bears, and stuffed soft sculpture items are also required to have a tag.

Fortunately, only twenty-nine states now have this law on the books, and even if your state is one of them, the law may be arbitrarily enforced. (One exception is the state of Pennsylvania, which is reportedly sending officials to craft shows to inspect merchandise to see if it is properly labeled.) The only penalty that appears to be connected with a violation of this law in any state is removal of merchandise from store shelves or craft fair exhibits. That being the case, many crafters choose to ignore this law until they are challenged. If you learn you must comply with this law, you will be required to obtain a state license that will cost between $25 and $100, and you will have to order special "bedding stamps" that can be attached to your products. For more information on this complex topic, see *The Crafts Business Answer Book*.

FTC Rule for Mail-Order Sellers

Even the smallest home-based business needs to be familiar with Federal Trade Commission (FTC) rules and regulations. A variety of free booklets are available to business owners on topics related to advertising, mail-order marketing, and product labeling (as discussed earlier). In particular, crafters who sell by mail need to pay attention to the FTC's Thirty-Day Mail-Order Rule, which states that one must ship customer orders within thirty days of receiving payment for the order. This rule is strictly enforced, with severe financial penalties for each violation.

Unless you specifically state in your advertising literature how long delivery will take, customers will expect to receive the product within thirty days after you get their order. If you cannot meet this shipping date, you must notify the customer accordingly, enclosing a postage-paid reply card or envelope, and giving them the option to cancel the order if they wish. Now you know why so many catalog sellers state, "Allow six weeks for delivery." This lets them off the hook in case there are unforeseen delays in getting the order delivered.

9. Protecting Your Intellectual Property

"Intellectual property," says Attorney Stephen Elias in his book, *Patent, Copyright & Trademark,* "is a product of the human intellect that has commercial value."

This section offers a brief overview of how to protect your intellectual property through patents and trademarks, with a longer discussion of copyright law, which is of the greatest concern to individuals who sell what they make. Since it is easy to get patents, trademarks, and copyrights mixed up, let me briefly define them for you:

- A *patent* is a grant issued by the government that gives an inventor the right to exclude all others from making, using, or selling an invention within the United States and its territories and possessions.

- A *trademark* is used by a manufacturer or merchant to identify his or her goods and distinguish them from those manufactured or sold by others.

- A *copyright* protects the rights of creators of intellectual property in five main categories (described in this section).

Perspective on Patents

A patent may be granted to anyone who invents or discovers a new and useful process, machine, manufacture or composition of matter, or any new and useful improvement thereof. Any new, original, and ornamental design for an article of manufacture can also be patented. The problem with patents is that they can cost as much as

$5,000 or more to obtain, and once you've got one, they still require periodic maintenance through the U.S. Patent and Trademark Office. To contact this office, you can use the following Web sites: www.uspto.com or www.lcweb.loc.gov.

Ironically, a patent doesn't even give one the right to sell a product. It merely excludes anyone else from making, using, or selling your invention. Many business novices who have gone to the trouble to patent a product end up wasting a lot of time and money because a patent is useless if it isn't backed with the right manufacturing, distribution, and advertising programs. As inventor Jeremy

A Proper Copyright Notice

Although a copyright notice is not required by law, you are encouraged to put a copyright notice on every original thing you create. Adding the copyright notice does not obligate you to formally register your copyright, but it does serve to warn others that your work is legally protected and makes it difficult for anyone to claim they have "accidentally stolen" your work. (Those who actually do violate a copyright because they don't understand the law are called "innocent infringers" by the Copyright Office.)

A proper copyright notice includes three things:

1. the word "copyright," its abbreviation "copr.," or the copyright symbol, ©

2. the year of first publication of the work (when it was first shown or sold to the public)

3. the name of the copyright owner. Example: © 2000 by Barbara Brabec. (When the words "All Rights Reserved" are added to the copyright notation, it means that copyright protection has been extended to include all of the Western Hemisphere.)

The copyright notice should be positioned in a place where it can easily be seen. It can be stamped, cast, engraved, painted, printed, wood-burned, or simply written by hand in permanent ink. In the case of fiber crafts, you can attach an inexpensive label with the copyright notice and your business name and logo (or any other information you wish to put on the label).

Gorman states in *Homemade Money,* "Ninety-seven percent of the U.S. patents issued never earn enough money to pay the patenting fee. They just go on a plaque on the wall or in a desk drawer to impress the grandchildren fifty years later."

What a Trademark Protects

Trademarks were established to prevent one company from trading on the good name and reputation of another. The primary function of a trademark is to indicate origin, but in some cases it also serves as a guarantee of quality.

You cannot adopt any trademark that is so similar to another that it is likely to confuse buyers, nor can you trademark generic or descriptive names in the public domain. If, however, you come up with a particular word, name, symbol, or device to identify and distinguish your products from others, you may protect that mark by trademark provided another company is not already using a similar mark. Brand names, trade names, slogans, and phrases may also qualify for trademark protection.

Many individual crafters have successfully registered their own trademarks using a how-to book on the topic, but some would say never to try this without the help of a trademark attorney. It depends on how much you love detail and how well you can follow directions. Any mistake on the application form could cause it to be rejected, and you would lose the application fee in the process. If this is something you're interested in, and you have designed a mark you want to protect, you should first do a trademark search to see if someone else is already using it. Trademark searches can be done using library directories, an online computer service (check with your library), through private trademark search firms, or directly on the Internet through the Patent & Trademark Office's online search service (see checklist and resources). All of these searches together could still be inconclusive, however, because many companies have a stash of trademarks in reserve waiting for just the right product. As I understand it, these "nonpublished" trademarks are in a special file that only an attorney or trademark search service could find for you.

Like copyrights, trademarks have their own symbol, which looks like this: ®. This symbol can only be used once the trademark has been formally registered through the U.S. Patent and Trademark Office. Business owners often use the superscript initials "TM" with a mark to indicate they've claimed a logo or some other mark, but this offers no legal protection. While this does not guarantee trademark protection, it does give notice to the public that you are claiming this name as your trademark. However, after you've used a mark for some time, you do gain a certain amount of common-law protection for that mark. I have, in fact, gained common-law protection for the name of my *Homemade Money* book and successfully defended it against use by another individual in my field because this title has become so closely associated with my name in the home-business community.

Whether you ever formally register a trademark or not will have much to do with your long-range business plans, how you feel about protecting your creativity, and what it would do to your business if someone stole your mark and registered it in his or her own name. Once you've designed a trademark you feel is worth protecting, get additional information from the Patent & Trademark Office and read a book or two on the topic to decide whether this is something you wish to pursue. (See checklist and resources.)

What Copyrights Protect

As a serious student of the copyright law, I've pored through the hard-to-interpret copyright manual, read dozens of related articles and books, and discussed this subject at length with designers, writers, teachers, editors, and publishers. I must emphasize, however, that I am no expert on this topic, and the following information does not constitute legal advice. It is merely offered as a general guide to a very complex legal topic you may wish to research further on your own at some point. In a book of this nature, addressed to hobbyists and beginning crafts-business owners, a discussion of copyrights must be limited to three basic topics:

> **what copyrights do and do not protect**
> **how to register a copyright and protect your legal rights**
> **how to avoid infringing on the rights of other copyright holders**

One of the first things you should do now is send for the free booklets offered by the Copyright Office (see checklist and resources). Various free circulars explain copyright basics, the forms involved in registering a copyright, and how to submit a copyright application and register a copyright. They also discuss what you cannot copyright. Rather than duplicate all the free information you can get from the Copyright Office with a letter or phone call, I will only briefly touch on these topics and focus instead on addressing some of the particular copyright questions crafters have asked me in the past.

Things You Can Copyright

Some people mistakenly believe that copyright protection extends only to printed works, but that is not true. The purpose of the copyright law is to protect any creator from anyone who would use his creative work for his own profit. Under current copyright law, claims are now registered in seven classes, five of which pertain to crafts:

1. *Serials* (Form SE)—periodicals, newspapers, magazines, bulletins, newsletters, annuals, journals, and proceedings of societies.
2. *Text* (Form TX)—books, directories, and other written works, including the how-to instructions for a crafts project. (You

could copyright a letter to your mother if you wanted to—
or your best display ad copy, or any other written words that
represent income potential.)

3. *Visual Arts* (Form VA)—pictorial, graphic, or sculptural
   works, including fine, graphic, and applied art; photographs,
   charts; technical drawings; diagrams; and models. (Also included in this category are "works of artistic craftsmanship
   insofar as their form but not their mechanical or utilitarian
   aspects are concerned.")

4. *Performing Arts* (Form PA)—musical works and accompany-
   ing words, dramatic works, pantomimes, choreographic
   works, motion pictures, and other audiovisual works.

5. Sound Recordings (Form SR)—musical, spoken, or other
   sounds, including any audio- or videotapes you might
   create.

Selling How-To Projects to Magazines

If you want to sell an article, poem, or how-to project to a magazine, you need not
copyright the material first because copyright protection exists from the moment you
create that work. Your primary consideration here is whether you will sell "all rights"
or only "first rights" to the magazine.

The sale of first rights means you are giving a publication permission to print your article, poem, or how-to project once, for a specific sum of money. After publication, you
then have the right to resell that material or profit from it in other ways. Although it is
always desirable to sell only "first rights," some magazines do not offer this choice.

If you sell all rights, you will automatically lose ownership of the copyright to your
material and you can no longer profit from that work. Professional designers often
refuse to work this way because they know they can realize greater profits by publishing their own pattern packets or design leaflets and wholesaling them to shops.

Things You Cannot Copyright

You can't copyright ideas or procedures for doing, making, or building things, but the *expression* of an idea fixed in a tangible medium may be copyrightable—such as a book explaining a new system or technique. Brand names, trade names, slogans, and phrases cannot be copyrighted, either, although they might be entitled to protection under trademark laws.

The design on a craft object can be copyrighted, but only if it can be identified separately from the object itself. Objects themselves (a decorated coffee mug, a box, a tote bag) cannot be copyrighted.

Copyright Registration Tips

First, understand that you do not have to formally copyright anything because copyright protection exists from the moment a work is created, whether you add a copyright notice or not.

So why file at all? The answer is simple: If you don't file the form and pay the fee (currently $20), you'll never be able to take anyone to court for stealing your work. Therefore, in each instance where copyright protection is considered, you need to decide how important your work is to you in terms of dollars and cents, and ask yourself whether you value it enough to pay to protect it. Would you actually be willing to pay court costs to defend your copyright, should someone steal it from you? If you never intend to go to court, there's little use in officially registering a copyright; but since it costs you nothing to add a copyright notice to your work, you are foolish not to do this. (See sidebar, "A Proper Copyright Notice, page 264.")

If you do decide to file a copyright application, contact the Copyright Office and request the appropriate forms. When you file the copyright application form (which is easy to complete), you must include with it two copies of the work. Ordinarily, two actual copies of copyrighted items must be deposited, but certain items are exempt from deposit requirements, including all three-dimensional sculptural works and any works published only as reproduced in or on jewelry, dolls, toys, games, plaques, floor coverings, textile and other fabrics, packaging materials, or any useful article. In these cases, two photographs or drawings of the item are sufficient.

Note that the Copyright Office does not compare deposit copies to determine whether works submitted for registration are similar to any material already copyrighted. It is the sender's responsibility to determine the originality of what's being copyrighted. (See discussion of "original" in the next section, under "Respecting the Copyrights of Others.")

Protecting Your Copyrights

If someone ever copies one of your copyrighted works, and you have registered that work with the Copyright Office, you should defend it as far as you are financially able to do so. If you think you're dealing with an innocent infringer—another crafter, perhaps, who has probably not profited much (if at all) from your work—a strongly worded letter on your business stationery (with a copy to an attorney, if you have one) might do the trick. Simply inform the copyright infringer that you are the legal owner of the work and the only one who has the right to profit from it. Tell the infringer that he or she must immediately cease using your copyrighted work, and ask for a confirmation by return mail.

If you think you have lost some money or incurred other damages, consult with a copyright attorney before contacting the infringer to see how you can best protect your rights and recoup any financial losses you may have suffered. This is particularly important if the infringer appears to be a successful business or corporation. Although you may have no intention of ever going to court on this matter, the copyright infringer won't know that, and one letter from a competent attorney might immediately resolve the matter at very little cost to you.

Mandatory Deposit Requirements

Although you do not have to officially register a copyright claim, it *is* mandatory to deposit two copies of all "published works" for the collections of the Library of Congress within three months after publication. Failure to make the deposit may subject the copyright owner to fines and other monetary liabilities, but it does not affect copyright protection. No special form is required for this mandatory deposit.

Note that the term "published works" pertains not just to the publication of printed matter, but to the public display of any item. Thus you "publish" your originally designed craftwork when you first show it at a craft fair, in a shop, on your Web site, or any other public place.

Respecting the Copyrights of Others

Just as there are several things you must do to protect your "intellectual creations," there are several things you must not do if you wish to avoid legal problems with other copyright holders.

Copyright infringement occurs whenever anyone violates the exclusive rights covered by copyright. If and when a copyright case goes to court, the copyright holder who has been infringed upon must prove that his or her work is the original creation and that the two works are so similar that the alleged infringer must have copied it. This is not always an easy matter, for "original" is a difficult word to define. Even the Copyright Office has trouble here, which is why so many cases that go to court end up setting precedents.

In any copyright case, there will be discussions about "substantial similarity," instances where two people actually have created the same thing simultaneously, loss of profits, or damage to one's business or reputation. If you were found guilty of copyright infringement, at the very least you would probably be ordered to pay to the original creator all profits derived from the sale of the copyrighted work to date. You would also have to agree to refund any orders you might receive for the work in the future. In some copyright cases where the original creator has experienced considerable financial loss, penalties for copyright infringement have been as high as $100,000. As you can see, this is not a matter to take lightly.

This is a complex topic beyond the scope of this book, but any book on copyright law will provide additional information if you should ever need it. What's important here is that you fully understand the importance of being careful to respect the legal rights of others. As a crafts business owner, you could possibly infringe on someone else's designs when you (1) quote someone in an article, periodical, or book you've written; (2) photocopy copyrighted materials; or (3) share information on the Internet. Following is a brief discussion of the first three topics and a longer discussion of the fourth.

1. **Be careful when quoting from a published source.** If you're writing an article or book and wish to quote someone's words from any published source (book, magazine, Internet, and so on), you should always obtain written permission first. Granted, minor quotations from published sources are okay when they fall under the Copyright Office's Fair Use Doctrine, but unless you completely understand this doctrine, you should protect yourself by obtaining permission before you quote anyone in one of your own written works. It is not necessarily the quantity of the quote, but the value of the quoted material to the copyright owner.

   In particular, never *ever* use a published poem in one of your written works. To the poet, this is a "whole work," much the same as a book is a whole work to an author. While the use of one or two lines of a poem, or a paragraph from a book may be considered "fair use," many publishers now require written permission even for this short reproduction of a copyrighted work.

2. **Photocopying can be dangerous.** Teachers often photocopy large sections of a book (sometimes whole books) for distribution to their students, but this is a flagrant violation of the copyright law. Some publishers may grant photocopying of part of a work if it is to be used only once as a teaching aid, but written permission must always be obtained first.

   It is also a violation of the copyright law to photocopy patterns for sale or trade because such use denies the creator the profit from a copy that might have been sold.

3. **Don't share copyrighted information on the Internet.** People everywhere are lifting material from *Reader's Digest* and other copyrighted publications and "sharing" them on the Internet through e-mail messages, bulletin boards, and the like. *This is a very dangerous thing to do.* "But I didn't see a copyright notice," you might say, or "It indicated the author was anonymous." What you must remember is that *everything* gains copyright protection the moment it is created, whether a copyright notice is attached to it or not. Many "anonymous" items on the Internet are actually copyrighted poems and articles put there by someone who not only violated the copyright law but compounded the matter by failing to give credit to the original creator.

   If you were to pick up one of those "anonymous" pieces of information and put it into an article or book of your own, the original copyright owner, upon seeing his or her work in your publication, would have good grounds for a lawsuit. Remember, pleading ignorance of the law is never a good excuse.

   Clearly there is no financial gain to be realized by violating the rights of a copyright holder when it means that any day you might be contacted by a lawyer and threatened with a lawsuit. As stated in my *Crafts Business Answer Book & Resource Guide:*

Changing Things

Many crafters have mistakenly been led to believe that they can copy the work of others if they simply change this or that so their creation doesn't look exactly like the one they have copied. But many copyright court cases have hinged in someone taking "a substantial part" of someone else's design and claiming it as their own. As explained earlier, if your "original creation" bears even the slightest resemblance to the product you've copied—and you are caught selling it in the commercial marketplace—there could be legal problems.

Crafters often combine the parts of two or three patterns in an attempt to come up with their own original patterns, but often this only compounds the possible copyright problems. Let's imagine you're making a doll. You might take the head from one pattern, the arms and legs from another, and the unique facial features from another. You may think you have developed an original creation (and perhaps an original pattern

The best way to avoid copyright infringement problems is to follow the "Golden Rule" proposed by a United States Supreme Court justice: "Take not from others to such an extent and in such a manner that you would be resentful if they so took from you."

Using Commercial Patterns and Designs

Beginning crafters who lack design skills commonly make products for sale using commercial patterns, designs in books, or how-to instructions for projects found in magazines. The problem here is that all of these things are published for the general consumer market and offered for *personal use* only. Because they are all protected by copyright, that means only the copyright holder has the right to profit from their use.

That said, let me ease your mind by saying that the sale of products made from copyrighted patterns, designs, and magazine how-to projects is probably not going to cause any problems *as long*

you might sell), but you haven't. Since the original designer of any of the features you've copied might recognize her work in your "original creation" or published pattern, she could come after you for infringing on "a substantial part" of her design. In this case, all you've done is multiply your possibilities for a legal confrontation with three copyright holders.

"But I can't create my own original designs and patterns!" you moan. Many who have said this in the past were mistaken. With time and practice, most crafters are able to develop products that are original in design, and I believe you can do this, too. Meanwhile, check out Dover Publications' *Pictorial Archive* series of books (see the "Things to Do" checklist and Resources). Here you will find thousands of copyright-free designs and motifs you can use on your craft work or in needlework projects. And don't forget the wealth of design material in museums and old books that have fallen into the public domain. (See sidebar, "What's in the Public Domain?" on page 278)

as sales are limited, and they yield a profit only to you, the crafter. That means no sales through shops of any kind where a sales commission or profit is received by a third party, and absolutely no wholesaling of such products.

It's not that designers and publishers are concerned about your sale of a few craft or needlework items to friends and local buyers; what they are fighting to protect with the legality of copyrights is their right to sell their own designs or finished products in the commercial marketplace. You may find that some patterns, designs, or projects state "no mass production." You are not mass producing if you make a dozen handcrafted items for sale at a craft fair or holiday boutique, but you would definitely be considered a mass-producer if you made dozens, or hundreds, for sale in shops.

Consignment sales fall into a kind of gray area that requires some commonsense judgment on your part. This is neither wholesaling nor selling direct to consumers. One publisher might consider such sales a violation of a copyright while another might not.

Whenever specific guidelines for the use of a pattern, design, or how-to project is not given, the only way to know for sure if you are operating on safe legal grounds is to write to the publisher and get written permission on where you can sell reproductions of the item in question.

Now let's take a closer look at the individual types of patterns, designs, and how-to projects you might consider using once you enter the crafts marketplace.

Craft, Toy, and Garment Patterns

Today, the consumer has access to thousands of sewing patterns plus toy, craft, needlework, and woodworking patterns of every kind and description found in books, magazines, and design or project leaflets. Whether you can use such patterns for commercial use depends largely on who has published the pattern and owns the copyright, and what the copyright holder's policy happens to be for how buyers may use those patterns.

To avoid copyright problems when using patterns of any kind, the first thing you need to do is look for some kind of notice on the pattern packet or publication containing the pattern. In checking some patterns, I found that those sold by *Woman's Day* state specifically that reproductions of the designs may not be sold, bartered, or traded. *Good Housekeeping*, on the other hand, gives permission to use their patterns for "income-producing activities." When in doubt, ask!

Whereas the general rule for selling reproductions made from commercial patterns is "no wholesaling and no sales to shops," items made from the average garment pattern (such as an apron, vest, shirt, or simple dress) purchased in the local fabric store *may* be an exception. My research suggests that selling such items in your local consignment shop or craft mall isn't likely to be much of a problem because the sewing pattern companies aren't on the lookout for copyright violators the way individual craft designers and major corporations are. (And most people who sew end up changing those patterns and using different decorations to such a degree that pattern companies might not recognize those patterns even if they were looking for them. See sidebar, "Changing Things," page 264.)

On the other hand, commercial garment patterns that have been designed by name designers should never be used without permission. In most cases, you would have to obtain a licensing agreement for the commercial use of such patterns.

Be especially careful about selling reproductions of toys and dolls made from commercial patterns or design books. Many are likely to be for popular copyrighted characters being sold in the commercial marketplace. In such cases, the pattern company will have a special licensing arrangement with the toy or doll manufacturer to sell the pattern, and reproductions for sale by individual crafters will be strictly prohibited.

Take a Raggedy Ann doll, for example. The fact that you've purchased a pattern to make such a doll does not give you the right to sell a finished likeness of that doll any more than your purchase of a piece of artwork gives you the right to re-create it for sale in some other form, such as notepaper or calendars. Only the original creator has such rights. You have simply purchased the *physical property* for private use.

How-To Projects in Magazines and Books

Each magazine and book publisher has its own policy about the use of its art, craft, or needlework projects. How those projects may be used depends on who owns the copyright to the published projects. In some instances, craft and needlework designers sell their original designs outright to publishers of books, leaflets, or magazines. Other designers authorize only a one-time use of their projects, which gives them the right to republish or sell their designs to another market or license them to a manufacturer. If guidelines about selling finished products do not appear somewhere in the magazine or on the copyright page of a book, you should always write and get permission to make such items for sale. In your letter, explain how many items you would like to make, and where you plan to sell them, as that could make a big difference in the reply you receive.

In case you missed the special note on the copyright page of this book, you *can* make and sell all of the projects featured in this and any other book in Prima's FOR FUN & PROFIT series.

As a columnist for *Crafts Magazine,* I can also tell you that its readers have the right to use its patterns and projects for money-making purposes, but only to the extent that sales are limited to places where the crafter is the only one who profits from their use. That means selling directly to individuals, with no sales in shops of any kind where a third party would also realize some profit from a sale. Actually, this is a good rule-of-thumb guideline to use if you plan to sell only a few items of any project or pattern published in any magazine, book, or leaflet.

What's in the Public Domain?

For all works created after January 1, 1978, the copyright lasts for the life of the author or creator plus 50 years after his or her death. For works created before 1978, there are different terms, which you can obtain from any book in your library on copyright law.

Once material falls into the public domain, it can never be copyrighted again. As a general rule, anything with a copyright date more than 75 years ago is probably in the public domain, but you can never be sure without doing a thorough search. Some characters in old books—such as Beatrix Potter's *Peter Rabbit*—are now protected under the trademark law as business logos. For more information on this, ask the Copyright Office to send you its circular on "How to Investigate the Copyright Status of a Work."

Early American craft and needlework patterns of all kind are in the public domain because they were created before the copyright law was a reality. Such old patterns may

In summary, products that aren't original in design will sell, but their market is limited, and they will never be able to command the kind of prices that original-design items enjoy. Generally speaking, the more original the product line, the greater one's chances for building a profitable crafts business.

As your business grows, questions about copyrights will arise, and you will have to do a little research to get the answers you need. Your library should have several books on this topic and there is a wealth of information on the Internet. (Just use your search button and type "copyright information.") If you have a technical copyright question, remember that you can always call the Copyright Office and speak to someone who can answer it and send you additional information. Note, however, that regulations prohibit the Copyright Office from giving legal advice or opinions concerning the rights of persons in connection with cases of alleged copyright infringement.

show up in books and magazines that are copyrighted, but the copyright in this case extends only to the book or magazine itself and the way in which a pattern has been presented to readers, along with the way in which the how-to-make instructions have been written. The actual patterns themselves cannot be copyrighted by anyone at this point.

Quilts offer an interesting example. If a contemporary quilt designer takes a traditional quilt pattern and does something unusual with it in terms of material or colors, this new creation would quality for a copyright, with the protection being given to the quilt as a work of art, not to the traditional pattern itself, which is still in the public domain. Thus you could take that same traditional quilt pattern and do something else with it for publication, but you could not publish the contemporary designer's copyrighted version of that same pattern.

10. To Keep Growing, Keep Learning

Everything we do, every action we take, affects our life in one way or another. Reading a book is a simple act, indeed, but trust me when I say that your reading of this particular book *could ultimately change your life.* I know this to be true because thousands of men and women have written to me over the years to tell me how their lives changed after they read one or another of my books and decided to start a crafts business. My life has changed, too, as a result of reading books by other authors.

Many years ago, the purchase of a book titled *You Can Whittle and Carve* unleashed a flood of creativity in me that has yet to cease. That simple book helped me to discover unknown craft talents, which in turn led me to start my first crafts business at home. That experience prepared me for the message I would find a decade later in the book, *On Writing Well* by William Zinsser. This author changed my life by giving me the courage to try my hand at writing professionally. Dozens of books later, I had learned a lot about the art and craft of writing well and making a living in the process.

Now you know why I believe reading should be given top priority in your life. Generally speaking, the more serious you become about anything you're interested in, the more reading you will need to do. This will take time, but the benefits will be enormous. If a crafts business is your current passion, this book contains all you need to know to get started. To keep growing, read some of the wonderful books recommended in the resource section of this book. (If you don't find them in your local library, ask your librarian to obtain them for you through the inter-library loan program.) Join one or more of the organizations recommended. Subscribe to a few periodicals or magazines, and "grow your business" through networking with others who share your interests.

Motivational Tips

As you start your new business or expand a money-making hobby already begun, consider the following suggestions:

- *Start an "Achievement Log."* Day by day, our small achievements may seem insignificant, but viewed in total after several weeks or months, they give us important perspective. Reread your achievement log periodically in the future, especially on days when you feel down in the dumps. Make entries at least once a week, noting such things as new customers or accounts acquired, publicity you've gotten, a new product you've designed, the brochure or catalog you've just completed, positive feedback received from others, new friendships, and financial gains.

- *Live your dream.* The mind is a curious thing—it can be trained to think success is possible or to think that success is only for other people. Most of our fears never come true, so allowing our minds to dwell on what may or may not happen cripples us, preventing us from moving ahead, from having confidence, and from living out our dreams. Instead of "facing fear," focus on the result you want. This may automatically eliminate the fear.

- *Think positively.* As Murphy has proven time and again, what can go wrong will, and usually at the worst possible moment. It matters little whether the thing that has gone wrong was caused by circumstances beyond our control or by a mistake in judgment. What does matter is how we deal with the problem at hand. A positive attitude and the ability to remain flexible at all times are two of the most important ingredients for success in any endeavor.

- *Don't be afraid to fail.* We often learn more from failure than from success. When you make a mistake, chalk it up to experience and consider it a good lesson well learned. The more you learn, the more self-confident you will become.

- *Temper your "dreams of riches" with thoughts of reality.* Remember that "success" can also mean being in control of your own life, making new friends, or discovering a new world of possibilities.

Online Help

Today, one of the best ways to network and learn about business is to get on the Internet. The many online resources included in the "Things to Do Checklist" in the next section will give you a jump-start and lead to many exciting discoveries.

For continuing help and advice from Barbara Brabec, be sure to visit her Web site at www.crafter.com/brabec. There you will find her monthly *Craftsbiz Chat* newsletter, reprints of some of her crafts marketing and business columns, recommended books, and links to hundreds of other art and craft sites on the Web. Reader questions may be e-mailed to barbara@crafter.com for discussion in her newsletter, but questions cannot be answered individually by e-mail.

You can also get Barbara's business advice in her monthly columns in *Crafts Magazine* and *The Crafts Report*.

Until now you may have lacked the courage to get your craft ideas off the ground, but now that you've seen how other people have accomplished their goals, I hope you feel more confident and adventurous and are ready to capitalize on your creativity. By following the good advice in this book, you can stop dreaming about all the things you want to do and start making plans to do them!

I'm not trying to make home-business owners out of everyone who reads this book, but my goal is definitely to give you a shove in that direction if you're teetering on the edge, wanting something more than just a profitable hobby. It's wonderful to have a satisfying hobby, and even better to have one that pays for itself; but the nicest thing of all is a real home business that lets you fully utilize your creative talents and abilities while also adding to the family income.

"The things I want to know are in books," Abraham Lincoln once said. "My best friend is the person who'll get me a book I ain't read." You now hold in your hands a book that has taught you many things you wanted to know. To make it a *life-changing book*, all you have to do is act on the information you've been given.

I wish you a joyful journey and a potful of profits!

"Things to Do" Checklist

INSTRUCTIONS: Read through this entire section, noting the different things you need to do to get your crafts business "up and running." Use the checklist as a plan, checking off each task as it is completed and obtaining any recommended resources. Where indicated, note the date action was taken so you have a reminder about any follow-up action that should be taken.

Business Start-Up Checklist

__Call City Hall or County Clerk

    __to register fictitious business name

    __to see if you need a business license or permit

    __to check on local zoning laws

    (info also available in your library)

*Follow up:*_____

__Call state capitol

    __Secretary of State: to register your business name;
    ask about a license

    __Dept. of Revenue: to apply for sales tax number

*Follow up:*_____

__Call your local telephone company about

    __cost of a separate phone line for business

    __cost of an additional personal line for Internet access

    __any special options for home-based businesses

*Follow up:*_____

__Call your insurance agent(s) to discuss

 __business rider on house insurance
 (or need for separate in-home insurance policy)
 __benefits of an umbrella policy for extra liability insurance
 __using your car for business
 (how this may affect your insurance)
 *Follow up:*_____

__Call several banks or S&Ls in your area to

 __compare cost of a business checking account
 __ get price of a safe-deposit box for valuable business records
 *Follow up:*_____

__Visit office and computer supply stores to check on

 __manual bookkeeping systems, such as the
 Dome Simplified Monthly
 __accounting software
 __standard invoices and other helpful business forms
 *Follow up:*_____

__Call National Association of Enrolled Agents at (800) 424-4339

 __to get a referral to a tax professional in your area
 __to get answers to any tax questions you may have (no charge)
 *Follow up:*_____

__Contact government agencies for information
relative to your business.

 (See "Government Agencies" checklist.)

__Request free brochures from organizations

 (See "Craft and Home Business Organizations.")

__Obtain sample issues or subscribe to selected publications

 (See "Recommended Craft Business Periodicals.")

__Obtain other information of possible help to your business
(See "Other Services and Suppliers.")

__Get acquainted with the business information available to you in
your library.
(See list of "Recommended Business Books" and "Helpful Library
Directories.")

Government Agencies

__Consumer Product Safety Commission (CPSC), Washington, DC
20207. Toll-free hotline: (800) 638-2772. Information Services:
(301) 504-0000. Web site: www.cpsc.gov. (Includes a "Talk to Us"
e-mail address where you can get answers to specific questions.)
If you make toys or other products for children, garments (especially children's wear), or use any kind of paint, varnish, lacquer,
or shellac on your products, obtain the following free booklets:

__*The Consumer Product Safety Act of 1972*
__*The Flammable Fabrics Act*

Date Contacted:_____Information Received:_____

*Follow up:*_____

__Copyright Office, Register of Copyrights, Library of Congress,
Washington, DC 20559. To hear recorded messages on the Copyright Office's automated message system (general information,
registration procedures, copyright search info, etc.), call (202) 707-
3000. You can also get the same information online at www.loc
.gov/copyright.

To get free copyright forms, a complete list of all publications
available, or to speak personally to someone who will answer
your special questions, call (202) 797-9100. In particular, ask for:

__Circular R1, *The Nuts and Bolts of Copyright*
__Circular R2 (a list of publications available)

Date Contacted:_____Information Received:_____

Follow up:_____

__Department of Labor. If you should ever hire an employee or independent contractor, contact your local Labor Department, Wage & Hour Division, for guidance on what you must do to be completely legal. (Check your phone book under "U.S. Government.")

Date Contacted:_____Information Received:_____

Follow up:_____

__Federal Trade Commission (FTC), 6th Street. & Pennsylvania Avenue., N.W., Washington, DC 20580. Web site: www.ftc.gov. Request any of the following booklets relative to your craft or business:

__*Textile Fiber Products Identification Act*

__*Wool Products Labeling Act of 1939*

__*Care Labeling of Textile Wearing Apparel*

__*The Hand Knitting Yarn Industry* (booklet)

__*Truth-in-Advertising Rules*

__*Thirty-Day Mail Order Rule*

Date Contacted:_____Information Received:_____

Follow up _____

__Internal Revenue Service (IRS). Check the Internet at www .irs.gov to read the following information online or call your local IRS office to get the following booklets and other free tax information:

__*Tax Guide for Small Business*—#334

__*Business Use of Your Home*—#587

__*Tax Information for Direct Sellers*

Date Contacted:_____Information Received:_____

Follow up _____

__Patent and Trademark Office (PTO), Washington, DC 20231. Web site: www.uspto.gov

For patent and trademark information 24 hours a day, call (800) 786-9199 (in northern Virgina, call (703) 308-9000) to hear various messages about patents and trademarks or to order the follow-ing booklets:

__*Basic Facts about Patents*
__*Basic Facts about Trademarks*

To search the PTO's online database of all registered trademarks, go to www.uspto.gov/tmdb/index.html.

Date Contacted:_____Information Received:_____

*Follow up:*_____

__Social Security Hotline. (800) 772-1213. By calling this number, you can hear automated messages, order information booklets, or speak directly to someone who can answer specific questions.

Date Contacted:_____Information Received:_____

*Follow up*_____

__U.S. Small Business Administration (SBA). (800) U-ASK-SBA. Call this number to hear a variety of prerecorded messages on starting and financing a business. Weekdays, you can speak per-sonally to an SBA adviser to get answers to specific questions and request such free business publications as:

__*Starting Your Business* —#CO-0028

__*Resource Directory for Small Business Management*—#CO-0042
   (a list of low-cost publications available from the SBA)

The SBA's mission is to help people get into business and stay there. One-on-one counseling, training, and workshops are avail-able through 950 small business development centers across the country. Help is also available from local district offices of the

SBA in the form of free business counseling and training from SCORE volunteers (see below). The SBA office in Washington has a special Women's Business Enterprise section that provides free information on loans, tax deductions, and other financial matters. District offices offer special training programs in management, marketing, and accounting.

A wealth of business information is also available online at www.sba.gov and www.business.gov (the U.S. Business Advisor site). To learn whether there is an SBA office near you, look under "U. S. Government" in your telephone directory, or call the SBA's toll-free number.

Date Contacted:_____Information Received:_____

*Follow up:*_____

__SCORE (Service Corps of Retired Executives). (800) 634-0245. There are more than 12,400 SCORE members who volunteer their time and expertise to small business owners. Many craft businesses have received valuable in-depth counseling and training simply by calling the organization and asking how to connect with a SCORE volunteer in their area.

In addition, the organization offers e-mail counseling via the Internet at www.score.org. You simply enter the specific expertise required and retrieve a list of e-mail counselors who represent the best match by industry and topic. Questions can then be sent by e-mail to the counselor of your choice for response.

Date Contacted:_____Information Received:_____

*Follow up:*_____

Crafts and Home-Business Organizations

In addition to the regular benefits of membership in an organization related to your art or craft (fellowship, networking, educational conferences or workshops, marketing opportunities, etc.), membership may also bring special business services, such as insurance programs, merchant card services, and discounts on supplies and materials. Each of the following organizations will send you membership information on request.

__The American Association of Home-Based Businesses, P.O. Box 10023, Rockville, MD 20849. (800) 447-9710. Web site: www.aahbb.org. This organization has chapters throughout the country. Members have access to merchant card services, discounted business products and services, prepaid legal services, and more.

Date Contacted:_____Information Received:_____

*Follow up:*_____

__American Crafts Council, 72 Spring Street, New York, NY 10012. (800)-724-0859. Web site: www.craftcouncil.org. Membership in this organization will give you access to a property and casualty insurance policy that will cost between $250 and $500 a year, depending on your city, state, and the value of items being insured in your art or crafts studio. The policy includes insurance for a craftsperson's work in the studio, in transit or at a show; a million dollars' coverage for bodily injury and property damage in studio or away; and a million dollars' worth of product liability insurance. This policy is from American Phoenix Corporation; staff members will answer your specific questions when you call (800) 274-6364, ext. 337.

Date Contacted:_____Information Received:_____

*Follow up:*_____

__Arts & Crafts Business Solutions, 2804 Bishop Gate Drive, Raleigh, NC 27613. (800) 873-1192. This company, known in the industry as the Arts Group, offers a bankcard service specifically for and tailored to the needs of the arts and crafts marketplace. Several differently priced packages are available, and complete information is available on request.

Date Contacted:_____Information Received:_____

*Follow up:*_____

__Home Business Institute, Inc., P.O. Box 301, White Plains, NY 10605-0301. (888) DIAL-HBI; Fax: (914) 946-6694. Web site: www.hbiweb.com. Membership benefits include insurance programs (medical insurance and in-home business policy that includes some liability insurance); savings on telephone services, office supplies, and merchant account enrollment; and free advertising services.

Date Contacted:_____Information Received:_____

*Follow up:*_____

__National Craft Association (NCA), 1945 E. Ridge Road, Suite 5178, Rochester, NY 14622-2647. (800) 715-9594. Web site: www.craft assoc.com. Members of NCA have access to a comprehensive package of services, including merchant account services; discounts on business services and products; a prepaid legal program; a check-guarantee merchant program; checks by fax, phone, or e-mail; and insurance programs. Of special interest to this book's readers is the "Crafters Business Insurance" policy (through RLI Insurance Co.) that includes coverage for business property; art/craft merchandise or inventory at home, in transit or at a show; theft away from premises; up to a million dollars in both personal and product liability insurance; loss of business income, and more. Members have the option to select the exact benefits they need. Premiums range from $150 to $300, depending on location, value of average inventory, and the risks associated with one's art or craft.

Date Contacted:_____Information Received:_____

*Followup:*_____

Recommended Craft Business Periodicals

Membership in an organizations generally includes a subscription to a newsletter or magazine that will be helpful to your business. Here are additional craft periodicals you should sample or subscribe to:

__*The Crafts Report—The Business Journal for the Crafts Industry,* Box 1992, Wilmington, DE 19899. (800) 777-7098. On the Internet at www.craftsreport.com. A monthly magazine covering all areas of craft business management and marketing (includes Barbara Brabec's "BusinessWise" column).

__*Craft Supply Magazine—The Industry Journal for the Professional Crafter,* Krause Publications, Inc., 700 East State Street, Iowa, WI 54990-0001. (800) 258-0929. Web site: www.krause.com. A monthly magazine that includes crafts business and marketing articles and wholesale supply sources.

__*Home Business Report,* 2949 Ash Street, Abbotsford, B.C., V2S 4G5 Canada. (604) 857-1788; Fax: (604) 854-3087. Canada's premier home-business magazine, relative to both general and craft-related businesses.

__*SAC Newsmonthly,* 414 Avenue B, P.O. Box 159, Bogalusa, LA 70429-0159. (800) TAKE-SAC; Fax: (504) 732-3744. A monthly national show guide that also includes business articles for professional crafters.

__*Sunshine Artist Magazine,* 2600 Temple Drive, Winter Park, FL 32789. (800) 597-2573; Fax: (407) 539-1499. Web site: www.sun shineartist.com. America's premier show and festival guide.

Each monthly issue contains business and marketing articles of interest to both artists and craftspeople.

Other Services and Suppliers

Contact any of the following companies that offer information or services of interest to you.

__American Express. For merchant account information, call the Merchant Establishment Services Department at (800) 445-AMEX.

Date Contacted:_____Information Received:_____

*Follow up:*_____

__Dover Publications, 31 E. 2nd Sreet, Mineola, NY 11501. Your source for thousands of copyright-free designs and motifs you can use in your craftwork or needlecraft projects. Request a free catalog of books in the *Pictorial Archive* series.

Date Contacted:_____Information Received:_____

*Follow up:*_____

__Novus Services, Inc. For merchant account information, call (800) 347-6673.

Date Contacted:_____Information Received:_____

*Follow up:*_____

__Volunteer Lawyers for the Arts(VLA), 1 E. 53rd Street, New York, NY 10022. Legal hotline: (212) 319-2910. If you ever need an attorney, and cannot afford one, contact this nonprofit organization, which has chapters all over the country. In addition to providing legal aid for performing and visual artists and craftspeople (individually or in groups), the VLA also provides a range of educational services, including issuing publications concerning taxes, accounting, and insurance.

Date Contacted:_____Information Received:_____

*Follow up:*_____

__Widby Enterprises USA, 4321 Crestfield Road, Knoxville, TN 37921-3104. (888) 522-2458. Web site: www.widbylabel.com. Standard and custom-designed labels that meet federal labeling requirements.

Date Contacted:_____Information Received:_____

*Follow up:*_____

Recommended Business Books

When you have specific business questions not answered in this beginner's guide, check your library for the following books. Any not on library shelves can be obtained through the library's inter-library loan program.

__*Business and Legal Forms for Crafts* by Tad Crawford (Allworth Press)

__*Business Forms and Contracts (in Plain English) for Crafts People* by Leonard D. DuBoff (Interweave Press)

__*Crafting as a Business* by Wendy Rosen (Chilton)

__*The Crafts Business Answer Book & Resource Guide: Answers to Hundreds of Troublesome Questions about Starting, Marketing & Managing a Homebased Business Efficiently, Legally, & Profitably* by Barbara Brabec (M. Evans & Co.)

__*Creative Cash: How to Profit from Your Special Artistry, Creativity, Hand Skills, and Related Know-How* by Barbara Brabec (Prima Publishing)

__*422 Tax Deductions for Businesses & Self Employed Individuals* by Bernard Kamoroff (Bell Springs Publishing)

__*Homemade Money: How to Select, Start, Manage, Market and Multiply the Profits of a Business at Home* by Barbara Brabec (Betterway Books)

__*How to Register Your Own Trademark with Forms* by Mark Warda, 2nd ed. (Sourcebooks)

__*INC Yourself: How to Profit by Setting Up Your Own Corporation*, by Judith H. McQuown (HarperBusiness)

__*Patent, Copyright & Trademark: A Desk Reference to Intellectual Property Law* by Attorney Stephen Elias (Nolo Press)

__*The Perils of Partners* by Irwin Gray (Smith-Johnson Publisher)

__*Small Time Operator: How to Start Your Own Business, Keep Your Books, Pay Your Taxes & Stay Out of Trouble* by Bernard Kamoroff (Bell Springs Publishing)

__*Trademark: How to Name a Business & Product* by McGrath and Elias (Nolo Press)

Helpful Library Directories

__*Books in Print* and *Guide to Forthcoming Books* (how to find out which books are still in print, and which books will soon be published)

__*Encyclopedia of Associations* (useful in locating an organization dedicated to your art or craft)

__*National Trade and Professional Associations of the U.S.* (more than 7,000 associations listed alphabetically and geographically)

__*The Standard Periodical Directory* (annual guide to U.S. and Canadian periodicals)

__*Thomas Register of American Manufacturers* (helpful when you're looking for raw material suppliers or the owners of brand names and trademarks)

__*Trademark Register of the U.S.* (contains every trademark currently registered with the U.S. Patent & Trademark Office)

Resources

▼▼▼

This resource guide includes several sections that present many sources for general interest topics and product lines relative to the art of decorative painting. Whether you paint for fun, for profit, or for both, I hope you will explore thse information sources—and others you may find along the way.

Using the Resources

Every effort has been made to insure validity of the information contained in this Resource Guide; all content has been consistently researched for accuracy. Realize, however, that in our fast-moving world, contact information (street names, post office boxes, e-mail and Web site addresses, and phone numbers) can and often do change.

Section A — Recommended Technique and Business Books
Section B — Recommended Magazines and Periodicals
Section C — Web Sites of Interest to the Decorative Painter
Section D — Helpful Information, Organizations, and
                 Business Contacts
Section E — Product Suppliers
Section F — Arts and Crafts Conventions, Shows, and Malls
Section G — Glossary of Terms
Section H — Business Contributors

Section A
Recommended Technique and Business Books

Acrylic and Fabric Painter's Reference Book, Fourth Edition, by Susan Adams Bentley (Jackie Shaw Studio)

Acrylic Decorative Painting Techniques by Sybil Edwards (North Light Books)

Anyone Can Paint — Book 1 by Pat Olsen (Grace Publications)

Anyone Can Paint — Book 2 by Pat Olsen (Grace Publications)

Art Marketing 101: A Handbook for the Fine Artist by Constance Smith (ArtNetwork)

Beginning Painter's Color Mixing Guide by John Gutcher (Plaid Enterprises)

Beginning Tole Painting — Level One by Linda Wright (LJW Publications)

The Book of Decorative Lettering by Jackie O'Keefe (Grace Publications)

Brush Strokes Made Easy (Plaid Enterprises)

Business and Legal Forms for Crafts (Allworth Press)

The Copyright Handbook: How to Protect and Use Written Works by Stephen Fishman (Nolo Press)

The Crafter's Guide to Pricing Your Work by Dan Ramsey (Betterway Books)

Crafting As a Business by Wendy Rosen (Chilton)

Crafting for Dollars: How to Establish and Profit from a Career in Crafts by Sylvia Landman (Prima)

The Crafts Business Answer Book and Resource Guide by Barbara Brabec (M. Evans)

The Crafts Business Encyclopedia by Michael Scott, as revised by L. D. DuBoff (Harcourt Brace Jovanovich)

The Crafts Supply Source Book by Margaret Boyd (Betterway Books)

Crafts Market Place: Where and How to Sell Your Crafts, edited by Angie Manolis

Creative Cash: How to Profit from Your Special Artistry, Creativity, Hand Skills and Related Know-How by Barbara Brabec, 6th Edition (Prima)

Decorative Painting Sourcebook (North Light Books)

Donna Dewberry's Complete Book of One-Stroke Painting by Donna Dewberry (Plaid Enterprises)

Floating Basics by Priscilla Hauser (Plaid Enterprises)

Glazing and Layer-Blending by Louise Jackson (Plaid Enterprises)

Handmade for Profit—Hundreds of Secrets to Success in Selling Arts and Crafts by Barbara Brabec (M. Evans)

Homemade Money—How to Select, Start, Manage, Market and Multiply the Profits of a Business at Home, 5th Edition, revised by Barbara Brabec (Betterway Books)

How to Show and Sell Your Crafts by Kathryn Caputo (Betterway Books)

How to Start Making Money with Your Crafts by Kathryn Caputo (Betterway Books)

How to Start Making Money with Your Decorative Painting by Dorothy Egan (North Light Books)

How to Survive & Prosper As an Artist, 4th Edition by Caroll Michaels (Owl Books/H. Holt)

Illustrated Guide to Fabric Painting, by Assorted Artists (Plaid Enterprises)

Living Your Life Out Loud: How to Unlock Your Creativity and Unleash Your Joy by Sallie Raspberry and Padi Selwyn (Pocket Books)

Marketing Online by Marcia Yudkin (Plume)

Marketing Your Arts and Crafts by Janice West

The Official Guide to Pricing Your Crafts by Sylvia Landman (Prima)

Paint the Basics by Priscilla Hauser (Plaid Enterprises)

Simply Paint It by Delta Design Staff (Krause Publications)

Small-Time Operator: How to Start Your Own Business, Keep Your Books, Pay Your Taxes, and Stay Out of Trouble by Bernard Kamoroff (Bell Springs Publishing)

Techniques for Beginning Painters (Plaid Enterprises)

Section B
Recommended Magazines and Periodicals

Following is a selected list of decorative painting–oriented magazines and periodicals. Not all of these publications have been listed in the text, but each is beneficial to both the hobbyist and professional painter. For other publications, check your local major booksellers or newsstands and your local library's magazine section.

The Artist's Journal, P.O. Box 9080, Eureka, CA 95501

The Decorative Artist's Workbook, P.O. Box 3285, Harlan, IA 51593-2465, 800-888-6880

The Decorative Painter (available only with membership in the Society of Decorative Painters), 393 McLean Blvd., Wichita, KS 67203, 316-269-9300

Decorative Woodcrafts, P.O. Box 54696, Boulder, CO 80326-4696

Let's Paint, P.O. Box 360, Stanford, KY 40484, 606-365-3193

Paint Works, 243 Newton-Sparta Road, Newton, NJ 07860, 800-877-5527

Painting, 2400 Devon, Ste. 375, Des Plaines, IL 60018, 847-635-5800

Quick & Easy Painting, 243 Newton-Sparta Road, Newton, NJ 07860, 800-877-5527

Tole World, 1041 Shary Circle, Concord, CA 94518-2407, 800-676-5002

In addition to periodicals dedicated to decorative painting, more and more magazines previously focusing mainly on crafting are including decorative painting projects. Several craft-oriented publications regularly include feature columns dedicated to decorative painting techniques, projects, and artists' products.

Aleene's Creative Living, 85 Industrial Way, Buellton, CA 93427, 800-825-3363

Arts & Crafts, 700 East State Street, Iola, WI 54900-0001, 715-445-2214, Fax 715-445-4087

Crafting Traditions, P.O. Box 5286, Harlan, IA 51593, 800-344-6913

Crafts Magazine, P.O. Box 56015, Boulder, CO 80322, 800-727-2387

Crafts N Things, 2400 Devon, Ste. 375, Des Plaines, IL 60018, 847-635-5800

Craftworks, 243 Newton Sparta Road, Newton, NJ 07860, 800-877-5527

Handcraft Illustrated, P.O. Box 7450, Red Oak, IA 51591-0450, 617-232-1000

Inspirational Crafts, 243 Newton-Sparta Road, Newton, NJ 07860, 800-877-5527

Wood Strokes/Weekend Woodcrafts,
1041 Shary Circle, Concord, CA 94518-2407,
800-676-5002

The following magazines and periodicals
provide information or listings for regional
and national shows, or offer a market to
advertise and sell your work through a
showcase publication. Some include inspirational and practical articles dealing with
hitting the show and fair circuits, promoting your business, and how to sell to a
variety of markets. Not all of these publications are mentioned in the text, but each
offers excellent information on show listings and product information.

ABC Art & Craft Event Directory,
P.O. Box 5388, Marysville, TN 37802-5388,
800-678-3566, Fax 423-681-4733. Features
detailed listings of approximately 3,500
events with detail on number of exhibitors,
expected attendance, and entry fees.

Arts & Crafts Show Business,
P.O. Box 26624, Jacksonville, FL 32226-
0624, 904-757-3913. A monthly publication
that includes festivals, fairs, and trade
shows covering several southeastern states
(Florida, the Carolinas, and Georgia).

*Better Homes and Gardens Crafts Show-
case,* P.O. Box 37228, Boone, IA 50010,
800-688-6611, www.bhglive.com/crafts.
An advertising and showcase publication.

Choices for Craftsmen and Artists,
P.O. Box 484, Rhinebeck, NY 12572,
914-876-2772. A quarterly publication
focusing on shows in the northeast region
(New York, New Jersey, Vermont, Pennsylvania, Massachusetts, and Connecticut).

*Country Business Newsletter, Sampler
Publications,* 707 Kautz Road, St. Charles,
IL 60174, 630-377-8000, www.sampler.com.

Country Sampler, P.O. Box 228, St.
Charles, IL 61074, 708-377-8399.
A showcase magazine.

Craft Marketing News, published by Front
Room Publishers. P.O. Box 1541, Clifton,
NJ 07015. Lists craft malls and shops seek-
ing artisans and craftspeople.

Craftmaster News, P.O. Box 39429,
Downey, CA 90239-0429. Show listing
focusing on West Coast events.

The Crafts Fair Guide, P.O. Box 688,
Corte Madera, CA 94976, 800-871-2341.
A periodical aimed at West Coast artisans.
Includes reviews of shows by participating
exhibiting artists.

The Crafts Report, P.O. Box 1992,
Wilmington, DE 19899, 800-777-7098,
www.craftsreport.com. Published
monthly. Features the more contemporary and trendy art styles plus articles on
business savvy and industry news. Also
includes show listings, announcements
of gallery openings, and calls for exhibit
entries.

*Directory of Craft Malls and Rent-a-
Space Shops,* Front Room Publishers,
P.O. Box 1541, Clifton, NJ 07015-1541,
973-773-42155, www.intac.com/~rjp.

Directory of Craft Shops and Galleries,
Front Room Publishers, P.O. Box 1541,

Clifton, NJ 07015-1541, 973-773-4215, www.intac.com/ ~ rjp.

Directory of Seasonal Holiday Boutiques, Front Room Publishers, P.O. Box 1541, Clifton, NJ 07015-1541, 973-773-4215, www.intac.com/ ~ rjp.

Directory of Wholesale Reps for Craft Professionals, Front Room Publishers, P.O. Box 1541, Clifton, NJ 07015-1541, 973-773-4215, www.intac.com/ ~ rjp.

Folk Art Treasures Country Marketplace, P.O. Box 1823, Sioux City, IA 51102, 800-398-5025. An advertising and show-case publication.

Hands On Guide, 1835 South Centre City Pkwy., #A434, Escondido, CA 92025-6544, 760-338-0025. A show listing publication focusing on better art and craft events over approximately 12 western states.

The Ronay Guides, 2090 Shadowlake Dr., Buckhead, GA 30625-2700, 800-337-8329, Offers listings of 1,500 shows, festivals, and fairs in several southeastern states (Georgia, Virginia, and the Carolinas); also has an Internet site (www.events2000.com) that provides information about exhibits held nationwide.

SAC Newsmonthly, P.O. Box 159, Bogalusa, LA 70429. A monthly newsletter featuring art and craft show opportunities.

Sunshine Artist, 2600 Temple Drive, Winter Park, FL 32789, 800-597-2573, www.sunshineartist.com. A monthly magazine that provides descriptions of approximately 2,000 events and includes articles and commentary on shows from participating artisans.

Section C
Web sites of Interest to the Decorative Painter

You can search for company names or products by using a search engine, such as www
.excite.com or www.altavista.com—or by looking for specific links within a Web site such
as www.tolenet.com/links/. The following Web sites may be of particular interest.

www.aleenes.com

www.tolenet.com/bb_brushes

www.loew-cornell.com

www.painting-books.com

www.paintingmag.com

www.pebeo.com

www.ebookcafe.com

www.justpaintit.com

www.ccsw.com

www.vikingwoodcrafts.com

www.plaidonline.com

www.daler-rowney.com

www.decorativeartist.com

www.chroma-inc.com

www.decoart.com

www.deltacrafts.com

www.painting.miningco.com

www.bhglive.com/crafts

www.onestroke.com

www.country.com

www.hgtv.com

www.icraft.com

Section D
Helpful Information, Organizations, and Business Contacts

Only a few of these organizations and business contacts have been mentioned in the text. Information sources for artists can be found at all levels from local communities to national and even international. Professional artisans appreciate the benefits of association memberships and the credentials afforded, which foster recognition for the serious artist and businessperson. The following listings represent a large cross section of organizations and business groups that may provide helpful information and source materials, including newsletters and optional professional benefits packages.

Amazon.com, 206-694-2952, www.amazon.com. Catalog and book resource hotline.

The American Association of Home Based Businesses, P.O. Box 10023, Rockville, MD 20849, 800-447-9710, www.aahbb.org. A large national organization. Membership provides access to discounts on products and services, tip sheets, and a newsletter.

American Craft Council (ACC), 72 Spring Street, New York, NY 10012, 800-724-0859 for membership, or 800-836-3470 for trade show information. An organization that provides members a bimonthly newsletter, group rates on credit card, and other programs.

American Professional Crafters Guild, 707 Kautz Road, St. Charles, IL 60174, 630-377-8000. An organization that offers such benefits as wholesale buying programs, credit-card processing, and dis-

counts on books and magazines. Members also receive a bimonthly publication. The group is sponsored by Sampler Publications, which publishes a magazine titled *Country Business.* Though aimed at the professional crafter in general, the business principles addressed in many of the articles apply also to the decorative painter.

The Craft & Art Show Calendar, P.O. Box 424, Devault, PA 19432, 610-640-2787. Information on top-ranked shows covering several eastern and northeastern states.

Decorative Artists Book Club, 1507 Dana Ave., Cincinnati, OH 45207, 513-531-8250. A specialty book club dedicated to the interests of the decorative painter.

eCraftsmall, 925-671-9852, Fax 925-671-0692, www.ecraftsmall.com. Web site for locating craft supplies; information for setting up your shop is also available within this cybermall.

International Faux Finishers Association (IFFA), P.O. Box 837, DeBary, FL 32713-0837, 407-668-9121, Fax 407-668-9121. An organization that focuses on preserving and promoting old and new processes of faux finishing techniques. The group holds an annual convention, which includes educational and business agendas.

International Guild of Glass Artists, 54 Cherry Street, P.O. Box 1809, North Adams, MA 01247, 413-663-5512, Fax 413-663-7167, www.igga.org. An organization for the glass artisan, including the decorative painter. Members receive the newsletter and are offered discounts from suppliers. Call or write for information.

Montclair Craft Guild, P.O. Box 538, Glen Ridge, NJ 07028. A regional organization focusing on artisans in the northeastern section of the United States. A newsletter, *Showcase,* is provided to members.

National Craft Association (NCA), 1945 E. Ridge Road, Ste. 5178, Rochester, NY 14622-2647, 800-715-9594, Fax 800-318-9410, www.craftassoc.com. Provides resources, contacts, and information for the small business. Free newsletter.

National Mail Order Association, 2807 Polk Street NE, Minneapolis, MN 55418-2954, 612-788-1673, www.nmoa.org. An organization offering information on how to start a mail-order business and utilize effective marketing techniques. Members receive the *Mail Order Digest* newsletter.

Society of Craft Designers, P.O. Box 3388, Zanesville, OH 43702-3388, 740-452-4541. An organization for the professional decorative painter, designer, author, craft teacher, and craftsman as well as others involved in the many facets of the industry. Affiliation includes an excellent bimonthly newsletter, a comprehensive listing of membership, and myriad opportunities to attend seminars and to network with manufacturers and promoters.

Society of Decorative Painters, 393 North McLean Blvd., Wichita, KS 67203-5968, 316-269-9300, www.decorativepainters.com. An organization dedicated to the decorative painter, whether hobbyist or professional. Membership includes a subscription to the society's high-quality full-color magazine, information about the annual convention, and opportunities to display designs at special events, which have included painting ornaments for the White House Christmas tree.

Stencil Artisans League, 386 East H Street, Ste. 209-188, Chula Vista, CA 91910, 619-477-3559, Fax 619-477-3559. An organization that, as the name implies, focuses the business applications of stenciling and related decorative painting. Membership benefits include a quarterly magazine, and the organization encourages education concerning product awareness and how to achieve certification. The annual convention features exhibitors and classes that publicize and teach new stenciling and decorative painting techniques.

Tolemarketplace, 10934 Eagle Lake Drive, Escondido, CA 92029, 760-746-0289, Fax 760-747-2167, www.tolemarketplace.com. Features Web site development and hosting to launch your decorative painting business on the Internet.

World Organization of China Painters, 2641 NW 10th, Oklahoma City, OK 73107-5400, e-mail: wocporg@theshop.net, 405-521-1234, Fax 405-521-1265. An organization for porcelain painters with established regional chapters. Recognized internationally, dedicated to preserving the art form and encouraging teacher certification.

Section E
Product Suppliers

Support your local craft and painting supply outlets whenever possible. If you don't see a product you like or want to try, ask the store whether they can order it from their wholesaler or supplier. The following list of suppliers and manufacturers represents a broad cross section of products from acrylic paints to portable exhibit booths to unpainted furniture. Note that some suppliers may require a minimum purchase or proof of a tax resale permit or vendor license before selling to an individual or home-based business. Several sell in small quantities upon request and some sell wholesale only. The majority of suppliers will advise you of their order requirements and will be helpful to ensure you are able to obtain their product lines, whether by direct shipment or by guiding you to your closest retailer.

Action Bag Company, 800-926-6100. Offers zip bags, corrugated boxes, and bubble wraps. Call for catalog.

A-1 Bags, 800-228-1922, 402-597-1922. "Call the bag lady" for information on zip bags and a variety of sizes of retail bags, printed and non-printed in a variety of colors.

A. Steele, W 12351 Long Lane, Stockholm, WI 54769, 800-693-3353, offers quick-in-place overhead canopies and battery-operated cash registers. Call or write for information.

Advanced Cleaning Technologies Inc., 2411 Lanside Drive, Wilmington, DE 19810, 800-323-9825. Offers non-chemical, untreated dust cloths for dusting decorative paintings and other art.

Allens Wood Crafts, 3020 Dogwood Lane, Rt. 3, Sapulpa, OK 74066, 918-224-8796. Paintable wood surfaces for home decorating and kitchen accessory pieces.

American Traditional Stencils, 442 First New Hampshire Turnpike, Northwood, NH 03261, 800-448-6656, www.amtrad-stencil.com. Source for wide variety of stencils.

Armstrong Products Inc., P.O. Box 979, Guthrie, OK 73044, 800-278-4279, 405-282-7584, Fax 405-282-1130. Suppliers of carpeted display panels for your exhibit booth. Call or write for a free catalog.

Art Craft Wood, 415 East 7th Street, Joplin, MO 64801, 800-537-2738, www.artcraftetc.com. Quality paintable wood products, including trunks, trays, lap desks, and furniture.

The Artists' Club, P.O. Box 8390, Vancouver, WA 98668-8930, 800-257-1077, www.ArtistsClub.com. "Shopping Made Easy for the Busy Painter" is the apt subtitle gracing their catalogs, which offer everything from new pattern books to exclusively designed music boxes.

Artograph, Inc., 2838 Vicksburg Lane North, Plymouth MN 55447, 612-553-1112. Manufacturers of the Lightracer light box and supplier of replacement lamps.

Back Street, 3905 Steve Reynolds Blvd., Norcross, GA 30093, 770-381-7373, Fax 770-381-6424. Manufacturers of Anita's acrylic paint, decoupage, and other products.

Bagsplus, 2907 Regner Road, Ste. 223, McHenry, IL 60050, 815-344-6700, Fax 815-344-6702, www.bagsplus.com. Offers variety of sizes and styles of zip bags, cloth drawstring, and retail bags. Call or write for free catalog.

BagWorks, Inc., 3301-C South Cravens Road, Fort Worth, TX 76119, www.bagworks.com. Online catalog or catalog by mail available for $2 (refundable) features paintable canvas bags, totes, aprons, and home decor.

Bayer Wood Products, 5439 Dorr St., Toledo, OH 43615, 800-323-0817, 419-536-1020, Fax 419-535-7117. Wood cutouts, turnings, paints, and craft supplies. Call for catalog.

Bear With Us, Inc., 3007 So. Kendall Ave., Independence, MO 64055, 816-373-3231, Fax 816-373-0705. Wood cutouts, including custom designs at the best competitive prices. Catalog available upon request.

Bentwood, Inc., P.O. Box 1676, Thomasville, GA 31792, 912-226-1223. Paintable specialty wood shapes, including piggins, scoops, canisters, wastebaskets, and keepsake bridal boxes.

Binney & Smith, 1100 Church Lane, Easton, PA 18042. Manufacturer of Liquitex paint lines and other products.

Brightman Design, 800-995-1723, www.displaybright.com. Providers of showcase lighting, pedestal and spot lights.

Catalina Cottage, 125 N. Aspan #5, Azusa, CA 91702, 626-969-4001, Fax 626-969-4451. Paints, brushes, artists' accessories, and paintable surfaces. Catalog available for $5; $50 minimum order.

Charm Woven Labels, 2400 W. Magnolia, Blvd., Burbank, CA 91506, 800-843-1111. Fabric labels for the decorative painter specializing in custom apparel or home decorating soft goods.

Color Fantasy, 215 Slater Avenue, Providence, RI 02906, 401-421-1116, Fax 401-421-0777. Offers blanks for posters, t-shirts, and puzzle kits, many with nature and environmental themes.

Colorful Images, 2910 Colorful Avenue, Longmont, CO 80504-6214, 800-458-7999, Fax 303-682-7148. Offers a variety of business cards, memo pads, and stationery items.

Country Wood Crafts, Ruth Wiest and Debbie Ricker, 132 Manor Road, Staten Island, NY 10310, 718-447-0163, e-mail: ruth718@earthlink.net. Specializing in 1/8-inch thick wood cutouts for the decorative painter, artisan, and crafter. Will custom cut from your patterns. Catalog available.

Craft Catalog, P.O. Box 1069, Reynoldsburg, OH 43068, 800-777-1442. Quality craft supplies at prices you'll love is their manifesto. Annual catalogs contain at least 200 pages, with pictures and prices of a full line of paints, brushes, painting surfaces including wood, tin, and papier-mâché, and a full line of worktable accessories, including drying boards, brush basins, and palettes.

Crafter's Choice Magnets, 11248 Playa Court, Culver City, CA 90200, 800-421-6692, Fax 310-390-4357. Provider of magnetic applications for painted ornaments and accessories. Available at major craft stores or call for retailer in your area.

Crafters Port-a-Palette, P.O. Box 161, Clarksboro, NJ 08020. Manufacturers of dual purpose paint and brush holder, which converts from a carrier to a worktable stand.

Crafts Galore, 1724 South Gold Street, Centralia, WA 98531 www.craftsgalore.com. General craft supplies available on the Internet.

Craftwood, 4611 W. Woolworth Avenue, Milwaukee, WI 53218. Wood products including split egg shapes, turnings, and more.

Creative Beginnings, 475 Morro Bay Blvd., Morro Bay, CA 93442, 800-367-1739, Fax 800-224-2767, www.creative-beginnings.com. Brass charms for embellishing wood ornaments and painted fabric creations. Available in most retail craft outlets, departments, and catalogs.

Creative Energies, 1607 N. Magnolia Ave., Ocala, FL 34475, 800-351-8889. Offers portable canopies for outdoor exhibits. Call or write for information.

Cridge, Inc., P.O. Box 210, Morrisville, PA 19067, 888-801-4438, Fax 215-295-6854. Supplier of glazed and bisque porcelain surfaces for the decorative painter.

The C-Thru Ruler Company, 6 Britton Drive, Bloomfield, CT 06002, 800-243-8419. Templates, straightedges, and designer letters for the decorative painter and crafter.

Cupboard Distributing, 119 Miami St., Rt. 36, Urbana, OH 43078-0148, 800-338-6388, www.cdwood.com. Wood cutouts, parts, and craft supplies. Call or write for a catalog.

Dalee Book Company, 129 Clinton Place, Yonkers, NY 10701, 914-965-1660. Paintable canvas surfaces for home and personal use.

Daler-Rowney/Robert Simmons, 2 Corporate Drive, Cranbury, NJ 08512-9584, www.daler-rowney.com. Manufacturer of fine decorative painting brushes, including Robert Simmons Folk Art and Expressions, and high-quality System 3 acrylic paints and compatible mediums.

Datile Crafts, 7834 C F Hawn, Dallas, TX 75217. Source for ceramic tiles.

Dealers Supply Inc., P.O. Box 717, Matawan, NJ 07747, 800-524-0576, Fax 732-591-8571, www.dirsupply.com. Featuring display supplies, showcases, lighting, folding tables, canopies, tote bags, and signs, as well as security supplies such as fire-retardant spray and

(MARK)
DESIGN WORKS
(800) 468-5487

counterfeit detectors. Call or write for a free catalog.

DecoArt Paints, P.O. Box 386, Stanford, KY 40484, www.decoart.com. Manufacturer of DecoMagic brush cleaner and a full line of high-quality acrylic paints, including Americana, Gel Stains, Heavenly Hues, Patio, No Prep Metal, Ultra Gloss Enamels, and control mediums including one specifically formulated for candles.

Decorator & Craft Corporation, *ID #* *TRISH* 728 S. Zelta, Wichita, KS 67207, 800-835-3013. Supplier of wide variety of papier-mâché surfaces, including boxes and seasonal shapes; rusty tin and other paintable surfaces. *REC'D*

Delta Technical Coatings, Inc. 2550 Pellissier Place, Whittier, CA 90601, 800-423-4135, www. deltacrafts.com. Manufacturers of Ceramcoat acrylics paints and paint supplies. *(800)*

Design Works, Inc., 170 Wilbur Place, Bohemia, NY 11716, 516-244-5749. Pre-glazed ceramic whiteware for decorative painting or use with marking pens or brush markers. Many home decor and cute paintables for bazaars. *REC'D* *631 (AREA CODE)*

Duncan Enterprises, 5673 E. Shields Ave., Fresno, CA 93727, 209-291-4444. Manufacturers of Aleene's products, including acrylic paints and other product lines such as Scribbles dimensional paints.

E & S Creations, P.O. Box 68, Rexburg, ID 83440, 208-356-6812. Offers originally designed craft hangtags. Write for catalog information.

Eagle Brush, Inc., 431 Commerce Park Drive SE, Marietta, GA 30060, 800-832-4532, 770-419-4855, Fax 770-419-1474.

Eclectic Products, 995 South A Street, Springfield, OR 97477, 800-693-4667. Manufacturer of E-6000 glue, which is excellent for attaching jewelry fittings and charms to painted wood.

Elaine Martin Company, 25685 Hillview Court, Ste. E, Mundelein, IL 60060, 800-642-1043, www.emartin.com. Offers a line of indoor booth and display systems, tables, and directors chairs. Call or write for free catalog.

Elegance in Easels, 800-325-8286, *REC'D* www.easels.com. Markets a variety of sizes and shapes of easels and stands for displaying painted planters, tiles, frames, and plaques. Call for wholesale catalog.

EverGreen Bag Company, 22 Ash Street, East Hartford, CT 06108, 800-775-3595, www.alcasoft.com/everbag. Offers retail packaging, poly bags, and shipping supplies, including bubble bags. Call for a free catalog.

EZ Dotz/Touch of Crafts, P.O. Box 849, Rancho Cucamonga, CA 91730, 909-944-8613, www.ezdotz.com. Simple-to-use dotting tool for accenting lettering and painted design work.

Factory Direct Craft Supply, 315 Conover Drive, Franklin, OH 45005, 800-252-5223, Fax 269-8741. Offers full line of painting and crafting supplies and accessories. Call or write for large $5 catalog.

Forster, Inc., P.O. Box 657, Wilton, ME 04294. Provider of wide variety of wood shapes for small pins, 3-D applications, children's painting craft projects, and imaginative embellishments.

General Pencil Company, P.O. Box 5311, Redwood City, CA 94063, 650-369-7169, Fax 650-369-7169, www.generalpencil.com. Manufacturers of The Masters TM brush cleaner and hand soaps. Removes paint, cleans and conditions your brushes—and your hands.

George's Woodcutting, 301 S.E. Bordner Dr., Lee's Summit, MO 64063, 816-525-2833, Fax 816-347-0028. Will cut from your own pattern, individual and wholesale. Write for information.

Grace Publications, 3819 N. Vermillion, Danville, IL 61832, 217-446-0224, Fax 217-446-0225. Offers how-to-paint books and more. Send a LSASE for free catalog.

Grumbacher, 100 North Street, Bloomsbury, NJ 08804, 800-346-3278, Fax 908-479-6762, www.grumbacher.com. Manufacturers of fine brushes and art materials.

Hang Up Bags from Monaco, P.O. Box 40, Bethel, CT 06801, 203-744-3398, Fax 203-744-3228. Suppliers of see-through hangup bags and racks for storing materials.

Heartland Industries, Fifty Visco Court, Nashville, TN 37210. Manufacturer of pre-assembled and installed non-permanent outbuildings suitable for conversion to studio and materials storage applications. Write for information.

Heartwood Creations, 6515 Hastings Drive, Colorado Springs, CO 80919, 719-531-9743. Offers "the Ultimate Painting Partner," a portable roll-up system that holds up to 100 paint brushes, water container, and paper towels.

Heritage Saw Company, 11225 6th St. E., Treasure Island, FL 33706, 813-367-7557. Offers steel saw blades with wood or plastic handles and circular saw blades for painting. Catalog available for $2.

HK Holbein, Inc., Box 555, Williston, VT 05495, 800-682-6686. Manufacturers of Holbein Duo Aqua Oil Color, an artist quality pigment in water-soluble linseed oil.

Hollywood Chairs, 5337 N. Cahuenga Blvd., #AB, North Hollywood, CA 91601, 818-505-0159. Suppliers of variety of directors chairs, custom logos, and other options.

Homespun Touch, 231 N. 7th Avenue, Sturgeon Bay, WI 54235, 920-743-8519, Fax 920-743-5345. Offers over 1,000 books on decorative painting, pre-cut wood and papier-mâché. Send $3 for large catalog.

Impact Images, 800-233-2630. Supplier of crystal-clear plastic bags for enclosing photos and small pieces of art. Call for a free sample and price list.

Innovative Solutions, 2220 Eastman Ave., #105, Ventura, CA 93003, 800-607-2462. Manufacturer of easy-to-use color wheel for value matching and accent color combinations.

JB Wood Products, 1285 County Street, Attleboro, MA 02703, 508-226-3217, Fax 508-222-9399. Unfinished wood for home decor, shelves, boxes, plaques, and seasonal items. Color catalog available.

Jackie Shaw Studio, 733 Peaks Street, Bedford, VA 24523, Fax 540-586-5732. Offers over 100 books and videos for self-teaching or classroom use.

Jerry Haines Sales Company, 1337 Donna Beth Avenue, West Covina, CA 91791. Source or information on the compressed Miracle Sponge TM.

John Mee Canopies, P.O. Box 11220, Birmingham, AL 35202, 800-987-3663, 205-967-1885. Offers canopies, directors chairs, and artists' print racks.

J.W. Etc., 2205 First Street, Ste. 103, Simi Valley, CA 93065, 805-526-5066, Fax 805-526-1297. Nontoxic wood sealers, stains, varnishes, brush cleaner, and wood filler.

Kemper Tools, 13595 12th Street, Chino, CA 91710, 909-627-6191, Fax 909-627-4008. Designer and manufacturer of art tools, in particular the "Spatter Brush" mentioned in the text. Many craft catalogs carry the spatter brush; or contact the manufacturer for sources.

Kimmeric Studio, P.O. Box 10749, South Lake Tahoe, CA 96158, 530-573-1616. Offering originally designed hangtags in a variety of themes, including seasonal.

Kirchen Brothers Crafts, P.O. Box 1016, Skokie, IL 60076. Offers general craft supplies. Send $1 for catalog.

Krafter's Kaddie, P.O. Box 43, Bridgeport, CA 93517, 888-552-3343. Paintable wooden binder covers and other surfaces.

Kreative Kanvas/Kunin Felt, 380 Lafayette Road, Hampton, NH 03842, 800-292-7900, Fax 603-929-6180, www.kuninfelt.com. Manufacturers of paintable non-fray surface for all decorative painting media. Call for local distributor or retailer.

Krylon, 31500 Solon Road, Solon, OH 44139. Manufacturer of spray sealers, varnishes, and paints. Available in most craft stores and home improvement centers.

Lamp Specialties, P.O. Box 240, Westville, NJ 08093-0240, 888-225-5526, Fax 800-722-7061. Paintable beveled glass ornaments, square glass tiles, and display easels. Free catalog available.

Lara's Crafts, 590 N. Beach Street, Fort Worth, TX 76111, 800-232-5272, www.larascrafts.com. Manufacturer of assorted wood pieces, including angels, cats, and Santa cutouts for ornaments and 3-D layering.

Loew-Cornell, 563 Chestnut Ave., Teaneck, NJ 07666-2490, www.loew-cornell.com. Manufacturers of quality artists' brushes and brush basins, including Brush Tub II.

Masterson Art Products, Inc., P.O. Box 10775, Glendale, AZ 85318-0775, 800-965-2675, www.masterson.com. Manufacturers of the Sta-Wet palette and the Rinse Well brush cleaning system.

Modern Postcard, 800-959-83665, www.modernpostcard.com. Offers reasonable postcard promotionals for marketing and advertising. Call for information and a sample kit.

Ott-Lite Technology, 1214 West Cass Street, Tampa, FL 33606, 800-842-8848. Manufacturer of true-color high-definition work lamps in desk, clamp-on, and floor models.

Pacific Chair Design, 730 Napa Avenue, Morro Bay, CA 93442, 805-772-7575. Manufacturer of exceptional quality flat-folding show chairs. Call or write for a free brochure.

Painting Goose Rackworks, 800-449-5473, Fax 909-693-2855. Vertical and rotating wire storage rack systems for acrylic paint bottles. Call for a brochure.

Paper Direct, P.O. Box 2970, Colorado Springs, CO 80901-2970, 800-272-7377, Fax: 800-443-2973, www.paperdirect.com. Offers preprinted designer papers for brochures, business cards, and flyers. Catalog available.

Paper Reflections, DMD Industries, Springdale, AR 72764, 800-805-9890, 501-750-8929, Fax 501-750-8937. www.dmdind.com. Paintable blank cards, book markers, and other paper products for the painter and crafter.

Pebeo of America, P.O. Box 717, Swanton, VT 05488, www.pebeo.com. Manufacturers of water-based paints especially formulated for glass, china, ceramic, and metal.

Plaid Enterprises, 1649 International Court, Norcross, GA 30091. 800-842-4197, Fax 770-381-3404. Manufacturers of acrylic paint products and publishers of how-to books.

Premiere Abrasives Company, 1626 Walker Road, Scott, LA 70583, 800-246-6460, Fax 714-529-5483, www.premiereabrasive.com. Offers sandpapers, sanding discs, and other products.

Promotion Factory, 815 Seymour Street, Monroe, NC 28110, 800-277-0031, Fax 800-309-4778. Manufacturer of novelty and baseball caps, aprons, tote bags, and other blank apparel and home decor items for the decorative fabric painter. Call for free catalog.

Provo Crafts, 285 E. 900 S, Provo, UT 84606, 801-377-4311. Assorted paintable wood surfaces and other products for the decorative painter, scrapbooker, and crafter.

Quick Grab, P.O. Box 15040, Scottsdale, AZ 85267-5040, 602-905-1446, Fax 602-905-0422. All-purpose excellent adhesive product for adhering jewelry fittings to painted wood and 3-D applications. Available in craft retail stores or call for nearest distributor.

Rings and Things, P.O. Box 450, Spokane, WA 99210, 800-366-2156, Fax 509-838-2606, www.rings-things.com. Brass charm assortments and jewelry fittings. Wholesale catalog available.

Royal & Langnickel Brush, 6707 Broadway, Merrillville, IN 46410, 800-247-2211, 219-660-4170, Fax 219-660-4181. Manufacturers of several lines of quality artists' brushes, including the AQUALON line mentioned in the text.

S&G Inc., P.O. Box 805, Howell, MI 48844, 517-546-9240. Paintable metal wind chimes.

Safe World International Inc., P.O. Box 1030, Ashland, OR 97520, 800-743-0115, Fax 888-482-6100. Offers a trigger handle that transforms spray cans into easy to use spray gun.

Sailor Corporation of America, Fayetteville, GA 30214, 800-248-4583, Fax 770-461-8452. Manufacturers of rolling ball pens in gold and silver for most surface applications.

Sakura of America, 30780 San Clemente Street, Hayward, CA 94544-7131. Permanent markers and paint pens in a variety of colors, points, and applications.

Schacht Lighting, 8407 Lot P. Coulver Road, Austin, TX 78747, 512-243-3444, Fax 512-243-3445. Supplier of show booth lighting, showcase lighting, and portable battery systems. Call for free brochure.

Silver Brush Limited, P.O. Box 414, Windsor, NJ 08561, 609-443-4900, Fax 609-443-4888. Offers fine quality artists brushes. Available through catalogs and better craft retail outlets.

Stan Brown's Arts and Crafts, 13435 SE Whitaker Way, Portland, OR 97230, 503-257-0559, Fax 503-252-9508. Painting books, art supplies, paints, and wood pieces. Catalog of 345 pages is available for $5.

Strathmore Paper, 39 South Broad Street, Westfield, MA 01085. Paper supplies including blank stock greeting cards for watercolor and acrylic wash applications.

Supply Source, P.O. Box 522, Forest Park, Dayton, OH 45405, 937-274-4650, 937-274-4668, Fax 937-274-8143. Offers single-framed overhead show canopies in a variety of styles.

Teaberry Farm, 7415 W. Ridgecrest Ave., Nine Mile Falls, WA 99026, 509-468-5985, Fax 509-468-7096, www.tea berryfarms.com. Wood kits and decorative woodcraft patterns; welcome signs, angels, ornaments. Online catalog or send $2 for color catalog.

Timber & Tole Canvas Collectibles, 9931 W. Skycliffe Avenue, Boise, ID 83704, 208-378-0569. Manufactures canvas painters' totes and over-the-door paint bottle holders.

Tombow, 2000 Newpoint Place Parkway, Ste. 500, Lawrenceville, GA 30043, 800-835-3232, www.tombowusa.com. Manufacturer of brush markers.

Trimline Canopy, 800-296-0049, www.flourish.com. Suppliers of exhibit canopies, backdrop curtains and frames, table covers, and display panel covers.

Tru-Color Systems, developer of the Color Match Sourcebook for color matching processes. Available in book form or computer software application.

Uchida of America Corporation, 3535 Del Amo Blvd., Torrance, CA 90503, 800-541-5877, www.uchida.com. Supplier of Marvy markers.

Unfinished Furniture Mart, 1820 Pacific Coast Highway, Lomita, CA 90717, 310-539-3631, Fax 310-539-4895. Source for unfinished paintable surfaces, including home decorator items.

USA Light and Electric, 800-854-8794, www.usalight.com. Offers clamp-on halogen light fixtures for art and craft shows. Call for a catalog.

Viking Folk Art Publications, Inc., 301 16th Avenue SE, Waseca, MN 56093, 507-835-8009, Fax 507-835-8541, www.viking-publications.com Distributors of quality decorative painting instructional books. Newsletter available through the Web site.

Viking Woodcrafts Inc., 1317 8th Street SE, Waseca, MN 56093, 800-361-0115, Fax 507-835-3895, www.vikingwoodcrafts.com. Offers wood pieces, papier-mâché, tin, acrylic paints, brushes, painting books, and packets. The 500-page catalog is available for $8.

Walnut Hollow, 1409 State Road 23, Dodgeville, WI 53533, 800-950-5101. Supplier of wide variety of high-quality paintable wood surfaces including plates, clocks, chairs, birdhouses, and tavern signs.

Walter Drake, Drake Building, Colorado Springs, CO 80940, 719-596-3853. Reasonable prices on stock business cards, return address and mailing labels, and novelty advertising items such as pencils, pens, and pocket calendars.

West Coast Wood Craft Supplies, 1256 Alderney Court, Oceanside, CA 92054, 760-721-8479, Fax 760-721-0481. Offers high-quality laser-cut wood shapes for ornaments and a variety of imaginative seasonal projects. Write for a catalog.

Wood Cellar Graphics, 87180 563rd Ave., Coleridge, NE 68727, 402-283-4725. Offers originally designed hangtags for pricing your projects. Write for catalog and information.

Woodcrafts, P.O. Box 78 Bicknell, IN 47512, 800-733-4820. Home decorating items and functional pieces, including wood sewing boxes.

Wood-n-Crafts, Inc., P.O. Box 140, Lakeview, MI 48850, 800-444-8075, Fax 517-352-6792, www.wood-n-crafts.com. Call for a free wholesale catalog.

Wood to Paint, P.O. Box 70, Mound, MN 55364-0070. Over 100 pre-cut ready-to-finish wood projects and fun kits for the beginner. Catalog available.

Wood Shoppe, 8009 Peak Drive, Garner, NC 27529, 919-550-1702. Manufacturers of carousel paint caddies in single-, double-, and triple-tier turntables, saving space on your painting table.

Woodworks, Ft. Worth, TX 76117, 800-722-0311, Fax 817-581-5235. Offers over 1,200 wood items. Call for wholesale catalog.

WOODWRKS.com
RGC's

Zim's, Inc., 4370 South 300 West, Salt Lake City, UT 84107, 800-453-6420, Fax 801-268-9859. Porcelain ornaments and a variety of wood characters, including nutcrackers and smokers.

Section F
Arts and Crafts Conventions, Shows, and Malls

The Society of Decorative Painters (SDP) hosts an annual convention, which is so well known among members that it is referred to simply as "the convention." Participants come from all segments of the decorative painting industry, including manufacturers, publishers, and suppliers, as well as nationally recognized teachers demonstrating hands-on techniques. There are also small-scale conventions sponsored by some regional or local chapters of the SDP. In addition, other organizations and private concerns sponsor conventions and trade shows directed toward the decorative painter and craftsman.

Association of Crafts and Creative Industries (ACCI) is an organization that sponsors a large well-publicized annual trade show event similar in scope to the Hobby Industry Association (HIA). While these events are not open to the general public, decorative painters who intend to launch a business may wish to inquire about requirements for admission and attend an event.

Belle Starr Outlaw Daze Arts and Crafts Show, P.O. Box 545, Carthage, MO 64836, 417-358-4974, Fax 417-358-5103. Call for information.

Bizarre Bazaar, P.O. Box 8330, Richmond, VA 23226, 804-673-7015, Fax 804-673-7017. The organization presents Christmas and Spring markets. Shows are juried. Write or call for exhibitor information.

Christmas Crossroads, P.O. Box 256, Lockport, IL 60441, 815-838-4900, presented by the Lockport Women's Club and billed as one of the Chicago area's largest craft shows since 1971. Call or write for exhibitor information.

Cimmeron Promotions, P.O. Box 2816, Ponca City, OK 74602, 405-765-1626. Promoter of several shows running from April through October in Texas, Kansas, and Missouri. Write or call for a show calendar and exhibitor information.

Cloud Productions, P.O. Box 586, Findlay, OH 45839-0586, 419-436-1457. Promoters of shows in Ohio and Indiana focusing on the holiday season and featuring Folk Art, Americana, Country, Southwestern, and Victorian arts and crafts. Call or write for information.

Coomers Incorporated, 6012 Reef Point Lane, Fort Worth, TX 76135. To inquire about Craft Malls, call 888-362-7238 and check out Coomers Global Gallery at www.coomers.com.

Country Peddler Shows/American Memories Inc., P.O. Box 160, Fort Myers, FL 33902, 941-479-5005, www.countrypeddlershow.com. or www.epeddle.com.
Write for exhibitor information.

Crafters Showcase, 414-250-0400, 414-327-0400, 414-376-0400

Creative Painting Convention, P.O. Box 80720, Las Vegas, NV 89180, 702-221-8234. Privately sponsored.

Deutsch Country Days, Luxenhaus Farm, 5437 Highway O, Marthasville, MO 63357-2357. Write or call for exhibitor information about this juried event.

Extrav—Painting Exposition, 2400 Devon, Suite 375, Des Plaines, IL 60018-4618, 800-272-3871. Two conventions annually; privately sponsored by *Painting Magazine.*

Harvest Festival, 601 North McDowell Blvd., Petaluma, CA 94954, 707-778-6300, 800-321-1213, Fax 707-763-5346, www.harvestfestival.com. Call for an application and schedules.

Heart of Ohio Tole, Inc. (HOOT), P.O. Box 626, Reynoldsburg, OH 43068-0626, 614-452-4541. Sponsored by an SDP chapter.

High Country Art and Craft Guild, P.O. Box 2854, Asheville, NC 28806, 828-252-3880. Features holiday (November and December) opportunities for marketing your traditional and contemporary works. Write or call for information.

Hillsboro Arts and Crafts Fair, 109 South Main, Hillsboro, KS 67063, 316-947-3506, Fax 316-947-3779. Thirty-one years in operation with public attendance approaching 40,000. Send SASE for schedule and fee information.

Hobby Industry Association (HIA) Large organization that sponsors annual trade shows. Employing guidelines similar to those of the Association of Crafts and Creative Industries (ACCI), events are open to professionals within the industry. While these shows at one time were intended to attract retailers, wholesalers, and product distributors, persons holding an HIA membership may attend the events. Decorative painters serious about launching a retail business may wish to inquire about events and admission or membership criteria.

Kaswood Expositions (Canada), 593 Main Road, Hudson, Quebec, JOP1HO, Canada for booth information or 70 Woodward Cresc, Halifax, NS, B3M1J7, Canada for teacher information; 902-443-7032, Fax 902-443-8783. Two shows annually; privately sponsored.

Keepsake Country Shows, 812 South Main Street, St. Charles, MO 63301, 314-949-6513, Fax 314-949-9644. Promotes shows in the Midwest. For exhibitor information, send a business-size SASE with 55 cents postage.

Madison Street Festival, Inc., 137 Steele Drive, Madison, AL 35758, 256-461-8181, www.madisonstreetfestival.org.

Merle Hay Mall Craft Festival, Stookey Companies, P.O. Box 31083, Des Moines, IA 50310. Juried show. Send SASE for information and schedule.

Mountain Magic, P.O. Box 681, Merrimack, NH 03054. Sponsored by an SDP chapter.

National Art and Craft Festival, 4845 Rumler Road, Chambersburg, PA 17201, 717-369-4810, Fax 717-369-5001. Three hundred exhibitors, 25 years in operation. Write for information.

Raindrop Chapter/Northwest Tolers, 3360 172nd Avenue NE, Redmond, WA 98052-5710, 206-861-9103. Sponsored by an SDP chapter.

Rio Grande Arts and Crafts Festival, 3709 Westerfield NE, Albuquerque, NM 87111, 505-292-7457. Write for application and information about show dates and fees.

Society of Decorative Painters, 393 N. McLean Blvd., Wichita, KS 67203-5968, 316-269-9300, www.decorativepainters.com

Tole Country, 3421 NW 68th Street, Oklahoma City, OK 73116. Sponsored by an SDP chapter.

Western Regional Decorative Painting Conference, Utah State University, Logan, UT 84322-5005, 801-797-0636. Privately sponsored.

Section G
Glossary of Terms

You will find glossary formats and a variety of descriptive labels in several painting magazines and most how-to paint publications. The following are some of the more commonly used terms as applied to decorative painting.

Acrylic Gouache: An opaque water-based paint, but binders are added other than water. Gouache is flexible and light-fast and can be used as general acrylics, including the ease of water cleanup.

Acrylics: Colored pigments mixed with water. Commonly available in ready-to-use squirt bottles. Acrylics are also available in tubes as pure pigments and are not pre-mixed with water. All acrylics are water-based, affording easy cold water cleanup.

Alkyd: Alkyds are pure pigment colors and are used like oil paints. They require cleanup with turpentine.

Antique: A technique of softening or shading different colors on a cured painting. Combine an antiquing mix (paint plus medium) and brush or rub mixture over the subject. Let sit and wipe off excess as desired for a soft look; or reapply mixture if the first application is not dark enough.

Base-in or Basecoat: Painting an object or a portion of a design before shading, highlighting, or adding other detail. Surfaces may require two or three basecoats, often with light sandings in between applications.

Basic Palette: Some artists specify colors they continually use and set up the palette uniformly as they begin each project.

Binder: An element, solution, or emulsifier mixed with paint to keep the product from separating.

Blend: Combining colors on your brush and stroking so that the values blend together before applying to a project.

Block-in: Applying colors side by side, leaving strong contrasts between areas, like a coloring-book application.

C-stroke: With a loaded paintbrush (round or flat), apply brush to surface at a slight angle, set down brush, and form an arc or 'c'-shaped stroke.

Cured: When paint is cured, it is completely dry. Dry to the touch may not indicate paint is dry beyond the surface. If acrylics feel cool on the surface, likely the paint has not completely dried, or cured.

Dirty-brush: Leaving a previously used color in the brush and blending in an additional color.

Distress: Deliberately scarring or marking a surface to lend an antique or heavily worn appearance.

Double-loading: Dipping half of the brush into a paint color; flipping the brush and dipping the other half into a second paint color; then lightly stroking the brush on a palette surface to blend colors.

Dry brush: A technique in which water is blotted out of the brush before dipping into the paint, and excess paint is also blotted out on a paper towel before applying to surface.

Drying board: A flat surface dotted with sharp points. Small painted projects are rested on the points for drying with little or no marring of paint applications.

Float: Applying color by picking up paint on a corner of a brush and softening the color with water or a floating medium before applying to a painted project. The term float may be used interchangeably with side-load or floated color.

Flyspeck: Spattering or spraying specks of paint onto a surface with a flyspeck tool or old toothbrush.

Glaze: Washing a color over a previously painted and dry basecoat, usually prepared with a wash of water or glazing medium.

Grain: Usually referred to concerning wood, fabric, or leather that denotes the direction of the fibers or pattern. Project instructions may include the words "sand with the grain."

Graphite: Non-waxy paper used for transferring patterns to a painting surface.

Grit: A term referring to grades of sandpaper (for example, very fine sandpaper is 220 grit and medium grade might be labeled 100 grit).

Highlight: Creating the illusion of a light source by using lighter values of paint to create contrast.

Loading the brush: Picking up paint from an edge of a paint puddle and applying slight pressure as you move the brush against the paint.

Medium: An element mixed with paint that changes its character or allows a special effect (such as crackle medium, flow medium). A term also used interchangeably with the types of paints (acrylic is referred to as a medium, as is watercolor or oil).

Oil-based: Products that are oil-based required turpentine or other solvent agents for cleanup and blending. Oil and alkyd paints are oil-based (petroleum-based) as are some varnishes.

Palette: The list of colors used in a painting project; also the surface on that you will squirt and mix your paints (wet-palette, Styrofoam tray, sheet of glass, or wax paper pad).

Pat-blend or pitty-pat: With a dry brush, pat or quickly pull soft strokes across colors for a blending technique.

Pigment: The coloring agent in paint; sometimes used interchangeably with the word paint.

Retarder: A medium used to slow the drying time of acrylic paints. It can be mixed with paint or used as an agent to moisten your brush.

Scruffy brush: An old worn-out brush with splayed bristles.

Sealer: A product used to prevent absorption, prevent wood grain from rising or leaking sap, or to protect a surface as a final protective application.

Shade: Applying a darker color value to effect contour of shapes to make areas recede as though in shadows.

Side-loading the brush: Dipping one corner of a flat brush into the paint and then blending until there is a gradation from dark to light (or none) color value to the other side of the brush.

Stipple: Pouncing a scruffy or stencil brush up and down with a minimum amount of paint to create a textured look.

Stylus: Tool used to trace over pattern lines (an old ballpoint pen serves the same purpose) and transfer the design to your painting surface. Usually one end of the stylus has a small tip and the other end is slightly larger. May also be used for making freehand filler designs and for embellishing lettering.

Tack: To remove sanding dust from a surface, usually with a tack cloth, but a damp paper towel or sponge can be substituted in most cases.

Tack cloth: A cheesecloth or muslin rag that has been saturated with solvents such as linseed oil and turpentine and is used to wipe sanding dust from wood projects. Note: Store in an airtight jar and observe safety procedures concerning odors and inflammability.

Tooth: The roughness of a painting surface that affects paint adherence (that is, smoothness, slickness, porosity).

Tracing paper: Thin paper that permits seeing lines of a design; used for tracing patterns.

Transfer paper: Coated paper used to transfer patterns to a painting surface. Products include Saral, Chacopaper, or graphite paper.

Transferring a pattern: Copying the lines of a design from tracing paper to your painting surface with transfer paper placed beneath the tracing paper.

Undercoat: Base-coating an area of a design prior to applying a pattern or designated color for the actual project (for example, before painting a red apple on a black slate, the apple portion may be undercoated in white acrylic in order to make the detail stand out from the black background).

Varnish: A medium that provides a protective coat while enhancing the vibrancy and detail of paint. Available in spray and brush-on applications.

Wash: Paint thinned to transparency, as much as four or five parts water to one part paint.

Wet-on-wet: A brush technique that allows a smooth blend of color values and creates a soft look. Shading or highlighting is added before the previously applied color has dried.

Section H
Business Contributors

The following professionals have provided contact information. Not all individuals mentioned in the text are listed.

Johnnie Elma Anderson, 3311 West Shandon, Avenue, Midland, TX 79707

Elizabeth Bishop, Seams So Creative Patterns, 212 E. St., Athens, AL 35611, 205-233-3834

Barbara Brabec, Barbara Brabec Productions, P.O. Box 2137, Naperville, IL 60567, 630-717-4188, www.crafter.com/brabec

Pama Collé, 3030 South Grand Avenue, #2, Glenwood Springs, CO 81601

Claire and Shaun Kelly, The Village Craft Gallery, 1660 Lakeside Drive, Bullhead City, AZ 86442

Linda and Ivan Maretich, Linda's Ewenique Boutique of Crafts, 12444 Lisbon Road, Salem, OH 44460, 330-533-6727, e-mail: taury@cboss.com

Susan Nelson, SCD-SDP, Cats 'n Stuff, 2316 13th Ave. NW, Rochester, MN 55901

Shirley Thomas, CRAFTMALL-WEB, 6000 LaSalle Drive, Fredericksburg, VA 22407, www.craftmallusa.com.

Ruby Tobey, Scribbles and Sketches Studio, 2305 W. 32nd Street South, Wichita, KS 67217-2044

Index

A

Accenting, 60–61

Accomplishment as benefit of decorative painting, 10–11

Accounting software, 226–227

Achievement Log to provide motivation, 281

Acrylic stain, applying, 54

Acrylic transparent wash, 55–56

Acrylics for decorative painting, 15–16

  airbrushing using, 17

  basic color set for, 18

  color-matching guide for, 19

  diluting, 54–55

  lengthening drying time of, 32

  as nontoxic, 41–42

  palette for, 27–29

  starting with, 16–19

  using acrylic finishes for, 68

Adoorables, 112, 113

Advance payment for custom orders, 208

Advertising for business. *See also* individual outlets

  in magazines, 177–178

  mailing list development for, 176

  media for, 214–216

  on Web, 215–216, 237

  word of mouth, 210, 216

Aerosol propellants, 42

Airbrushing using acrylics, 17

Alkyds versus oils for decorative painting, 16

American Craft Malls, 251

Anderson, Johnnie Elma

  catalysts for sales of, 162

  fairness stressed by, 156

  getting feel for pricing at shows described by, 153

  goals of, 119, 123

  gratitude attitude journal of, 88, 89, 218

  professionalism advocated by, 195–196

  search for ideas by, 87

  successful selling tip from, 192

Angel project, 94–98

Antiquing effects, 62–64

Attorney, deciding when to retain, 242–244

Audience for pieces, assessing, 205–206

Auto insurance during business use of car, 257–258

Automotive wax on outdoor projects, 69

B

Bad checks

  avoiding customers', 252–253

  collecting, reasons for, 253–254

Balance sheet for each sales event, 184

Basecoating

  alternatives to, 56–72

  brushes for, 23

  candles, 71

  canvas, 71

  crackling as, 64

  metal, 70

  new wood, 56, 108, 110

  opaque paints for, 19–20

  outdoor projects, 68

  sealing before, 56

  terra cotta, 100

  under crackling effect, 64

  under glazing, 61

About the Author

DENNIS YOUNG, PHOTOGRAPHER

SUSAN YOUNG, author, artist, and designer, purchased her first three paint brushes in 1975. Since then, her painted and written works have been featured in scores of publications and on national television. Susan is a member of the Society of Decorative Painters and the Society of Craft Designers. She writes and paints from her Peach Kitty Studio, where hundreds of projects are on display—along with those first three brushes.

About the Series Editor

BARBARA BRABEC is one of the world's leading experts on how to turn an art or crafts hobby into a profitable home-based business. She regularly communicates with thousands of creative people through her Web site and monthly columns in *Crafts Magazine* and *The Crafts Report*.

To Order Books

Please send me the following items:

Quantity	Title	U.S. Price	Total
_____	Decorative Painting For Fun & Profit	$ 19.99	$ _____
_____	Holiday Decorations For Fun & Profit	$ 19.99	$ _____
_____	Woodworking For Fun & Profit	$ 19.99	$ _____
_____	Knitting For Fun & Profit	$ 19.99	$ _____
_____	Quilting For Fun & Profit	$ 19.99	$ _____
_____	Soapmaking For Fun & Profit	$ 19.99	$ _____
_____	_____	$ _____	$ _____
_____	_____	$ _____	$ _____

Subtotal	$ _____
Deduct 10% when ordering 3–5 books	$ _____
7.25% Sales Tax (CA only)	$ _____
8.25% Sales Tax (TN only)	$ _____
5% Sales Tax (MD and IN only)	$ _____
7% G.S.T. Tax (Canada only)	$ _____
Shipping and Handling*	$ _____
Total Order	$ _____

*Shipping and Handling depend on Subtotal.

Subtotal	Shipping/Handling
$0.00–$29.99	$4.00
$30.00–$49.99	$6.00
$50.00–$99.99	$10.00
$100.00–$199.99	$13.50
$200.00+	Call for Quote

**Foreign and all Priority Request orders:
Call Customer Service
for price quote at 916-632-4400**

This chart represents the total retail price of books only
(before applicable discounts are taken).

By Telephone: With American Express, MC, or Visa,
call 800-632-8676 or 916-632-4400. Mon–Fri, 8:30–4:30.
www.primapublishing.com
By E-mail: sales@primapub.com
By Mail: Just fill out the information below and send with your remittance to:
Prima Publishing • P.O. Box 1260BK • Rocklin, CA 95677

Name _____

Address _____

City _____ State _____ ZIP _____

MC/Visa/American Express# _____ Exp. _____

Check/money order enclosed for $ _____ Payable to Prima Publishing

Daytime telephone _____

Signature _____